This book is dedicated to anyone who wants to do something good.

~ ~ ~

A massive thanks to James Kerr for his time and his inspirational book "Legacy" for starting this whole journey. "Legacy" has been a game changer for me.

~ ~ ~

A massive thanks also to, Lee Peck, Jason Rhodes, Mike Ford and Tim Walker for reading the developing versions of this book for me. I really appreciate your help.

I would also like to thank Dave Davies at Blue Frontier for all his creative design input.

~ ~ ~

As this is a work of opinion, any references to real people, places or events may include factual inaccuracies, adaptations or omissions. If that is the case, I apologise unreservedly for any offence or upset caused.

~ ~ ~

# BUILD YOUR SUPER-TRIBE

## HOW TRIBAL RITUALS AND TRADITIONS CAN CHANGE THE MODERN WORLD

SIMON J. RHODES

# CONTENTS

1. The importance of tribes ..................................... 1

2. The Signs and Rituals of Tribes................................. 24

3. Building your tribe ...................................... 51

4. Generating Tribal Power.................................... 1

5. Super-tribes ................................................. 31

6. How I've learned what matters ............................. 30

# 1. THE IMPORTANCE OF TRIBES

Tribes have dominated our history. Every great civilisation has been a tribe. So has every great organisation, whether that's a sports team, business or charity. Tribes still dominate our modern world. The most successful organisations are invariably tribes.

However, simply assembling a group of people is not enough to get something great done. Tribes require much more than that. Tribes need to be built.

> *"United, united, united we stand.*
> *United we never shall fall.*
>
> *United, united, united we stand.*
> *United we stand one and all."*[1]

## 1.1 WHY CHOOSE THE HARD WAY TO SUCCESS?

Every organisation is searching for the quickest and easiest route to achieve success. Whether your organisation is a business, sports team, school, political party or charity, being successful matters. But what 'success' really means and how you sustain it matter even more.

If you're a business, achieving success could mean increasing your market share, recruiting the best people or improving your profit margins. If you're a sports team, success could mean winning the league, the cup or gaining promotion to the league above. If you're a

---

[1] From United by Judas Priest on the album British Steel. Arnold H. Glascow.

charity, success might mean significantly increasing your charitable donations or raising your public profile. If you're a volunteer group, success could mean increasing the number of hours of volunteering you deliver each year.

Whatever it's trying to achieve, every organisation needs success every year just to survive. Beyond that, regular and sustained success is needed in order for any organisation to thrive. Getting winning results matters to every single organisation. But how is success achieved? How is winning done?

In order to win and keep winning, to grow and keep growing, every organisation needs to constantly adapt and improve itself. And that leads straight to a fundamental fork in the road. There is an easy way and a hard way to achieve that improvement.

> *"Success is simple. Do what's right's,*
> *the right way, at the right time."*[2]

The most-travelled route towards perceived improvement is the drive to ever greater efficiencies. That's the hard way. It's done by asking staff to work ever harder for the same money or less, driving operating costs ever lower; and demanding ever higher sales and production figures. Each squeeze of an organisation's resources might produce more "juice" but that squeeze comes at an organisational and a human cost. Each time an organisation ramps up its demands it might get a short-term performance spike. But that is always at an engagement cost, causing longer term problems. In the World of efficiencies, organisational expectations and demands on workers are becoming more and more unrealistic.

For many organisations, every new financial year brings the task of getting even more blood from the same stone. Demanding greater improvements from even less is a flawed methodology with a finite limit. Unrealistic and unrewarding goals kill employee engagement and flatten a workplace culture. Even if you manage to achieve the impossible, next year's targets simply go up again. Pushing your

---

[2] Arnold H. Glascow.

people to fear, stress and illness creates an ever-decreasing spiral towards total organisational failure. When collective engagement has gone, there is no tribe left. In stark contrast, super-tribes provide the opposite. Super-tribes they are about building social and commercial successes.

> *If the soul of your organisation*
> *has been crushed, there is no*
> *more winning to be done*

Too many employers are caught up in the success at all costs mentality. How many managers have sold their souls for their organisations? How many go home and become a different person? How many feel pressurised into doing absolutely anything they have to, just to deliver a bit more profit?

Building a successful organisation should be a positive and enjoyable experience. It shouldn't be about doing down the competition, bad mouthing the referee, polluting the environment, cheating donors, setting out to injure an opponent, fleecing your customers or refusing to pay your suppliers a fair price. Building a successful organisation shouldn't be about oppressing or burning out your workers[3] either. Yet how many jobs have become depressing, oppressive and soulless? How many managers are under hideous pressure and afraid of losing their jobs? How many organisations have devalued their people to the point of contemptuous disinterest? Are your organisation's workers people or are they merely statistics on a spreadsheet? Is your organisation too focused on 'success' to see what success really looks like? Is it sliding inexorably towards this hidden cliff edge?

David Graeber has written a book[4] about "bullshit jobs" which sets out categories of jobs that he believes are largely meaningless and pointless. There are too many plenty of these thankless jobs, but worse than that, every job becomes a "bullshit" job if you're disengaged whilst you do it. The more crappy jobs your organisation

---

[3] I am using the words employees, workers and staff interchangeably to help with the flow, rather than for their specific legal definitions.
[4] This is a 2018 book called "Bullshit Jobs: A theory."

has, the less engaged its workforce will be. How can any organisation expect uninspired and disengaged workers to magically create success? Ironically, those jobs mighty escape the coming technological advances, as they are not worth automating. That means the future of work still includes workers carrying out duties that leave them devalued and disinterested. That's a depressing thought and it's utterly avoidable.

~~~~~

The better and easier way to achieve sustainable success requires a longer-term, open-minded and more inclusive approach. That's because sustainable organisations plan and operate collectively. They protect and value their key assets. They don't risk burning them out. And yet too many working people are close to burn out. A blinkered look at the current financial year might somehow 'justify' this 'cash now' approach, but that justification is built on sand. Any sensible view would reject this obsessional short-termism out of hand. Super-tribes wouldn't dream of treating their key people badly.

## Let us put our minds together and see what life we can make for our children[5]

By positively involving all of your stakeholders and harnessing all of their collective efforts, an organisation has a far greater chance of achieving its goals. That is not as easy to do as it is to say, but it is unquestionably true. Very few organisations manage it. Truly sustainable organisations do. These super-tribes do three things really well. They stick to their purpose, they involve all their stakeholders; and they think in the past, present and future.

~~~~~

Working groups come in all shapes and sizes. Each business, club or third sector organisation has a different combination of assets and resources, made up of: office buildings, factories, warehouses, machinery, technology, fixtures and fittings, staff, customers,

---

[5] Lakota, Hunkpapa Chief Sitting Bull.

vehicles, suppliers, tenders, contracts, leases, office furniture, cash, stock, work in progress and vehicles. The most valuable asset class of them all is people, whether those people are in research and development, production, sales, training, human resources, finance, logistics, distribution or management.

Every organisation is unique, with a different mix of challenges. Every organisation gets to choose how to address its challenges in its own way, through deciding how best to deploy all its assets and resources. Many organisations make single-person decisions, trusting or at least accepting the views and opinions of a Chief Executive of Managing Director alone. Too often feedback and debate is stifled. Super-tribes are different. They make collective and inclusive decisions.

There are so many opportunities to make good and bad choices. All those choices matter. Good leadership involves getting the best out of all the available assets and resources, whilst also protecting them for the future. Good leadership seeks the views of all the organisation's stakeholders, in the knowledge that the organisation's most valuable asset is its people.

Do organisations with more engaged employees produce better results? Common sense says yes. More engaged employees work harder, smarter and more efficiently than unhappy ones. Engagement brings us social belonging, which can bring us sustained and long-term enjoyment. Fully engaging provides us with a much longer term 'fix' than the instant gratification we get from eating chocolate or drinking wine. Committing to our tribes offers us the chance of a happier life.

Some organisations want proof of a link between staff happiness and performance. Three published studies have provided evidence of that link. A 2011 study[6] found employee attitudes in different branches of a bank could be positively associated with the higher sales per employee in that branch (without being able to prove a direct correlation). A separate 2012 study[7] found that the higher mean

---

[6] A study by Bartel et al across 193 branches of US bank.
[7] A study of manufacturing firms in Finland by Bockerman and Ilmakunnas.

workplace job satisfaction in engaged workplaces could be independently associated with greater value added per employee. In 2019, Oxford University's Saïd Business School 1,793 BT workers across 11 call centres were found to make more calls and improve their selling rates when their mood was happier. In all three cases the studies found that highly engaged workplaces performed better than less engaged ones.

Science helps to provide the explanation. If our work causes stress, we become subject to a constant drip-feed of cortisol which suppresses the release of oxytocin. That's the hormone which makes us social and collaborative. Stress is catching too. We automatically respond to cortisol in others, meaning that stress is contagious. Happy employees have low cortisol and high oxytocin levels. Happy, unstressed employees perform better in a team environment. What more evidence are we waiting for?

Whilst many businesses increasingly rely on technology, virtually every organisation's prize asset remains its people. Every organisation gets to choose how to treat its own people. When I say every organisation gets to choose, I really mean the people inside each organisation get to choose how to treat each other. Managers and owners can't hide behind an inanimate corporate structure and claim it is the "company" deciding to do something. Organisations don't make decisions, the officers and employees in them do. Business decisions are always made by people.

Throughout the course of history workers have been treated very differently depending on the attitude of the employer and what was on offer. Some have trusted, rewarded and encouraged their workers. Others have held them back, treated them unfairly and paid them poorly. The latter approach is fractured if not completely broken. Which of these approaches is more likely to achieve the better results?

*"If everyone is moving forward together, then success takes care of itself."*[8]

---

[8] Henry Ford.

For some senior managers the essence of "leadership" is about personally driving success through their seniority, power and status as the leader. Perhaps the military aside, that approach misses the open secret. It is not through command and control, or fear and obedience that organisations are successful. Good leadership is not about being a "strong" leader either. It's about combining all the organisation's resources and harnessing the efforts of all of the organisation's stakeholders. It's about creating a working environment where everyone cares about everyone else and for everyone else.

This unification process is much easier to say than it is to do. That's because building a tribe is a wicked problem. Every day organisations fail to create the collective will and effort that's needed for their cause. But a tribe and even a super-tribe can be built.

It should be obvious, but a group of people working together can generate far more power than a single individual can. A collective approach creates a shared energy and sustainable momentum that makes winning much more likely. Good leaders accept that there is a limit to what they can personally do and go from there. Building something good takes a tribal philosophy. Building something even bigger takes a super-tribe. This book is about building a super-tribe of people and generating super-tribe power.

# 1.2 THE ESSENTIAL ELEMENTS OF TRIBE

The essentials of a modern tribe can be summarised into 6 core concepts.

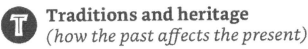

**Traditions and heritage**
*(how the past affects the present)*

**Rules, ceremonies and rituals**
*(how things are done)*

**Illustration through stories, songs and art**
*(expressing the special and unique)*

**Brand and symbols**
*(how the tribe is presented to the outside world)*

**Establish a clear vision, purpose and values**
*(reason for being and direction of travel)*

**Stakeholder alignment**
*(how tribal power is generated)*

This book explores all these concepts in the context of real tribes and the effects of the World around us. As every tribe is formed within its own context, for its own reasons, we need to look at deeper at what makes a tribe. But first, an example of a great modern tribe.

~~~~~

The Royal National Lifeboat Institution (RNLI) exists to provide the UK and Ireland with a 24 hour search and rescue service. Founded in 1824, brave crew members immediately began saving lives by rowing out to help sailors in distress. Extraordinarily it wasn't until thirty years later that the first life jackets were invented.

The RNLI has a proud heritage. Originally known as Royal National Institution for the Preservation of Life from Shipwreck, its name changed to the RNLI in 1854. Its website states "We are proud of our history, the affection in which people hold our traditions, and the RNLI's achievement of saving lives over nearly two centuries." And they should be proud. The RNLI saves an average of 22 people a day, every day. All of this has work been achieved by volunteers who risk their own lives every time a lifeboat leaves the shore.

In 1884, Leonora Preston designed the RNLI flag we know today, after her brother was rescued by Ramsgate lifeboat volunteers. That helped to establish the RNLI's colours, logo and brand. Ever since that flag has flown, lives have been saved.

The RNLI is a tribe with a safety culture. Its primary purpose is saving lives at sea. Its vision is one of ending preventable loss of life at sea. Its four core values are inherently tribal. Trustworthy, Courageous, Selfless and Dependable are all characteristics based on looking out for each other.

The 2019 RNLI calendar has a photo and quote from a volunteer on its June page "As soon as I turned 17, I joined the lifeboat – I followed in my dad's footsteps. They're like my second family, the crew." Isobel Tugwell, Trainee Crew Member, Shoreham Lifeboat station.

## Many, many lives have been saved

With 238 lifeboat stations and 348 lifeboats, the RNLI provides an extraordinary and selfless service. Costing over £400,000 a day to run, the tribe's stakeholders include the army of volunteers raising money to keep it going. Without them, more lives would be lost.

The RNLI doesn't just protect the UK and Ireland's coastline it educates on safety and builds community partnerships beyond its lifeboat stations. The RNLI will "always work to identify, grow and maintain effective partnerships and coalitions to further the cause of the wider lifesaving community." That additional step of working with others to achieve a collective tribal power is what makes the RNLI a super-tribe.

When you are trying to emulate a strong modern tribe in action, you could do much worse than take a close look at the RNLI. We can all learn lessons from its purpose, camaraderie and selflessness.

## 1.3  WE NEED TRIBES

As human beings we all have basic fundamental needs and other more sophisticated ones. Abraham Maslow created a priority list, putting those needs into their order of importance. Drawn as a pyramid, this is known as Maslow's Hierarchy of Needs.[9] From the base upwards our needs are:

- **Physiological** *(including air, food, water, clothing, shelter and reproduction)*
- **Safety** *(from war, poverty, disease, accident and pollution)*
- **Social Belonging** *(being part of a group of people)*
- **Esteem** *(being valued, respected and accepted)*
- **Self-actualisation** *(the realisation of a person's full potential); and*
- **Self-Transcendence** *(where the self finds its actualisation by giving itself to some higher goal in altruism or spirituality).*

Every single one of those needs is better met by being part of a tribe. At the most basic level, a tribe can use its collective resources to feed, clothe and shelter everyone in it. So a tribe that includes farmers and builders should survive. A builder living alone may not fare as well.

*"Talent wins games, but teamwork and intelligence win championships"*[10]

---

[9] The hierarchy of needs is the psychology theory of Abraham Maslow, contained in his 1943 paper "A Theory of Human Motivation" which was published in Psychology Review. Michael Jordan

[10] Michael Jordan of the Chicago Bulls.

Many people are trying to find meaning and purpose in their lives. At its highest level, a tribe can collectively find its self-actualisation (if not its self-transcendence) through living to its tribal values and achieving its tribal purpose. An organisation's leaders have to ensure that their tribe meets all of its collective needs, so that it can sustain itself. By doing so, tribes can help all their individual members to meet their individual needs.

~ ~ ~ ~ ~

Our basest needs are physiological. At work, offering everyone free drinks helps to meet a core physiological need. Providing free drinks costs relatively little and scores a brownie point with every re-usable mug or bottleful. However, that brownie point opportunity is immediately lost by providing cheap or tasteless tea and coffee, because it repeatedly disappoints, every single drink, every single day. Employers should always provide a choice of high-quality drinks. Never let your finance team choose your tea bags.

## Why not live your best life?

Creating a clear vision, purpose, set of values and strategy for the whole organisation, produces a tribal plan. That allows each member to become part of something much larger and more meaningful than they can be as an individual.

Aligning your own interests with your tribe's interests can, in its best form, help you to reach a higher plain of happiness. In modern terminology, belonging to tribes allows you to live your best life. Your potential grows faster inside a tribe and it grows exponentially inside a super-tribe.

~ ~ ~ ~ ~

Wolves typically live in packs of between two and twenty family members. Being a member of a wolf pack helps each individual wolf to meet its basic needs for food and safety.

Based around a dominant pair of wolves who mate for life, a pack includes other family members such as their children, parents and siblings. Each pack lives and hunts together, operating as one unit. Wolves think and act as a collective group. When a pack is on the move the oldest, weakest wolves walk at the front of a single-file column. They set the pace for the journey. That's deliberate. It helps to ensure that no wolf is left behind.

When hunting, each wolf plays a different role, depending on its age, experience and ability. Before the hunt begins, each wolf knows exactly what's expected of it and of everyone other pack member. That means that the pack can operate in silence giving it the element of surprise. The youngest wolves tend to observe from the sidelines learning how hunting is done. The faster females take on herding roles, driving the prey towards a suitable place to attack and preventing it from escaping. The slower but heavier males head straight towards the trap that the female wolves have set and then take down the prey. This way the pack works together as a team to feed every member in it. The pack plays to every wolf's strengths and uses them to create a collective super-strength as a combined hunting force.

Wolves communicate with each other through scent, sound and physical posturing. To help a wolf find its pack, nature gives the wolf a howl which can be heard up to ten miles away. The different noises used; and the number of wolves howling can change the meaning of each message. That creates a unique language. Only the wolves in the pack know it. So only the wolves in that pack can use it and benefit from it.

By living, playing and hunting together a wolf pack builds bonds of mutual trust, reliance and collaboration. Those bonds are absolutely vital to meeting the pack's needs and to securing its future. As with human families, eventually young adults known as 'dispersers' strike out on their own to find mates and establish new packs. But they leave with those pack lessons and experiences ingrained into them. Then the cycle begins all over again.

*"When the snows fall and the white winds blow, the lone wolf dies but the pack survives."[11]*

Meeting all the individual human needs of its people will always provide the foundations of a stable environment for a tribe to grow and flourish in. Organisations have needs too. They need peace and stability in order to develop and establish themselves.

There are exceptions such as the war-like city state Sparta, but most organisations need the following to thrive: a settled structure, stable leadership, little (if any) corruption, a fair distribution of resources, an acceptance of the rights of others; and good relationships with its neighbours.

Businesses, sporting clubs, charities and other organisations draw strength from the skills, energy and experience of their employees, members, supporters, donors and supporters. Successful organisations look for the common purposes that pull them together and they use that human power to achieve them. Successful organisations focus on meeting every stakeholder's basic and complex needs. That way they can call all their people to action.

~~~~~

Like individual human beings and organisations, society as a whole has needs too. According to a 2018 report entitled "Is Britain Fairer?"[12] the UK has a several groups that need urgent help.

"Child poverty has increased and the inequalities resulting from socio-economic disadvantage are seriously affecting many people's lives. Women are still not benefitting from equality in practice and there are increasingly large gaps between the experiences and outcomes of disabled people and some ethnic minorities and the population as a whole. The persistent disadvantages faced by certain

---

[11] George R.R. Martin - A Game of Thrones
[12] Commissioned by the Equality and Human Rights Commission; and sub-titled The state of equality and human rights in 2018.

groups raise significant concerns that some people are being left behind."

A tribal society wouldn't willingly leave its own people behind unless they wanted to be left. As that is what's happening in the UK, it means the UK is not yet a super-tribe. It is a place where many tribes co-exist without coming together to resolve all their collective needs. Not everyone cares and not everyone is being cared for.

If parts of society feel that their basic needs are not being met, then they will demand change until all those needs are being met. Driving change can take several different forms, including for example voting to change the government or voting to leave the European Union. It could be evolutionary or revolutionary change. The less that the public cares about the society they're part of, the more random, extreme and inconsistent those changes might be.

The more that governments and society care about all of their people, the less chance there is of anyone being "left behind". Caring about our communities helps to preserve them and preserve our way of life. A government and society that cares for everyone in it appeals to everyone. An uncaring government runs a much higher risk of revolutionary change that ousts it from power. Every tribe needs to apply this same core principle. Stop caring and you'll stop mattering.

## 1.4 WHY TRIBES MATTER

We all experience life from our own personal perspectives. We view the World from our inside out. As a result, no one else sees things precisely like we do. No one ever has done and no one ever will. Our view of the World is unique for two key reasons. Firstly, no one else occupies the identical point in space and time as us. Take where you are sitting or standing right now. No one else is sitting or standing exactly where you are, at exactly the same time. It's not physically possible. So, if an incident happened close by, you would be the only person to see it from the exact spot that you're in. That literally gives you a different perspective to anyone else. Your view of the World is therefore always unique to you. But that doesn't mean you need to be alone. Tribes give us a safe and practical way to pool our perspectives for everyone's benefit.

Secondly, we interpret everything we experience differently to anyone else. That's because we all have a unique combination of DNA, life experiences and personal relationships. Our neurodiversity makes us different from everyone else. So, no one else interprets what happens in the World in quite the same way that we do. Every experience is reflected through our own individual prism of history, influencers, mental scars and biases as we alone interpret them. Each particular life experience (or quale) we experience is unique.

We can all go for a walk in the same park, but how we experience it is specific to each of us. So, every piece of information we receive is automatically self-influenced as you consciously analyse it. But that doesn't mean we have to face the World alone. The existence of tribes means that you don't.

Our minds are always looking after our selfish interests. Why else would people hog the middle lane on a clear motorway? We are in effect pre-destined to believe what suits us best. Our own interests are 'front and centre'. Legendary Roman leader Julius Caesar understood this well, saying that "Men are nearly always willing to believe what they wish." Some people need help finding common ground to work in, to help themselves and help others too. Tribes can offer a common purpose to get behind.

## We need help finding common ground with others

As we see and understand things uniquely, every one of us lives a truly individual life. That level of uniqueness also depends on how our brains work. If we are lucky, we are neurotypical and see the World in a similar way to most of society. Approximately 85% of people are neurotypical, which leaves one in six (15%) people who are neurodivergent. Their brains work very differently to the majority. Neurodivergence includes conditions like Autism, Attention Deficit Hyperactivity Disorders, Dyslexia and Dyspraxia. Having any of those conditions adds another layer of difference. Each person's cognitive reserve is different too. How much learning we do, how much exercise we take and how well we sleep we get are all factors that affect our brain power as we age. The more of each we do the better our brains perform. There are so many forms of difference between people, but that make us the individuals we are. Interestingly, regardless of the differences between us, we often end up thinking similarly to other people.

Despite all our individualism we are all human and we are all part of society. We all benefit from social interaction. As social interaction is far harder for some people than for others, neurodivergent people need help to 'fit in'. Tribes can offer that assistance.

~~~~~

Whether or not we are neurotypical, we are constantly reminded of our unique perspective. It happens every time that we interact with other people. That means that we notice our own points of difference as a matter of routine, multiple times every day. Often that prompts a subconscious reaction, but sometimes it provokes a conscious reaction which can shock, unnerve or concern us. The more alone we fare, the more vulnerable we feel.

## *Tribes can help us to find our place in the World*

In the modern World we live in, difference is entirely normal. Finding someone just like us is far harder than finding someone who's different. As a result, working with other people requires us to work with people who are different to us. We need to be tolerant, understanding and appreciative of those people and their differences. We can acquire that understanding and tolerance in part by 'looking' through the perspectives of others. By investing time getting to know other people we can improve our understanding and appreciation of other people's differences. By accepting other people's differences, we can make our own lives less arduous and stressful. So, rather than fearing what's different, we should embrace it. We should encourage others to embrace it too. Tribes help us to be part of something with a collective perspective that we can fit into.

Gathering the knowledge and insights that other people have to offer, helps us to understand and develop ourselves better. We can constantly learn new ideas and points of view from our encounters with other people. Observing can be insightful, but we can't truly understand other people without speaking to them. That's because we're limited to seeing other people from their outside in. We are reliant on what we are told. So, we need to listen really well. We also need to share our learning. Tribes allow us to receive teaching from and share our learning with other tribe members.

~~~~~

We only really understand ourselves because we see ourselves from the inside out. As a result, we are aware that there is more depth to us than anyone else can see. It frustrates us when other people judge us too superficially. Why can't they understand us better? And yet how do we judge others? If we don't take the time to appreciate their view of the World, then the answer will be "Superficially". All too often we take the selfish and lazy option of judging other people from our own perspective. And yet, our own frustration should teach us that other people are deeper and more interesting than their exteriors give away. We shouldn't judge them hastily, by their physical characteristics. That's because if we can get past the obvious differences that we might have with another person, we ironically discover a hidden secret. We have more in common with other people than first seems likely. Joining tribes allows us to find that out.

There is much that connects us and gives us shared ground. The more we have in common with anyone else, the more we agree with them and accept them. That makes us more likely to call them our friends and choose to spend time with them. Just as we can feel threatened by people who are different, we feel reassured by people who are like us. With the great truth being that there are many people out there who think similarly about the things that matter to us. Getting to know other people usually increases our chances of getting on with them. Tribes allow us to quickly and safely get to know other people.

We have high expectations of how we'd like to be treated. We hope that others will give us their time, patience and understanding. So, to be fair, we should do the same in return. Unfortunately, we don't always. Difference still freaks people out. Those points of difference can be easy to detect[13] and people are often too quick to judge them. Tribes allow us to be with people who behave in the same way we do. Tribes can treat us in the way that we want to be treated.

## We can feel threatened by difference

Our inbuilt and unconscious bias means that we instinctively judge other people as strangers. If someone has contrasting views to us, we don't just see them as different we tend to see them as wrong. The more dissimilar to us someone is the more of an outsider they appear; and so the less we instinctively like them. As humans we find it easier to casually stereotype other humans rather than spending the time needed to get to know them properly. With such a binary approach, the more that someone appears to threaten our values and interests, the more we repel them. We react as if our very survival feels threatened. As a result, being superficially different to someone can put us off becoming their friend, wanting to work with them or looking out for them. Tribes can help us to get past the superficial levels of many relationships and find common themes to work on.

Somehow, despite our natural in-built reluctance, we develop new interactions and relationships every day. Somehow, we cope with the fear and threat of other people and we thrive. Our instincts are our self-defence mechanisms, protecting us around the clock. The best ways to get around our controlling instincts are working harder at understanding other people and calling-out our unconscious biases more. That way we can flag up our own limitations and address them. We can improve ourselves and increase our chances of success. The more we can appreciate what other people have to offer us and each other, the larger and more useful our network can become. Joining tribes give us the time to get to know what other people have to offer.

---

[13] The World is global but only 3% of the World's population lives outside the country of its birth.

~~~~~

Despite being born individuals we don't want to be on our own. The evidence is all around us. Our World is full of groups. Everywhere people get together in all walks of life. We know that we like being together because we have so many words and expressions for being in groups. They include: company, partnership, team, fellowship, mateship, alliance, togetherness, camaraderie, brethren, comradery, sisterhood, brotherhood, fraternity, sorority, affiliation, solidarity, esprit de corps and tribe amongst others. All these group words have a positive ethos and spirit to them.

*"Great things in business are never done by one person; they're done by a team of people."*[14]

Our words for being on our own or acting in our interests have much more negative connotations. They include: single, individual, alone, lonely, loner, isolated, solitary, outcast, forsaken, unaccompanied, selfish and abandoned. The word 'autonomous' is perhaps an exception, but even that doesn't sell lone working particularly hard.

~~~~~

Alone we are subject to our own personal weaknesses. As David Bowie once said "I'm feeling like a society in myself, so broken up and fragmented.[15]" We cannot always spot our flaws or cover for them. We need help. So rather than accepting the theory of "rugged individualism"[16] and striving on alone, we need to ask for help and let other people to help us. Some people claim that they are "self-made" or that they don't need to rely on anyone else. But that is so rarely true as to be a myth. Modern living means that even when we think we are

---

[14] Steve Jobs.
[15] From the book 'Interviews and Encounters – Bowie on Bowie'.
[16] This was the philosophy on which Herbert Hoover won the 1928 U.S. Presidential election. Everyone should stand on their own two feet and provide for themselves. Its weakness was revealed by the 1929 Wall Street Crash which led to the Great Depression. America only recovered when rugged individualism was ditched in favour of the help offered by President Roosevelt's New Deals.

struggling on alone, we rarely are. At the most basic level we don't grow or hunt all our own food, we go to a local market or supermarket. We don't refine our own fuel, we buy it from a petrol station. We don't make all our own clothes, fully educate ourselves or build every component for our house. We need to disavow ourselves of the illusion that rugged individualism is sustainable. We need other people and they need us. There is a good trade to be done. Alone is almost never truly alone anyway. When Greta Garbo famously said "I want to be alone" she probably meant alone in a fully stocked and furnished house or hotel, with room service.

## *We are not truly self-made, we all need other people*

We may be born into a divided World, but we don't have to accept a life of division and self-interest. We don't have to struggle tirelessly on our own. As human beings we are instinctively sociable, despite our fears of difference. We are wired-up to live with and work with other people. But our unconscious biases and fears will get in the way if we let them.

By seizing the opportunity to collaborate with others and holding our unconscious bias to account, we can satisfy our base needs far more readily and increase our own performance level at the same time. Exaggerating our mutual similarities and working through our collective differences can really help a tribe to gel. Working together for mutual benefit isn't automatic or easy. It requires an open mind and focused thinking. But when a group clicks, it is far stronger than the sum of its parts.

# 1.5 WORK TRIBES

Armed with this knowledge, employers need to provide a work tribe for their people to join. Employers need to work very hard at on-boarding and assimilating new workers into their tribe. That's because on arrival every new joiner will be perceived as different. Every outsider needs to become an insider before they will be accepted. This fear and threat is at its highest when a new joiner comes direct from a competitor. The label "competitor" immediately arouses greater suspicion and invokes questions of disloyalty. So organisations should make a point of emphasising each new recruit's similarities (rather than differences) when announcing their arrival. That will help to speed up their integration. After all they are moving from foe to friend. The sooner they become an insider, the more efficient their working relationships will be. Performance increases when co-workers understand each other's needs and limitations. Tribes allow co-working to flourish.

~~~~~

Whist it is inherently difficult to build teams of people, but with a caring mindset we can do just it much better than our competitors. We need to use every trick in the book to assimilate a group of different people into a single joint enterprise. But it's worth it, because the hard truth is that by chasing our own dreams by ourselves, we have far less chance of achieving them. By going it alone we may not have to help anyone else chase their dreams, but we aren't helping ourselves. Together we are more powerful.

~~~~~

When tribal leaders "get it" and bring a collaborative approach, their organisations can really thrive. Jürgen Klopp is the Manager of Liverpool Football Club. Having won the 2019 Champions League trophy, his team is more successful than most. Jürgen describes his philosophy in what are inherently tribal terms.

*"What is right, what is wrong? If you think it is good for all of us, then it is probably right. I do everything in order that everyone feels better. The main thing is to make each other stronger. That is how I understand life, but in a football team it is especially like that. Help your mate to be the best he can be; and he will help you to be the best.[17]"*

Working as a team has been repeatedly proven to work for human beings in every generation, whether that's in construction, agriculture, warfare, business, emergency services or sport. Teamwork can help a whole group of people achieve their goals simultaneously. By combining multiple skills and resources, huge super-structures can be constructed, the British Army can defend us, our schools can teach us, the NHS can save our lives; and teams of sportsmen and women win matches that one player alone could not.

~~~~~

Just like people, organisations focus on what's important to them. Commercial and sporting organisations want to beat every organisation that competes with them. When that purpose suits the group's common interests, its stakeholders can unite to produce a tribal power. By playing on external threats and a sense of crisis or adversity, organisations can enhance the feeling of togetherness and tribalism within their group. By creating a 'siege mentality' a tribe pitches itself against the rest of the World, using phrases like "Everyone else wants us to lose, so we have to stick together." This sense of common fear or danger helps to tighten a group around its shared purpose. All tribes need to give themselves a united purpose that binds all their stakeholders together.

---

[17] These quotes formed part of an interview with Jürgen Klopp in the sports section of the Telegraph newspaper in 2018.

In March 2019 former Conservative Party MP Heidi Allen was appointed the interim leader of the new political party Change UK. Her opening remarks were to declare a vision and sense of togetherness. "We in Change UK, as we hope to be known, don't just dream about a fairer and better future for our country, we are determined to unleash it through hard work, passion and shared endeavour." Whilst some people rallied to the new party, because it offered something different, it's not at all clear what that different actually is. Having a name and a leader is not enough. To say that Change UK didn't catch the public's imagination is a massive understatement. The other political tribes clearly held far more loyal appeal. To me that's because it lacked a core purpose and place in the political spectrum.

## *A united purpose is the engine room of a tribe*

The obvious comparison is the Brexit Party which formed around former UKIP Leader Nigel Farage in 2019. Pushed away by the traditional parties, which hadn't listened, 31.6% of the voting population voted against the traditional 'status quo'. Pulled in by the simplicity of the message (the UK must leave the EU for its own good) and by the down to earth charisma of its leader, those same voters actively chose the change offered by the Brexit Party. As a result, with almost no backswing, the Brexit Party thrashed the traditional Conservative-Labour axis in the 2019 European Parliament elections. That was remarkable. A single issue cause can focus minds more than a mixture of policies. A compelling call to arms can catch a wave of dissatisfaction and ride it to election success.

Then came Boris Johnson with his "Get Brexit done" and "One Nation Conservatism" campaign slogans. By taking the initiative on the key issue of Brexit away from Nigel Farage's Brexit Party; and simultaneously taking the centre-ground from the Liberal Democrats, the Conservatives secured the biggest overall majority for over thirty years.

~~~~~

Where businesses are able to harness the power of the whole organisation to achieve common goals, then they can be truly successful. But organisations can be too restricted in their thinking. In business, companies can focus too narrowly on short-term financial rewards and concentrate too hard on the current year's profit and loss account. Not enough organisations direct enough energy into delivering rewards for all of their stakeholders and into planning for their long-term sustainability.

No person is economically independent. No business is either. If you are making goods or providing services, you need people to sell them to. If you need a component or product that you can't make yourself, you have to buy it from someone else. That inherent reliance on others applies to every company and every nation. Every organisation is directly or indirectly inter-connected to many other organisations. Even America's periods of protectionism have still involved trading overseas. As David Smith the Economics Editor of the Sunday Times puts it "The UK is an open economy. What happens in the rest of the World matters to us too."

# 1.6  BANDING TOGETHER IS NATURAL

Each country, city and organisation operates as the product of the collective behaviours and values of its people. Cities would never have been created without society working towards that. Plato [18] appreciated this inherent need when speaking of Athens "This City is what it is, because our citizens are what they are."

This is not to say that every group is good for us or good for society at large. There are positive, negative and neutral versions of grouping together. The nature of the group's vision of the future, its purpose for being together and its values will tell us the answer. Selfish,

---

[18] Plato was a Greek philosopher. He studied under Socrates and was influenced by the works of Pythagoras. In 387 BC he created the Academy which was a free study group for teaching others. Aristotle became his most famous student. The word academy is till found in education today.

discriminatory or violent groups are not good for society. They also create a need for other groups to exist, in order to hold them to account.

## Not every group is good for society

Whether you are inside or outside a group heavily influences how you feel about it. The term "old-boys club" tends to be used about a disproportionally male or public school environment, such as a business, club or society where someone's gender and background seem more important than their ability or work ethic. If you are on the inside, you might mistakenly see that elitist and insular thinking positively as it protects you. However, if you are on the outside, "old boys' club" becomes a very critical term. Instances of men giving jobs to other men, simply to avoid giving them to women are thankfully reducing by the day. Whilst members may perceive strength in belonging to an "old boys' club" its exclusivity is precisely what makes it vulnerable.

~~~~~

The bonds of fellowship within a tribe are evident across the animal kingdom. There are lessons there for us to follow. Prides of lions, herds of wildebeest, mobs of meerkats, bloats of hippos, towers of giraffes and cackles of hyenas all live, feed and defend themselves by working together. Another example of natural group strength comes from the sea.

Dolphins are a very sociable marine mammal, living and working together for feeding, self-defence and play. Dolphin groups are known as pods and range in size from two to several hundred dolphins, depending on the availability of food. They communicate with each other by a mixture of whistling, posture and touching. This combination of communication methods gives dolphins a unique form of language that allows them to function underwater. Without that collective understanding, they would all get lost or get in each other's way.

Dolphins use echolocation to find their prey. They send out high-pitched sounds hoping to bounce them back off a passing shoal of fish. When a dolphin detects an echo it swims off towards it, hoping to find fish. When a shoal is discovered, the pod is summoned. The dolphins then work hard to surround the shoal on all sides. When the shoal has been trapped, the dolphins take it in turns to swim through the shoal with their mouths open. A single dolphin couldn't hunt like this in the open sea. When fish are hard to find, dolphin pods cleverly follow seabirds, whales and trawlers to help them find food. Dolphins constantly have to adapt to changes in their "market".

Almost every group in the animal kingdom has a predator. Dolphins are no exceptions. Sharks, orcas and killer whales all hunt and eat dolphins. Individually dolphins are vulnerable, but living together means they can aggressively defend their pod from attack. Fully aware of the dangers that the pod might face, adult male dolphins swim on the outside of the pod to explore the sea and protect the group from attack. Alone they are vulnerable but together they provide a strong defensive force. When a pod does come under attack, the adult males work together as a team to force the predator away. If a fellow dolphin is injured in an attack, the other members of the pod will help lift it up to the surface to allow it to breathe. Dolphins maximise the benefits of being in a pod to every dolphin's joint benefit.

## Alone we can be vulnerable

Dolphins journey together for very long distances, migrating as the seasons change. They cleverly save their energy by swimming in the slipstream of ships, which is known as bow-riding. They often synchronise their movements as a pod, spy-hoping out of the water in unison. All the time they are checking on each other and keeping their pod safe.

Despite their tribal nature, dolphins aren't tied to one pod for life. They are very pragmatic and can change their pod whenever they like, especially if another pod offers a better chance of giving them food. But dolphins will always choose to be within a pod rather than being on their own.

Humans band together in businesses because of the financial security that companies provide them with. But like dolphins, workers leave their jobs where there are sustainability concerns about their current employer. Some will also leave where there are greater rewards on offer at another organisation. Leaders should always be aware of the market forces in play. Unless your organisation offers all its workers enough "fish" they will be on the look out for another pod to join. And by "fish" I don't just mean money.

~~~~~

We may still deny it, but the truth is that we don't operate very well on our own. But too much of modern interaction is superficial and doesn't fulfil us. Too many of our relationships are virtual or transient. Not everyone we know cares about us.

If you had a crisis how many people would offer you help? Wouldn't it be great to say everyone you know? The truth is likely to be far from that ideal.

Similarly, if everyone you know had a crisis, how many of them would you help? Everyone you know? It's probably fewer than you'd care to openly admit. Many of our relationships lack depth and warmth. Shallow, narrow lives aren't enjoyable or not healthy for us. We are closer to being alone than we think we are.

Statistically, people living alone suffer a greater risk of depression and live shorter lives. Researchers in Finland[19] found that during an eight year period of study, people living alone bought 80% more anti-depressants than the people who lived with someone else.

In the UK, living alone is a growing phenomenon. Due to higher divorce rates and increasing life expectancy[20] there were 2.43 million

---

[19] The study was conducted by the Finnish Institute of Occupational Health in 2000 and was published in BioMed Central's public health journal.
[20] According to the Office of National Statistics a male born in 2014 to 2016 had a 21% chance, and a female a 32% chance, of surviving to at least age 90.

45 to 64-year-olds living on their own in the UK in 2017, compared with 1.59 million in 1996[21]. More people are lonely than ever before. More people than ever need to find a new tribe to belong to.

## *Shallow, narrow lives aren't enjoyable*

The benefits of people working in groups are there for all to see. Incredible feats have been achieved by teams of people focused on a single project, feats that one individual couldn't have achieved alone. Could one person have single-handedly built a pyramid during 2,600 B.C. in Ancient Egypt? Or could one person have constructed the Colosseum in Rome in AD 70? The answer is an emphatic no.

With modern engineering and technology, it's debatable whether that's even possible now. One person can operate machinery but that's a false premise. To truly build a pyramid alone, you'd have to design and build a digger and a crane yourself first (without any existing plans or parts). Otherwise you would be using learning obtained from other people. One person simply couldn't invent and build everything needed within their lifetime.

~~~~

However strong we are as an individual, we already rely on the assistance of strangers every day. We get daily help from a multiple sources like shops, restaurants, petrol stations, businesses, schools and colleges, hospitals, local authorities and the emergency services amongst others. Virtually no one can manage alone.

Did anyone really achieve anything great without any help from someone else? Just because you don't give credit to other people for their contributions, doesn't mean they didn't help you. We work quicker, better and for longer, when we work with other people.

We can join tribes and work for common goals with people who seem similar. We can also involve others who at first appear different to us, by checking our unconscious bias and concentrating on establishing

---

[21] According to the Office for National Statistics (ONS).

a joint purpose. We are more likely to succeed in a joint enterprise because of the social benefits, as well as all the shared ideas and energy. Groups of people find another level entirely when they operate as tribes (and not just a disparate collection of individuals).

~~~~~

Tribalism is sometimes wrongly perceived as representing aggression, exclusion and violence. Those are just characteristics displayed by some extreme tribes, not tribes in general. Those same unpleasant traits can also be found in any individual. Any person could be aggressive, selfish or violent. These traits are not unique to tribes. They are human.

But defining tribalism as just a synonym for aggression is completely wrong. Tribalism is the search for common good. Super-tribalism is where every single stakeholder works towards that common good.

# 1.7 TRIBES ARE MORE THAN JUST A SWARM

Swarming is the collective behaviour of self-propelled, free thinking insects. Flocking, herding and shoaling are other terms for the same form of collective movement. These are all known as emergent behaviours because they don't have a coordinating or controlling mind behind them.

Despite travelling rapidly in close proximity, shoals of fish are able to move as part of the same flow. Rather than being chaotic, every individual fish somehow avoids colliding with every other one. When a shoal swims off, a sense of order forms instantly. Driven by a need to escape from a predator or to look for food, a collective structure occurs. Each fish takes constant reference points from the position of the other fish around it. By controlling and regulating its own movement in relation to those nearby, the whole shoal becomes aligned and appears to move as one.

Humans don't naturally display the same swarming or shoaling pattern as insects, birds, fish or animals. Our freedom to think as individuals and our focus on meeting our own personal needs naturally propels us all in separate directions. That is unless there is a united purpose which acts as a magnet and pulls us all together as one. Then we have a reason to regulate our movement and form part of the flow. We need to choose to be part of a flow.

~ ~ ~ ~ ~

Tribalism really represents a group of people who are bonded by unity and togetherness. Tribalism is the glue that makes us belong to something bigger. Coming together as a group with a common vision, purpose and set of values can generate tribal power and get big things done. Tribal power requires each member of the tribe to be united and committed to the tribe's collective purpose. That's a question of choice. Joining a tribe means willingly becoming part of something bigger and greater than you are as an individual. That wider tribe could be made up of family members, or friends, work colleagues, gym buddies or neighbours. Some people call this collaborative working. To be tribal, a group needs to be more than just a loose connection of collaborators. And it is only through a tribe that you can generate the strength of tribal power.

> *Joining a tribe means willingly becoming part of something bigger and greater than you are as an individual.*

Tribes will have their own natural energy once they are up and running. But getting a tribe moving off in the right direction takes a concerted and sustained effort. Choosing a purpose with mass appeal is likely to make much faster and easier progress that a niche purpose which only benefits a few people. Where a tribe's purpose has a wider benefit for society that can be more motivating and rewarding than a purely business benefit alone. Whatever purposes your tribes have, you won't stay a member of any of them if there's nothing in them that motivates you.

~ ~ ~ ~ ~

When people work on a joint project they can either act independently, or they can choose to coordinate their actions. Independent action might bring coincidental success. But it risks major conflicts, collisions and gaps. Coordinated action is more likely to bring intended success.

The process of taking reference points from everything around you isn't automatic for humans. Rather than just setting off and trying to avoid bumping into each other, there needs to be a controlling philosophy in place first. To streamline anything, there needs to be clarity over who is doing what, how and when it needs to be done. Human movement can be controlled by reaching agreement over the direction and pace of travel. By choosing to coordinate our operations, we can create a tribal flow that allows everyone to move as one together.

Being prepared to invest your time and effort in something is an essential commitment to any project, especially when no one else can see what you're doing. It is hard work just to keep on track and stay within the flow. It's even harder if you have no clear direction or outcomes in mind. That's why much greater things can be achieved if a project team has the same vision, purpose, values in mind. Does your organisation share those things?

## Create a tribal flow

Artistic swimming (formerly known as Synchronised Swimming) is a sport which involves aspects of swimming, gymnastics and dancing. Despite taking a good deal of criticism over the years Artistic Swimming is now acknowledged to be a fully fledged sport. With competitors unable to touch the bottom of the swimming pool, it is extremely demanding, as the routines can last up to four minutes in length.

Artistic swimming requires a combination of precision timing, physical strength, aerobic endurance, athleticism and artistic merit. The team events require all of those individual skills, together with excellent synchronisation. The flow of movement is the visible end result of all the planning, training and co-ordination of every team member. An artistic swimming team needs to recruit the strongest possible individuals, create a tribal culture and environment, agree a set of routines; and put in many hours of purposeful practice, all set to music and time. The result is supposed to look effortless. When everything gels, it looks like it's easy. However, the work required to get an artistic swimming team to that point is anything but easy. Creating a flow of movement takes hard work from everyone.

Employers can help themselves by creating the culture, environment and vision, purpose and values to achieve a common flow. In the human world co-ordination rarely happens automatically or accidentally. Organisations have to facilitate and create their own unique swarming effect.

~~~~~

Marvel is the biggest movie franchise of all time, having grossed over $17 billion. The Marvel Comic Universe (MCU) contains dozens of super-heroes. The most famous are probably Iron Man, Captain America, Spiderman and the Hulk. Each character has super-human abilities (through the use of technology in Iron Man's case). Each super-hero is repeatedly tested by powerful enemies. The list of Marvel's super-heroes is long and also includes Thor, Scarlet Witch, Black Widow, Vision, Iron Patriot, Falcon and Ant-Man amongst many others.

When a super-hero faces a threat that's too big to cope with individually, Marvel evens the odds up, by teaming that hero up with other super-heroes. They form groups like the X-Men, the Fantastic Four and the Avengers. Despite clashing egos and differences of opinion, the need to defeat a shared enemy creates a united purpose they can all get behind. Alone they will all die. Together they can become almost unbeatable.

That is until Thanos comes to the Earth in search of the Infinity stones. At that point the Avengers cannot match him alone. So Marvel then raises the odds even further and draws together super-heroes from right across the MCU to fight the Infinity War, including Black Panther, Guardians of the Galaxy and Dr. Strange. In Avengers: Infinity War and Avengers: Endgame the clear underlying message is that even super-heroes are more powerful when they work together.

## Tribe members assemble

As Tony Stark (Iron Man) says to Loki in Avengers Assemble[22] "Yeah, takes us a while to get any traction, I'll give you that one. But let's do a head count here: your brother the demigod; a super soldier, a living legend who kind of lives up to the legend; a man with breath-taking anger management issues; a couple of master assassins, and YOU, big fella, you've managed to piss off every single one of them."

Every organisation should aim its recruitment high, super high. Assemble the best characters you can, teach them the skill-sets they need; and give them a united purpose to swarm around. Tribe members assemble.

---

[22] Marvel's 2012 film Avengers Assemble was the first of its Avengers films.

## 1.8  WE ARE FUNDAMENTALLY TRIBAL

The World isn't populated by eight billion nomads, hermits and wanderers. We don't live our lives alone. We live together, side by side, with other people. Whether we immediately accept it or not, we already belong to tribes. Many are benign and co-exist together quite happily. Others are in direct geographical, sporting or commercial conflict. We are probably members of both kinds of tribes.

Some of our tribes are more obvious than others. Some of them are much more important to us than others. Your family is the most obvious tribe and it may be your most important one. Where you were born created a series of tribes for you, based on the communities of the town or city, county and country of your birth. The schools you went to and the organisations you've worked for provide more of your tribes. Then you can add your politics, religion and each of the sports teams that you support. Your tribes probably don't stop there. You may have other beliefs, interests and passions.

Your tribes can also include the people who go to the same gym, coffee shop, church or pub as you. They may also be groups of people from the same trades union, charity, or voluntary group. Then there are fellow users of your social media channels and vlogs you watch, as well as fan groups around the films, television programmes or bands you really like. They can be people you meet in person, people you meet online or members of a WhatsApp group that keeps you all in touch 24/7/365.

### *We are fundamentally tribal*

The needs of others can also motivate people to pull together to achieve a common goal. Good causes can create a tribe that reaches far beyond family, birthplace, work and geographical boundaries. Female Emancipation, Free Nelson Mandela, Feed the World, Save the Whale, Save the Planet and End Poverty are just a few examples of where groups of people have formed around a cause and become a tribal movement. Each one can bring positive and lasting change. You may belong some of these tribes too.

There are always local causes to get involved with too, whether that's community allotments, gardening for the disabled, city regeneration or political independence for your region. At work you can champion causes with a wider stakeholder focus, such as supporting local charities, or, reducing carbon emissions by doing things like using sustainable energy, becoming paper-less or bringing in low-energy lighting.

Each group of people you belong to could be a separate tribe. Each one of us belongs to a unique set of tribes. Everyone does, but no one else shares exactly the same combination as you.

## *We can all be influenced and inspired*

Tribes are everywhere. What clothing brands we wear, what cars we drive and what coffee we drink could add us into more tribes. Even tea has got into the action. Yorkshire Tea has created its own tribe. This retail tribe phenomenon has been because we can be influenced and inspired by all the brands pitching to us. Once we start to follow the crowd and adopt a new brand or cause, we join another movement. Successful commercial organisations work tirelessly to create tribes around their products and services. They are constantly trying to persuade their regular customers to stay loyal and new consumers to join their tribes.

We live in a society where people have quick, shallow opinions. We can be judged by the brand labels that we wear and the personal labels that people attribute to us. But our lives should be about more than that. Whilst some tribes can be limited to superficial brand followers, other more meaningful tribes can tap into much deeper motivations to power themselves. Many could be far more successful.

~~~~~

A 'tribe' could be said to be an artificial construct is entirely man-made. But the collective attraction to be together is more natural and magnetic than that. Tribes form around shared needs. They are the obvious end product where resources are limited and have to be fought for. Tribes can take the away the loneliness of single living and remove the boredom of lone working. Tribes add a form of social sustenance, feeding our hunger to belong to something beyond ourselves.

The word 'tribe' comes from the Latin word tribus. It is used synonymously with the Greek word phyle, which means tribe, race, or clan. Each word describes a group of people who are linked together by common history, purpose, symbols and rituals. Historically, tribal life was characterised by geographical and cultural isolation, where small groups lived in harmony with the land and natural world around them. Those tribes worked together for the mutual protection, survival and common benefit of the whole group. Those were the hallmarks of a traditional tribe.

Many modern tribes still operate in a close geographical area. But increasingly often, modern tribes live separately amongst the wider population, operating together as a collective but living remotely from one another. Tribes can reach out locally or right across the World. You may belong to both traditional and modern tribes. We are naturally and fundamentally tribal, but why?

It's because, without our human relationships we are vulnerable. We tend to turn inwards on ourselves, lose our self-confidence, become insecure and limit the lives we lead. Being part of a tribe, but Co-dependency is generally better than sole dependency.

~~~~~

By focusing on joint and common goals, we can trick our unconscious bias into seeing similarity instead of seeing diversity. By thinking "we" instead of thinking "me" people can overcome their narrow, singular thinking. That change of perspective isn't easy for everybody. There's a sliding scale of openness to new things and some people struggle to ever think beyond themselves. The more focus an organisation has on joint thinking, joint decision-making and joint goals the more chance there is of affecting the change from "me" to "we". A clear, joint goal can focus everyone's minds on achieving the same end result.

Having a unifying purpose can bind individuals and even strangers together. That can happen at all levels and in all sizes, for example by setting up a local orchestra, creating a national charity or rallying to the defence of your country in wartime.

Tribes can form around all sorts of causes, for example around re-wilding, which is a form of nature conversation. Amazing work is being done on the American Prairie Reserve in Montana. The American Prairie Reserve is a wildlife conservation area that has been created by gradually acquiring private land that bordered onto public land. By stitching contiguous land together, tract by tract, the American Prairie Reserve now spans over three million acres. All this work has been funded by millions of dollars of donations. The non-profit organisation that runs the APR has saved this land for generations to come.

## Look for similarity of thinking

Another example of how a tribe can be pulled together around a cause is Common Goal, the initiative launched by Juan Mata. The Common Goal website explains its purpose "The idea is simple. Common Goal's members pledge 1% of their earnings to a central fund. And together we allocate this fund to high-impact organisations that harness the power of football to advance the United Nations Global Goals." Over 100 male and female players have signed up, as well as Liverpool's Manager Jürgen Klopp.

To see the difference between a tribe and a bunch of people, you only need to compare the European and American Ryder Cup teams over the last ten years. One is a fully fledged tribe, the other is barely even a team. The passion and influence of talisman Ian Poulter cannot be underestimated. Like athlete Kriss Akabusi, Ian Poulter has found another level of performance from a team dynamic. Not only does he play his best golf as part of the Ryder Cup team[23], but he also inspires his teammates to raise their games too, by convincing them to putt[24]

[23] Ian Poulter has never lost a singles match at a Ryder Cup.
[24] A poor pun. Sorry.

the team ahead of themselves. Ian Poulter is not the Ryder Cup Captain (yet) so it is not for him to drive[25] others yet, but he inspires them. Known as the Postman "because he always delivers" Ian Poulter is also nicknamed "Mr. Ryder Cup" because of his influence on five wins out of the six Ryder Cups he's played in. Ian Poulter is a superb Ryder Cup golfer because he is tribal.

We can also have power and influence within our own tribes, helping to shape the pathway ahead. We just need to understand what our tribes are and how we can influence them.

Your existing tribes may offer you an opportunity to get involved and promote your own values, purposes and beliefs. However, if your tribes have purposes or values that you don't agree with, you could always join a different tribe or start your own.

~~~~~

So can we freely choose which tribes we're part of? The truth is that we are all subject to mental and physical limits and constraints. Our birth family, birthplace, work, marriage and hobbies 'rule in' certain tribes for us and by definition 'rule out' certain others. We all have statutory and contractual obligations that we are legally required to comply with. We also have moral and financial obligations to other people that influence our decision-making. As well as those external constraints we also have our own internal controls, beliefs and motivations that drive our actions. We are individuals, but heavily influenced individuals. Without a clear path ahead to follow, we can all get lost.

Knowing that our obligations can control and restrict us, we have to stay vigilant. If their power and influence has a negative effect we should reject it. For example, our tribes should never use force, fear or intimidation on us. If you ever find yourself inside a tribe that rules by oppression, you need to change your tribe or change your tribe.

Alone we can make a difference, but as part of a group we can help to achieve the purposes and visions that we have in common with other

---

[25] This pun was unintentional so I left it in.

people. Our hearts and minds could be won over by something much bigger and more powerful than we ever thought. We just need to find something inspirational to believe in. We need to be alert to the possibilities and benefits within a tribe. We mustn't rule anyone out as a fellow tribe member based simply on our own internal assumptions and biases.

*"The World is closing in. Did you ever think that we could be so close, like brothers?"*[26]

So what can we take from all this? Which tribes will help us be successful? How can we adapt our own organisations to make them more successful?

We can learn a great deal from studying other groups in society and applying that learning to our own tribes. That insight can teach us how best to adapt and evolve our own group. But that's not all we can learn. Understanding another tribe's place in the World teaches us about the World that our tribe is part of. That insight helps us to position our tribe in the best possible place to sustain its future.

As Charles Darwin famously observed, it's the ability of a species to adapt to change that sets it apart. It's not just about who is the strongest now, it's about who can keep on adapting and improving. Generating sustainable tribal power can give a successful present and future. Sadly not every tribe has a future to match its present or its past.

The Maasai people live in Southern Kenya and Northern Tanzania along the Great Rift Valley as they have done for centuries. Their society is very structured, comprising sixteen sections (IIoshon). The Maasai live in circular kraals, protected by a fence of acacia thorns to keep lions and other wild animals out. Everyone in Maasai society has a set role to play. The warriors build the kraal and provide the security. The women build the houses (Inkajijik), collect the water

---

[26] A lyric from Wind of Change by The Scorpions.

and firewood, milk the cattle and cook for the family. The boys herd the cattle. The elders act as the advisers and directors for their Inkang (which is the basic Maasai unit where the elders and their families live). There is a simplicity and order about their way of life. One Maasai prayer neatly sums up Maasai society "Meishoo iyiook enkai inkishu o-nkera." The English translation is "May Creator give us cattle and children".

Even though the Maasai are semi-nomadic, they still live in their sections for the most part. However in drought years the Maasai take a more communal approach to land. In times of drought, section boundaries are ignored and everyone is free to roam and graze their livestock where they wish. According to Maasai tradition and values, no one should be denied access to natural resources such as water and land. Sadly those drought years are becoming increasingly common due to global warming, the lack of access to water and the impact of major commercial projects which are syphoning off more and more water.

## External pressures and influences are shrinking the land and resources around them

Maasai society is rich with ceremonies and rites of passage. They include Enkipaata, Emuratta, Eunoto, Eokoto e-kule, Enkang oo-nkiri and Olngesherr. Of all the Maasai initiations, circumcision is the most important rite of passage as it moves a person from childhood to adulthood. But with rising global opposition to genital mutilation, many young Maasai women no longer undergo genital circumcision.

This traditional rite of passage for both sexes gave tribe members their place in Maasai society. Now a new approach is taking over, due to intense Western pressure. This clash of cultures is gradually being won by the outsiders. As a result, Maasai culture is being eroded, just like its land. Many would say this change is for the better. They might say that genital mutilation is unnecessary and humiliating. Others would argue that each organisation should be free to choose its own way.

Despite its proud heritage and culture, the Maasai Association website reports troubled times. "Maasai society, which once was a proud and self-sufficient society, is now facing many social-economic and political challenges. The level of poverty among the Maasai people is beyond conceivable height. It is sad to see a society that had a long tradition of pride, being a beggar for relief food because of imposed foreign concepts of development. The future of the Maasai is uncertain at this point. One thing, however, is certain that the Maasai culture is quickly eroding at the expense of civilisation".

The Maasai approach to life doesn't please everyone, especially on the contentious issue of female circumcision. But circumcision isn't the only Maasai tradition that's being driven out of existence. It seems somewhat ironic that "civilisation" is crushing the Maasai people's way of life.

*Every tribe with a clear vision, purpose*
*and values can attract and repel*
*depending on how much you agree*

The challenges faced by the Maasai raise the important question 'What makes one civilisation more "right" than another one?' Maybe the test is one of religion, morality and legality? Or maybe the tribe that's "right" is simply the most aggressive and demanding one of all. The more powerful you are, the less anyone tells you what to do. That form of hierarchy may work for you if you are part of the strongest tribe. But what if you belong to the outmoded tribe? What if you're the victim of heavy external pressure to change your culture? How would you react to having your traditions removed, eroded or banned?

If strength is the ultimate arbiter of what is "right" then theoretically the most powerful tribe will eventually swallow up every other tribe, forcing them all to abandon their heritage, culture and traditions. The threat of that increases with every advance in weaponry, but so far no one tribe has reached the tipping point of lasting dominance. The success of tribes and empires has proven to be cyclical because no tribe has adapted fast enough to the threats around it to stay permanently in front. The inherent power within tribes has stopped us being forced to become one bland, homogenised, vanilla-flavoured nation of peoples. That tribal power and resilience has also helped the World stand firm against oppression.

The World is full of multi-coloured, multi-purpose and multi-cultural tribes providing checks and balances on each other, just like nature does in the wild. Despite all the challenges, some tribes have always done better than others. But what sets each of them apart? What makes some successful and others struggle or die out?

## 1.9 TRIBAL ACTION PLAN

Your team, project group or organisation may already be high-performing. If it is, then understanding why that's the case will help you to keep it up at that level. If it isn't high-performing then understanding why it isn't will allow you to improve its performance level. Understanding produces insight and opportunities. Failing to understand your own tribe will mean standing in failure.

- Have you thought about what everyone else in your tribe wants? Are every stakeholder's needs aligned or do they conflict? How can you align everybody's needs better?

- If your tribe needs to grow, then spread the word about the 'needs' that your tribe can meet. Who else can you meet those needs for? Tell them and they may want to join.

- What other needs can your tribe meet? How can it look after its members better? The more your tribe means to each and every member, the more engaged in it they'll be.

~~~~~

There are a number of differentiating elements in any tribe and I will now describe and illustrate each one. Afterwards we need to look at how tribal power is generated and what makes tribes become super-tribes. Like life, tribes are what we make of them.

*"There is no destiny.*
*There is only free will."*[27]

---

[27] Artorious Castus (Arthur) in King Arthur 2004.

# 2. THE SIGNS AND RITUALS OF TRIBES

## 2.0 EVERY TRIBE IS UNIQUE

Every organisation sees the World from its own unique perspective, just like every person does. Businesses, sports teams, schools, political parties, charities and every other organisation has its own unique combination of elements, stakeholders and ways of working. Over time, each organisation develops its own hierarchy, behaviours, signs and rituals. Its traditions begin and are repeated through time. Organisations acquire a form of personality, based on their vision, purpose and values. People who join either conform to the tribe's social norms, or they leave.

Organisations at their basic level are just a group structure. In that form, they cannot have sustainable success. Winning organisations are groups that have become something much greater than the sum of their parts. They have become an entity which makes its own tribal footprint on the World. At that point, organisations become identifiable as tribes from their specific blend of tribal elements. Each one is unique. No two tribes look, sound or operate in quite the same way. The fewer tribal elements your group has, the less it will look, sound or feel like a tribe.

Overall tribes can have up to twenty distinguishing features. Without a good majority of them, it is difficult to call any organisation a tribe. Each feature helps to create and maintain a sense of tribe. Each of them should support the Tribe's purpose, vision and values (VPV) and each one should be aligned and incorporated into the tribe's strategy.

A tribe's traditions, signs and rituals are the glue that binds people together. They provide a sense of routine belonging and homeliness. They bring a feeling of safety, comfort and reassurance from their togetherness. An organisation with positive, healthy and inclusive signs and rituals is in a good place. An organisation where everyone does their own thing is not. That type of organisation is definitely not a tribe.

Historically, being born into a tribe meant a lifetime of commitment. It was inconceivable that a Spartan would want to be Athenian, or a Sioux warrior would want to become Cheyenne. In centuries past, changing tribes was an anathema. These days' people will change almost anything about themselves and their lives to be 'happy'.

Nowadays our commitment is more voluntary. We can choose to stay or leave almost anything, including our job, marriage and even our gender. In truth the length of our commitment is the length of our notice period, or the time it takes to make a change. So if anyone can quit a tribe at any point, how can you build one and hold it together?

~~~~~

As I mentioned earlier, the essentials of a modern tribe can be summarised into six core concepts. They are all immensely powerful to any organisation. They are:

**(T) Traditions and heritage**
*(how the past affects the present)*

**(R) Rules, ceremonies and rituals**
*(how things are done)*

**(I) Illustration through stories, songs and art**
*(expressing the special and unique)*

**(B) Brand and symbols**
*(how the tribe is presented to the outside world)*

**(E) Establish a clear vision, purpose and values**
*(reason for being and direction of travel)*

**(S) Stakeholder alignment**
*(how tribal power is generated)*

Asking how your tribe deals with each of them, gives you six themes to address. But underpinning these six tribal concepts are the twenty elements which help to set each tribe apart from very other. They are the twenty signs of tribe.

To really understand a tribe we need to break it down into all of its constituent parts. Those elements will be of varying importance depending on the tribe in question, but they may all have a role to play. Each tribe can be analysed according to these elements and how aligned they all are. Your tribes can be analysed in exactly the same way.

The twenty elements of a tribe are: purpose, heritage, structure and hierarchy, rules, nicknames, values, spiritual homeland, language, stories, art, songs, colours/uniform, ceremonies, badges/logos, symbols, brand, routines, opposition, records and fragrance/flavour. Each combination of these elements makes and distinguishes each tribe from any other. I will now explain and illustrate each one using examples of historical and modern tribes.

## 2.1 TRIBAL PURPOSE

Tribes form in order to fulfil a purpose. Tribal purposes vary enormously, whether they are narrow and local or vast and global in their aspirations. They can include bringing up children, winning a cup or championship, building a successful business, driving global change or just forming a friendship group to make gym visits more pleasurable. Tribes can be well-planned and highly organised, or they n be an instant response to a crisis. The reason for a tribe's existence ld explain what it is all about. The purpose should act as a call to

A tribe's purpose should be the control dial for every tribal decision, the hand on the tribal tiller. A tribe's purpose should be its driving force, its fuel. "If you build it, he will come.[28]"

But too often that central purpose is blunted by disinterest, self-interest, failing management, greedy ownership or selfish leadership. These can all gradually eat away at an organisation's core purpose until they can be battled and defeated. What has got in the way of your tribe's core purpose?

*A tribe's purpose should be*
*its driving force, its fuel*

If a tribe is worth forming and holding together that must be because its purpose is still valid and intact. Stating its purpose and sticking to it is absolutely crucial, or it won't be achieved. There are many examples of tribal purpose throughout this book. Your organisation needs to know its own purpose. It could adopt or adapt another tribe's purpose, but would anyone engage with it? Why was your tribe formed? Why does it exist? For whose benefit? What is its tribal purpose? Is it clear to everyone? Is it still relevant? Do you still believe in it?

~~~~~

Sir Alex Ferguson was the Manager of East Stirlingshire, St. Mirren and Aberdeen FC in Scottish football and then the Manager of Manchester United in England. His purpose was to win every championship and every cup. Within that wider purpose, he aimed to win every single football match. Sir Alex is quoted as saying "I never played for a draw." His philosophy demanded consistence and unrelenting excellence. His two purposes fitted neatly together. One was a sub-set of the other. They became the combined purposes at both Aberdeen and Manchester United, creating strength and unity at those clubs.

---

[28] From Field of Dreams and about "Shoeless" Joe Jackson.

Distilling his purpose down to winning matches and trophies allowed him to focus on the top end of the table and the business end of the season year after year. Sir Alex fought for every single win and together they added up to cups and championships. Sir Alex Ferguson wanted to dominate Scottish, then English and European football. As a Manager he won 3 Scottish League Championships, 1 UEAFA Cup and 4 Scottish Cups as the Manager of Aberdeen. He then went on to win an astonishing 38 trophies as Manager of Manchester United including 13 Premier League titles, 2 Champions League trophies and 5 F.A. Cups. Sir Alex Ferguson stuck to his purpose and it made Aberdeen and Manchester United greater than ever before.

Since Sir Alex's retirement, David Moyes, Louis Van Gaal and Jose Mourinho have all tried to continue the same purpose at Manchester United. Jose Mourinho won the F.A. Community Shield, EFL Cup and Europa League in his first season, but even he couldn't keep it going for a second season. By the time he left United, the culture at the club had become dysfunctional and under-performing. But however dysfunctional things are within a tribe, a period of Winter can always lead into Spring.

In December 2018 Ole Gunnar Solskjaer was appointed Manchester United on a temporary basis. As a former Manchester United player and scorer of the winning goal in the 1999 Champions League final, Ole knew how the club had worked under Sir Alex Ferguson and what its supporters now expect. By appointing Mike Phelan, Sir Alex Ferguson's former right-hand, Ole helped to reinforce the old messages and standards. The team is once again trying to dominate its opponents. It is no surprise that United's results immediately improved.

Former Manchester United player Teddy Sheringham was interviewed on Radio 5Live about why things might have improved. He started by explaining that there is a "Manchester United Way" of playing. In a phrase Manchester United "take the game to the opposition". The emphatic way Teddy said it showed how deeply ingrained it was. In Sheringham's day Manchester United believed they could beat any other team in the World. United's players were full of confidence in themselves, their Manager and each other. In every single game the Manchester United players backed themselves to win. There was no time or space for self-doubt. In Sir. Alex Ferguson's era, Manchester United never, ever gave too much respect to the opposition. Why? Because that reduces your own strength. You can almost hear Sir. Alex saying "If we play the United way, we can beat anyone".

Both David Moyes and Louis Van Gaal struggled to live in the vast red shadow of Sir. Alex Ferguson (especially as Sir. Alex is still at the club). After their failures the next appointment was critical to restoring United's fortunes. Jose Mourinho was the most successful candidate with major trophies in Portugal, England, Italy and Spain. Jose Mourinho also had the personal self-confidence to step out of the Ferguson shadow. But to many his appointment was a surprise. Jose Mourinho is a winner but he is also appears to be a destructive force. His trophies have come at a wider cost.

*A group's self-confidence is more important than a leader's self- confidence.*

Mourinho's approach to attacking football is to defend first and counter-attack when you can. Stopping the opposition from scoring does keep a game tight, but it doesn't strike fear. It doesn't yell 'We are Manchester United'. The Ferguson and Mourinho styles of football are diametrically opposed. That clash in styles might have been glossed over at a lesser club, but Jose Mourinho was following a Manager with an equally extraordinary history; and he was joining England's leading club.

When it came to how to get the best out of the players The "Manchester United Way" and the "Jose Mourinho Way" were also incompatible. Ferguson's 'Father' figure used a parental style. The players and staff personally felt his support and his disappointment. The players felt he cared about them as people and they wanted to please him above anyone else. Mourinho appears to have an 'every man for himself' approach with each player being responsible for delivering their part of the game plan. There doesn't seem to be any sense of caring or togetherness. Mourinho appears to see himself as a 'Benevolent Demi-God' whose kindness in selecting a player should be enough to make any player grateful. Not enough of his players seem to feel he cared about them as people. It seems that too many of them felt like pawns on his Chess board. Some of the notable exceptions seem to be the Chelsea players from his first stint in England. There is a closeness there that Mourinho hasn't been able to replicate since. What did he do there that was different? It was successful and felt like a whole of something. If Jose Mourinho could replicate those relationships elsewhere he could have a period of sustained success.

Let's be clear. Everyone respects what Jose Mourinho has achieved. You cannot write off his trophy haul because he is a difficult person. His success is extraordinary. In fact, it's all the more impressive because of his character flaws. However, just like Sir. Brian Clough at Leeds, his way wasn't his United's way. Jose Mourinho was following a Manager with an equally extraordinary history. One approach had to give. In short, the "Manchester United Way" would have had to fundamentally change if Mourinho was to be successful over a long period. That unnatural tension raised two big questions. Which type of football is more enjoyable to play? Which type is more successful? In the highly competitive World we live in, the second is almost impossible without the first.

After the Ferguson era, Manchester United supporters were used to 'no fear football' where attacking was always the way to defeat the opposition. 'Attacking' is a positive way to win matches rather than a weakness in your defence. Which players wouldn't prefer to attack all game and outscore the opposition to win? Which type of football is more enjoyable to play?

Inside Mourinho's head his tactics and approach was right. But his communication made some of the Manchester United players bristle and rebel. The results quickly stopped coming for Mourinho. After the success and enjoyment of the Ferguson era, why should United settle for a focus on defence? That shows weakness and fear. It respected the opposition too much. It gave the opposition too easy a time. It was not the "Manchester United Way." Who accepted it? The players didn't. The supporters didn't. The club didn't.

The most striking differences between Mourinho and Ferguson are firstly that Ferguson is truly loved and secondly that his legacy lived on in his former players and club officials. Ole Gunnar Solskjaer is one such former player. When United appointed him it was effectively re-appointing Sir. Alex Ferguson. The "Manchester United Way" is now once more the "Manchester United Way" once again.

~~~~~

The Pantomime is an eccentric British institution. For a few weeks at Christmas every year, Pantomimes take place in theatres and local halls up and down the country. The basic premise takes a well known fairytale like Cinderella or Aladdin and twists it for comedy value. Gender roles are swapped for comedic effect, so the Dame is played by a man; and the principal boy is played by a woman[29]. Audiences are encouraged to cheer, boo and sing along. A pantomime is a short-lived season of fun.

Each pantomime has its own cast and crew, formed from a mix of well-known stars, unknown professionals and local amateurs. Their joint purpose is to put on a particular show and entertain their audiences for the show's brief run. That one-off group of actors and crew bonds tightly for a brief period. For the time they're together they have an intense working relationship doing rehearsals and two shows a day seven days a week. Their combined reliance on each other gives them a single, temporary purpose. Comedian Bobby Davro regularly works in pantomime. For the duration of the show he describes the team's relationship as being "like a family". After the pantomime finishes, that family bond is permanently broken and everyone goes their own separate way. That repetitive process of bonding and separating must be hard.

~~~~~

The Finnish have a history of gathering together for accomplishing communal tasks and fundraising. This community purpose is called a talkoot. In times gone by, a communal talkoot provided manual

---

[29] An idea taken from the Tudor "Feast of Fools".

labour to others for major projects they couldn't achieve on their own. Examples included field clearing, crop planting and barn raising.

Subbotniks are a form of semi-compulsory community service which is almost expected. The concept began in Russia after the 1917 Revolution. Voluntary weekend working was effectively a Government requirement. Modern subbotniks can help to collect rubbish or recyclable material from the streets.

Restricting a tribal purpose to a single project can help to keep that project well-focused and get it Finnished[30].

~~~~~

The importance of purpose cannot be overstated. A common purpose is the cornerstone of a modern tribe. Without a defining and unifying purpose there is no tribe. Most organisations start with good intentions. They set out to create an inclusive tribe. But without conscious monitoring, many lose their way and drift into a single financial purpose, making profit for the owners. Nearly every organisation could do more to review, clarify and agree its purpose.

A genuinely tribal purpose needs to pass seven tests:

1. **Is it inclusive to all the tribe's members and stakeholders?**

2. **Does it offer a fair and equitable distribution of the benefits it offers?**

3. **Is it motivational to all the tribe's stakeholders? The positive effect of (1) & (2) will help.**

4. **Is it succinct and memorable? A single phrase or sentence is best.**

5. **Is it clear and unambiguous?**

---

[30] Deliberate misspelling.

6. **Is it aspirational and still achievable? It needs to be worth doing & worth trying to do.**

7. **Is it dynamic and exciting enough to persuade new people to join the cause?**

What is your tribe's purpose? Is its meaning clear? Is there a need for it? Does the whole tribe know and understand what it means in practice? Is everyone fully committed to the same purpose? Is the tribe's decision-making properly tested against its purpose? Is your tribe's core purpose front and centre of everything? If not, why not?

## 2.2 TRIBAL HERITAGE

Heritage is something that's both handed on from the past and which is still important and relevant today. Heritage has a value, although it's not necessarily financial. It could be in the form of a language, building, symbol or tradition.

Tribal heritage is the path and inheritance that has led the tribe to where it is today. If a tribe has been around for decades or even centuries, its heritage is likely to play a big part in how it operates now. Oxford and Cambridge Universities have built their heritage over successive decades. The mere mention of their names is enough to conjure a sense of educational excellence.

If a tribe is brand new, then there is no tribal heritage yet. That is a vulnerability and weakness. The glue offered by a strong heritage needs to be mimicked and built at pace by any new organisation. The present quickly needs to become the past, so that the immediate present and future have roots.

As human beings we have the ability to think about the past, present and the future. A tribe's heritage speaks about its past, in its present. The energies, investments and successes of the past can give a tribe a better present and a leg-up into its future. But it if a tribe has under-invested or lost its way in the past, its heritage will make its present weaker and more vulnerable than it should be. Inheriting a negative heritage legacy puts a new leader immediately on the back foot.

Although the past can be a burden as well as a benefit, the present can always change that. A re-invention and re-positioning of a tribe's vision, purpose and values can make an immediate and positive impact. A range of new investments and recruitments that are focused on the tribe's purpose can aid the present and the future, as well as wiping away the mistakes of the past.

## Review and re-position your tribe's vision, purpose and values

Re-living events of the past can act as a powerful emotional trigger. They can re-set our loyalty, remind us of our traditions and spark greater energy for our current challenges. That's why sporting clubs keep replica trophies in glass cabinets and tell past stories through their Hall of Fame. Shinto or kami-no-michi is a Japanese religion which focuses on connecting modern Japan with its ancient past. By creating a spiritual path, a tribe's heritage can power its future.

Heritage is set in the past, but today is tomorrow's past. Like the human brain, an organisation's heritage changes and adapts to its circumstances every day. What we do today can almost instantly improve our tribe's heritage for tomorrow and beyond. So rather than just looking at this year's profit and loss account, tribes should reflect on their past and plan for the future. Positively developing a tribe's heritage makes it more appealing to its stakeholders, more attractive to future stakeholders and more sustainable.

~~~~~

Sticking with Manchester United, its former Manager Jose Mourinho has described 'football heritage' in terms of the recent successes and the playing staff that you currently get the benefit of now. The further in the past a trophy was won and the fewer current players that have won trophies, the less football heritage a club has. Jose has pointed to Manchester City having had more recent success and boasting more players with winning experience than his United team did. Some people, remembering the extraordinary success of Manchester United under Sir Alex Ferguson, dismissed his views. They look at heritage over a longer period. But although Joe Mourinho is a master at down-playing his difficulties, he has a point. However it is assessed, heritage matters. Time move son and now Jose has to tap into Tottenham's heritage.

Sporting success is transitory, even the greatest runs of success come to an end when the club's heritage is lost. Manchester United and Bath Rugby have both had long trophy winning periods. Neither of these clubs is currently in that same dominant position. Both of them still have a heritage that is more historic than current. Each of them has to fight to create a new dynasty of winning players and coaches, which will bring with it a greater heritage for their future players and managers to benefit from.

The top club trophy in football is the Champions League. Any knock-out cup competition is difficult to win. One missed shot, or one lucky deflection could make all the difference. Winning cups takes great belief. Belief grows as a club's heritage grows. Real Madrid won the Champions League in 2014, 2016, 2017 and 2018. Before that Real Madrid won it in 2000 and 2002. Before that the club had won the top European club competition on eight other occasions.

Between 2002 and 2014, Real Madrid did not win the Champions League. Jose Mourinho was the Manager during part of that period from 2010-2013. Despite winning the Champions League with Porto and Inter Milan and league titles in four countries, Jose didn't win the Champions League with Real Madrid. From 2003 to 2013 no Real Madrid Manager did. The club's heritage was threatened. But the club found a way to dig into its past to generate a winning mentality. How? The appointment of its former player Zinadine Zidane as Manager in

2016 provided a heritage bridge between the past and present. Zinadine Zidane had won the Champions League playing for Real Madrid in 2002. Using his experience of winning and his love of the club, he drove Real Madrid back to its heady heights. From 2016 to 2018 Zidane won the Champions League three times in two and half seasons as a Manager. Since he left Real Madrid is no longer the same force. Real Madrid needs to re-establish its heritage again.

~~~~~

Generational family businesses can have an advantage over other corporate brands. They are more likely to build customer loyalty. That's because they tend to treat their customers better, for two reasons. Firstly, it's their family name and reputation that's at stake. People will fight harder to protect and maintain their own personal reputation, than they will for a faceless corporate brand. Secondly, they want the next generation of the family to inherit the business in a good state. All round sustainability is crucial to keep the business going through the family generations. With more skin in the game, family businesses have a heritage which values longevity, customer service and positive relationships with all of their stakeholders. There are hundreds of great examples to name them all.

J.M. Armitage Limited is a Tool and Equipment Hire company in Batley, West Yorkshire. The business sells and hires out a wide range of tools and equipment including diggers, saws, power tools and wood chippers. The tool and equipment hire market is very competitive. To win repeat business J.M. Armitage Limited has had to provide great value for money and excellent customer service time after time, hire by hire, over many years. Formed in 1966, the business has built a strong reputation over fifty years, trading on the Armitage family name. Managing director Mark Armitage explains the importance of that heritage. "My Dad created a business and built it really well. Then I joined him in it after I left school. Together we ran it as a family. That was a wonderful time for me. Now that Dad's retired, we still run it with the same family feel and customer focus that it's always had."

# A family tribe can make a strong business tribe

York House Leisure operates six holiday caravan and residential park home sites in North Yorkshire. It's another second generation business which is managed by two brothers, Tim and Phil Brierley. The focus of the business is holiday home and residential park home sales, with some of their parks offering touring facilities as well as holiday home and lodge hire. The company has continually invested in its holiday parks as part of its long-term commitment to providing a premium customer service within the tourism and leisure sector. The Company ethos centres on excellent customer service and the provision of superbly maintained parks, with the objective being to create the best possible customer experience.

Phil Brierley explains the company's heritage "My parents started the business in 1965 with the purchase of a park in Northern Ireland, this started as a hobby as my Father's profession was actually dentistry." Although Dentistry was Mr. Brierley Senior's main profession, the holiday and residential parks industry has formed a fundamental part of the family's life. As a family we have lived and breathed the business all of our lives. Working with my brother Tim is brilliant. We both feel the same way about how to run the business. As a result of our family approach, we now have six holiday parks with over 500 pitches and we look forward to seeing this figure continue to grow."

Timpson is a second generation family key cutting and shoe repair business. With a very strong brand based around the family name, the business has grown to over 2,000 outlets nationwide. The Timpson family connection has given the business a strong set of values that make it an attractive place to work. One is supporting the rehabilitation of ex-offenders. Turning around a life in this way provides a super-tribe effect, with the employer, employee and the wider society all benefitting simultaneously. This all comes down to mutual trust and respect. Sir John Timpson says "The most important way you can offer good customer service is to trust your people and give them the freedom to get on and do it the way they think best."

Timpsons' excellent customer service has been key[31] to its success. In 2000, Sir John Timpson published his debut business book Dear James, in which he passed on the lessons he'd learned in thirty years as a Chief Executive to his son. James Timpson is now the Timpson Group CEO).

All of these businesses have clear family values and a sustainable future. Their family essence is core to them. Many other businesses have tried to mirror the values and focus of a family business. Those that have genuinely adopted family business values will have seen the benefits. The ones that just talk about it won't.

~~~~~

Heritage isn't just found in family businesses. Every organisation can develop a heritage using strong positive values, a long-term approach to investment and people development, CALM recruitment[32] and a focus on excellent customer service.

The Body Shop has a specific section on its website for Heritage. It says "Our story started in Brighton, England in 1976. Never afraid to stand out from the crowd and stand up for what's right, we search the world for the finest ethically-sourced ingredients to create a range of naturally-inspired beauty products. Today our dedication to business as a force for good is stronger than ever. As part of our Enrich Not Exploit™ Commitment, we've made it our mission to enrich our products, our people and our planet. That means working fairly with our farmers and suppliers and helping communities thrive through our Community Trade programme, being 100% vegetarian and always and forever being firmly against animal testing. Together we can do it, it's in our hands."

~~~~~

If your tribe's heritage is negative, you may be able to re-position it with time and new publicity. There are exceptions where a tribe's history and perceptions are too heavy to carry forwards positively.

---

[31] Apologies for the pun.
[32] More later.

But generally as long as the tribe is prepared to change positively, its heritage can do too.

Dope Black Dads is one example. Concerned about the lack of positive and constructive conversations around black fathers, a group of black dads based in London, New York and South Africa have come together to provide a progressive discussion around male parenting experience. Fed up with stories about absent fathers and poor role models, a number of black fathers starting to form and change perceptions.

By discussing the highs and lows of what it means to be a black father in today's society, Dope Black Dads have created a new and positive dialogue about black fathers.

~~~~~

Does your tribe know its own origin story? Who are its heroes and heroines? What are its historic events? What traditions and customs are based on its story so far? Is your tribe tapping into its past in order to build its future?

# 2.3 TRIBAL STRUCTURE AND HIERARCHY

Like many organisations, a tribe's basic structure is split into three main elements. They are its hierarchy, its decision-making processes; and its roles and responsibilities. Tribes can be successful in all shapes and sizes, but the most successful tribes have a well-established structure to them. The smaller the tribe and the tougher the sector, the more nimble the decision-making needs to be.

A tribal structure will create a sense of order, hierarchy and control. That helps tribes to operate quickly, calmly and efficiently, reducing the chances of tribal conflict and disharmony.

~~~~~

In 19th Century America, the Sioux were labelled violent savages by the white soldiers and settlers who invaded their lands. These Native Americans weren't savages. They were tribal. The Sioux were forced to protect everything that mattered to them. Under threat they defended their villages, their sources of food (meat such as Buffalo, wild fruit and wild vegetables), their sources of clothing (such as Buffalo hide); and their sacred land (the Black Hills). But when they acted in self-defence of their people, land and way of life they were feared and vilified for it.

The Sioux were a settled and tribal people with a clear structure and hierarchy. The Great Sioux Nation was the highest level of Sioux society and included all thirteen political sub-divisions. There were seven Sioux nations, the Wdewakanton, Sisseton, Teton (or Lakota), Wahpekute, Wahpeton, Yankton, and Yanktonai.

Each summer until 1850, the Seven Fires Council brought together the Chiefs of all seven nations. The Seven Fires Council made decisions which applied to every part of the Great Sioux Nation. Each of the seven Sioux Nations had its own structure, from village to tribe and finally up to nation. At the smallest level, each Sioux village had a Village Council which debated issues, made decisions and ran the village.

Each Village Council chose a Chief, who was given the role for life. That is an extraordinary act of faith. Other than monarchies, it is very unusual for a modern leader to hold any role for life. According to a PWC survey, top UK bosses spend an average of 4.8 years in the job[33]. Leaders must be able to lead and to serve simultaneously. Electing a leader who does both of these jobs well is critically important.

Every organisation has a different culture, set of needs and list of available candidates, so guidance on leadership terms is probably better than fixed rules. It probably takes two to four years for any leader to understand enough about their organisation, its stakeholders and themselves to hit their peak. There may be a peak period from three to seven years when a leader's best work is typically done. After leading the same organisation for seven years or more there is a risk that the leader loses the humility, curiosity and relentlessness that are needed to be highly effective. Some leaders will lose their mojo and effectiveness earlier than others.

## Get clarity in your structure and hierarchy

Every senior leader will eventually hold office for too long, so that they lose their edge or abuse their authority. How long that takes will depend on the character of the person and the organisation's circumstances. Equally, some leaders aren't given long enough to do their best work. Too many leaders are given insufficient authority to implement their vision for change. A healthy balance of authority and time is needed. The right balance of autonomy and close supervision

---

[33] Reported in the Financial Times in May 2017 as being a survey of the three hundred biggest UK companies.

is also needed. Each Sioux Chief had the tribe's elders to turn to for guidance.

The Sioux social structure reached down to village level. Every village council was divided into groups. The village Chief allocated each different group its responsibilities for the year, including hunting for food or keeping law and order in the village. Each group's responsibilities changed over the years, so that no group became too powerful within the Council. That approach helps to keep a healthy balance within any tribe.

Sitting Bull's Hunkpapa and Red Cloud's Oglala were Sioux tribes that formed part of the Lakota Nation. They were both made up of several villages. Each tribe had a tribal council formed with members from each of its villages. Each tribal council chose a tribal Chief and organised itself into functional groups, just like at village level. The Sioux social and political structure was essentially the same at all levels of its hierarchy.

Within each Sioux village, there was a Chief, a Medicine or Holy Man and a War Chief. This gave the tribe a clear sense of who was responsible for what. One hundred and fifty years later, many modern businesses use a structured hierarchy like the Sioux. The Native American concept of Chief is still used for many leading roles such as Chief Executive, Chief of Staff, Chief Finance Officer, Chief Medical Officer and Chief Operating Officer.

~~~~~

The Vikings were a seafaring people, whose prominence came during the 8th to 11th Centuries AD. They were raiders, explorers and traders, although they are perhaps best known for their longboats and fighting skills. Viking raiding parties plundered and pillaged through over thirty of today's countries including Britain, Iceland and Russia, reaching as far away as Canada and Afghanistan.

The Vikings were a military society. In battle they fought like berserkers using extreme violence, which may have been fuelled by alcohol and psycho-active mushrooms. The Vikings believed in dominating and devastating their enemies. They struck suddenly with great brutality, which made them deeply feared. Military victory should have been enough. Instead the Vikings deliberately chose to use fear to spread panic amongst their enemies. It was a tactical military decision. By today's moral standards they were horrifically brutal, violent and barbaric. There were many aspects of Viking life which are utterly inappropriate for the modern World. In other regards the Vikings were centuries ahead of their time.

But a broader picture emerges if we can look behind the extreme violence they showed towards other cultures. Somewhat surprisingly the Vikings were not a lawless mob. Viking society was ordered. It had three clear classes, a religion and rights for its women and children. Reeking havoc and violence on other cultures cannot be condoned, but some other aspects of Viking life can be.

The Jarls were the major landowners and politicians of Viking society. Below them were the Karls, who were free men and women that typically owned a farm and a few animals. The Karls were the middle class and had to work their land hard to make ends meet. At the bottom of Viking society were the Thralls who were slaves, often captured from raids abroad. They acted as servants to both the Jarls and Karls. Their lives were of little value. Indeed when a Jarl died his thralls were sometimes killed and buried next to him.

The Vikings were a religious people. They believed in the Norse Gods, with a particular focus on Thor and Odin their gods of war and death. Death played an important part in Viking society. All Viking warriors wanted to earn themselves a glorious death and take their place in the hall of their ancestors (Valhalla) which waited for them in Asgard (heaven).

*In some regards the Vikings were*
*centuries ahead of their time*

The institution of marriage existed, but there was no such thing as an illegitimate child. All children were allowed to inherit from their parents. Viking women were free women from the age of twenty and had the same rights as Viking men to divorce and remarry. They could cohabit rather than marry if they wished. Married women could also have children outside of their marriage. This social freedom was born from a practical need. Without sufficient warriors to fight for it, Viking society was under threat. Having a relaxed view about personal relationships allowed Viking society to produce a steady stream of future warriors. These rules supported their central purposes of surviving and thriving.

Despite its violent nature Viking culture had a clear social and religious structure at its centre. The incredible geographical reach the Vikings achieved would not have been possible without a sense of tribal order outside the chaos of battle.

However successful an organisation is, it should always have a clear structure and hierarchy. The Viking's fixed three class system is questionable as it held back social movement, but three or more tiers of management is common in modern organisations. The key question is Does everyone know who is responsible for every activity? The Vikings did. Clarity is hugely important.

Like the Vikings, every organisation should structure itself up to be sustainable for years to come. Succession planning is often overlooked as businesses and sports teams chase short-term glory. Owners demand results now, rather than planning for sustained results later.

~~~~~

Every organisation needs to decide how best to operate. One way of assessing structure is to look at where control lies. In the military, if the authority and direction for a task come from the same central leadership it's termed Command and Control. If instead the central leadership delegates authority and direction to a sub-leader on the ground, it's called Mission Control.

Command and control can allow one mind to make all the decisions, which can lead to greater consistency and efficiency. But the downside is that decisions are made remotely. So they can be based on incomplete or out of date information. Mission control gives faster, real-time decision-making. As long as all leaders are fully briefed, well-trained and given genuine authority, mission control can be much more immediate and effective.

Many leaders aren't good at trusting other people or delegating real authority to them. Leaders typically like to keep a firm grasp of what they're responsible for. Driven by a sense that control means power, leaders often limit the trust they give to their teams. So rather than allowing their people to learn and fail (in a controlled environment) most leaders prefer to hold all the reins and use command and control. Building a tribe comes from people breaking down their barriers, trusting and being trusted. That collective trust is grown through regular and consistent interactions over a period of time. Leaders can facilitate those interactions, but they cannot fake trust.

## Mission control or command and control?

Some leadership claims to offer mission control but is in fact command and control in disguise. That loses hearts and minds rather than gaining them. It is grossly unfair to delegate a hollow responsibility for a project or function without also giving the necessary authority and resources to deliver it. Organisational charts should reflect where the real authority (namely budget, influence and resources) sits, not where the nominal responsibility rests. Many organisations have organigrams with titles and hierarchies which look the part, but they often belie the reality.

Whether your tribe operates on a command and control, or a mission control basis, it is vital that its structure is agreed and consistently applied. In either case, it is also important that there are substitutes ready to step in and take over from the leaders. Bad leaders tighten their grip on power by holding everyone else back. Good leaders loosen their grip and work to create more good leaders.

There should always be a healthy balance between the existing leaders, elders and the up and coming leadership candidates. Organisations should try and avoid the situation where a Board or Executive Committee retains the entire organisation's authority and only rarely changes its composition.

~~~~~

On a first appearance, ants seem to wander round the World quite randomly. But every ant is part of a well-structured society with specialist sub-groups.

Inside each colony, every single ant has a defined role which it carries out without objection. All ants are capable of communicating with every other ant in their colony, allowing each colony to operate as one well-organised team. By employing all the skills and resources of the colony, ants are able to solve much bigger problems than they could solve alone. Through their collective efforts ants have managed to colonise virtually every landmass in the World, ironically except for Antarctica.

How is ant society organised? Each colony has a Queen ant that lives up to thirty years. She mates with the male drones and lays eggs. The female worker ants (ergates) build the underground nest, protect the colony and go out into the wider World foraging for food. Female worker ants live for up to three years. Male drones only exist for mating and they die shortly afterwards. Male soldier ants (dinergates) help to defend the colony from attack. They typically only live for a few weeks before being replaced by new soldiers.

## The colony always comes first

How is ant society controlled? Ant colonies don't use a command and control structure. The Queen doesn't give out orders. Ants are theoretically autonomous insects, but their genetics and environment hugely influence their behaviours. They are genetically born to be team players and they live their lives as team players, so they always behave as team players. As a result the colony always comes first.

Each individual ant reacts to its own genetic coding (which helps to set its role in the colony) and to every stimulus around it. When an ant travels, it leaves behind its own individual chemical trail. Ants use their two antennae ("feelers") to detect chemicals, air currents, and vibrations. They also use them to transmit and receive signals through their sense of touch. All of the stimuli around an ant influences its behaviours and next steps. Those stimuli can include communications from other ants from the same colony, invading strangers or locating suitable food sources. Ants are therefore highly flexible and reactive to their circumstances.

~~~~~

In friendship groups, members can sometimes assume a role for the group. As a result of the individual contributions of its members, friendship groups can fulfil their collective needs. The roles can include the organiser, the parent, the defender, the competitive one, the sounding board, the persuader, the peacemaker, the party animal, the daredevil, the therapist, the entertainer, the carer and the child. People can play one role in one tribe and completely role in another tribe. What roles do you play?

~~~~~

Like ants, every tribe needs a clear way of operating that everyone understands. Whether it's more like a swarm, herd, cluster, pack, unit, club, troop, regiment, brigade, group, team or a band, every different collection of people needs a framework of some kind to become a tribe. The structure of a tribe is important in setting its ways of working and its culture, as each tribe has a unique method of operation. Whatever that structure is, order usually better than chaos. The more aligned that the structure is to the tribe's vision, purpose and values, the more successful it is likely to be.

Ants put the colony first and foremost working forwards from that premise. Most people start from the other end of the telescope, asking themselves the question "Is this job working well enough for me?" Whichever view of your tribe you have, every tribe member needs to know where they stand. That comes from having clear communication paths leading to every other tribe member. Organising and monitoring a tribe's communication methods is vital. The transfer of information is what allows a tribe to learn and adapt. With so many options for hierarchies and control structures available, internal communication methods need to be tailored to match the organisation's needs. Too many businesses prepare an organisational chart and assume that the people on it will do all the rest. Poor role definitions, unclear responsibilities and inconsistent communications will always stifle an organisation's potential.

## Order is better than chaos

Many organisations have a full-time marketing or PR team working on its external communications. But far fewer have an internal communication strategy. Why is that? Both are equally important. A flow chart of a tribe's responsibilities and communication paths would be of more practical use than a chart merely containing job titles in neat boxes. The hierarchy of an organisation merely tells you who has nominal authority for that organisation. Whereas the way a tribe communicates tells you who has real influence over the organisation's performance.

If organisational control is heavily centralised (for example if one person signs off every decision) then the organisation needs to establish excellent communication paths up as well ad down, so the decision maker is well-informed. Without good communication pathways a centralised structure is making decisions in the half-light.

Where organisational decision-making is delegated to others then there needs to be a well-functioning reporting process, so that the leadership knows exactly what's going on. Without being given good information and feedback about what's happening on the ground, an organisation's leadership can't see the big picture.

Focusing too much on your organisation's structure and hierarchy could therefore be missing the real target. That's because hierarchies promote impersonal relationships and top down thinking. The real target is a clear set of responsibilities and an effective communication flow. Just like ants, organisational communication has to move freely between every point of the decision-making, back and forth in a continuous flow. Without it, an organisation will misunderstood, mistrust and misfire.

Ask yourself:

- **Who needs to make decisions in my organisation?**
- **What decisions do they need to make, for what and when?**
- **What information does each decision-maker need to receive, from whom and when?**
- **What reports do they need to produce, for whom and when?**
- **What information flows are needed and between whom?**

Then create a communications chart to help that decision-making process be effective.

Personal communication is also very important in every organisation. That's the one to one communication between a manager and each member of their team. Hierarchies can strangle the humanity out of working relationships. Rather than sending generic all team emails, managers need to develop a positive, warm, two-way communication path with every employee that they need to manage. Developing person to person relationships will create a functioning hierarchy, rather than a purely nominal one.

~~~~~

There will always be messages that any organisation needs to get across to its staff. But they shouldn't all be focused on the "worker hard" messages that the organisation wants to give out.

More importantly, they should include the information that the employees need to know. That is:

- **What is our collective purpose?**
- **How does that help us?**
- **Who benefits?**
- **What's the plan?**
- **Which elements am I responsible for?**

- **Who gives me my instructions?**
- **Who gives me training and guidance?**
- **Who do I ask if I need extra time or resources?**
- **Who do I ask for more authority or budget?**
- **Who do I escalate any concerns to?**
- **When I'm finished who do I get sign off on my work from?**
- **Who decides whether I'm doing a good job?**
- **What am I rewarded for?**
- **Who decides whether I get pay rise or bonus?**

Do all your employees know how your World really works? Every employee should have a clear list of what they are responsible for. Their rewards should be built around their responsibilities. Are they? Unless someone is motivated by direct responsibility and personal reward things rarely get done as well as they could.

~~~~~

Does your tribe's structure and hierarchy constrain or empower it? Does its form allow it to achieve its purpose? Is it too hierarchical so that too many initiatives get stuck or lost? Is it too flat, so no one leads? Are your tribe's structure and hierarchy trapping its progress or helping to drive it?

# 2.4 TRIBAL RULES

In addition to every organisation's structure and hierarchy, a series of rules, regulations and conditions shape the way it operates in practice. Each tribe will have a different blend and format for its rules.

Specific tribal rules can include which membership criteria apply to join (for example requiring an application, interview or a vote), what needs to be done to remain a member (for example following rules of good conduct or paying an annual subscription), how to elect new leaders (for example by requiring a presentation or a vote) and how to expel a member (for example after a disciplinary hearing).

A tribe's rules should support its purpose and uphold its tribal values. The rules should be aligned with the tribe's vision, purpose and values. Do yours?

~~~~~

Leaders can often get to influence and enforce their own tribe's rules. Sometimes leaders can persuade their tribe to fundamentally change its rules. They need to be changed when they aren't supporting the tribal purpose. How much choice a leader has over the rules depends on how much autonomy the leader has. Sometimes the rules are bigger than the tribe.

Poker is a card game that's played right across the World. Playing cards at home for fun you can choose any rules you like. But if you want to play Poker you need to play the conventional rules. Those have become established over time. Players agree to play by universally accepted rules, such as standard Poker or Texas Holdem so that Poker players know exactly where they stand before the game begins. Whilst there is a degree of unpredictability about which cards are dealt to which player, the rules for playing Poker are anything but random. Clear rules create transparency and fairness. Everyone gets an equal chance to win.

In Poker each hand of five cards is ranked depending on the combination of cards in it. There is a precise pecking order which dictates which hand of cards wins. Top of the pile is a Royal Flush, where all the five cards are in the same suit and in consecutive order, made up of the Ace, King, Queen, Jack and 10 in the same suit. Then it's a Straight Flush with the King, Queen, Jack, 10 and 9 in one suit and so on down until it's the five lowest cards in the same suit. Then in descending order of importance after a Straight Flush there is Four of a Kind, Full House, Flush, Straight, Three of a Kind, Two pairs, a pair and lastly where no player has even a pair of cards there is a High Card. The rules take some learning, but you need to learn them as they are rigidly applied. There is no flexibility or leeway. They are the rules. Rules that are enforced remain rules.

Some games of Poker also rank the suit of cards, so that if two players have the same basic hand they can still be separated into a winner and a loser. So, if both players draw a Royal Flush, the suit they are in will dictate who wins the hand. The standard priority order of suits is Spades followed by Hearts, Clubs and Diamonds. So, a Royal Flush of the Ace, King, Queen, Jack and 10 of Spades is the perfect hand and cannot be beaten. Other orders are used but that would need to be agreed in advance. Then there are other rules depending on who is dealing the cards. If you change card game completely, all the rules change too. Whichever rules are being used for whichever game, they should be agreed in advance and stuck to. Everyone plays Poker in the same way so that there's a level playing field and an equal chance to win.

The more complex rules are, the more important it is to write them down. The more likely it is that any rules will be enforced, the more you need to memorise them and follow them to the letter. So if you're operating in an environment with rules, regulations, traditions or expectations, you need to invest the time finding out what those rules are, how they work and when they are enforced.

## Know the rules, follow the rules

In sport, business and public services, as well as Poker, you need to know all the rules of engagement before you start. If there are no rules at all, you need to know that too. Sometimes there is a set of agreed rules, but the people you're dealing with have no intention of following them. In The Pirates of the Caribbean[34], there is right of Parley under the Pirates' Code. When asked to respect the right of Parley (from the French meaning to speak) Captain Barbosa replies "The code is more what you'd call 'guidelines' than actual rules."

Knowing where you stand in any environment or walk of life can be difficult. That's why it is so important for tribes to have agreed rules and regulations. Otherwise the tribe's purpose, vision and values could be jeopardised. Members can choose to comply with the rules, or face the consequences.

Risk plays a key part in Poker. Gambling can be done with relative caution, or with reckless abandon. Some players change how they approach the game depending how the cards are dealt, who their opponents are; and how much money they are up or down. Like every other aspect of Poker, the level of risk is still subject to the rules.

Unless an organisation has clear rules and a clear hierarchy, there will be disorder and chaos. Businesses cannot perform at their peak without order. Every leader should invest time in setting and communicating how their organisation needs to operate. Everyone else should educate themselves about what their own role and responsibilities involve. "Learning the ropes" is a nautical phrase used by sailors to mean learning the skills of the job and the rules for working together.

~~~~~

The Guardian Angels have been patrolling the New York Subway since 1979, helping to reduce violent crime. They wear their

---

[34] The successful film franchise starring Johnny Depp, Orlando Bloom, Keira Knightley and Geoffrey Rush.

distinctive uniform of a red beret, red jacket and white t-shirt with the logo of an eye inside a pyramid on a winged shield. Group members are trained in martial arts but they operate unarmed. Their purpose is to protect other people. As a result, the Guardian Angels only accept volunteers who don't have recent or serious criminal record. By way of contrast the Hell's Angels won't accept volunteers with any connections to the Police.

~ ~ ~ ~ ~

On 11 November 1620, the Mayflower dropped anchor in Plymouth Harbour, just off what is known today as Cape Cod, Massachusetts. Sailing from Southampton and then Plymouth in England, the ship had set out for a new World to escape religious persecution. Unable to land in Virginia Company land as planned, the ship drifted into unknown territory. Threatened with rising disquiet and complaints, forty-one of the Puritans and other passengers decided to sign the Mayflower Compact on board. The Compact created a body of laws for the new Plymouth Colony.

Without this agreement to regulate themselves in their new country, there could have been anarchy and chaos when they disembarked. This act of self-governance began the process that eventually led to American Independence. By agreeing the Mayflower Compact, the colonists made a commitment to one another. Each tribe of people needs to agree its own set of rules.

~ ~ ~ ~ ~

Religions tend to have prescriptive rules and laws governing their religious observances. Religious rules relate to who should be worshipped, what acts of worship are required, how religious services and ceremonies should take place and what behaviours are forbidden. For example, Canon law is the body of laws and regulations made by or adopted by ecclesiastical authority for the government of the Christian Church of England.

Religions offer a well-established set of rules and regulations. Believers don't get a free choice in deciding which rules to adopt and which to reject. If you adopt a religion you have to accept the whole package. If you don't like it, you have to choose a different religion, or start your own.

## *Are you all in?*

In Poker you can't decide to have more cards than anyone else, or create new kinds of winning hands. But you choose how much to commit with each hand of cards you're dealt. There are some rules and some freedoms. By contrast, with religion you have to go "all in" every hand. That kind of approach has a fixed mindset at its heart, which doesn't appeal to everyone.

~~~~~

Golf and other sporting clubs tend to operate with strict rules. As well as applying the rules of golf, golf clubs also have their own rules on course etiquette, speed of play, behaviour in the clubhouse, permissible equipment, dress code (on and off the course), joining fees; and annual membership fees. How the club captains are chosen, how you can book tee-off times; and when someone can be expelled from the club are examples of other golf club rules.

The sport of golf is more regimented and formal than others. There are rules for almost every aspect of the game and golf club life. Whether or not you like that approach, it offers clarity for club members and visitors alike.

~~~~~

Who chooses a tribe's rules is important. Rules are just words unless you believe in following them. Having a set of rules imposed on you can really put you off following them. If an organisation tells you what to do and doesn't listen to your feedback, your attachment to that tribe becomes weaker.

Organisations that involve all their stakeholders in creating their rules will get much greater engagement from those stakeholders. People who help to make the rules are more likely to stick to the rules. So even if an organisation's rules change and develop, its members are far more likely to stay part of the tribe if they've had a say those changes.

~~~~~

Do your tribe's rules set it up for success? Do they follow and support its values? Do they encourage the actions required to make the tribe's vision become a reality? Or are your rules, policies and procedures restricting your tribe's development? Is too much red tape preventing your tribe from achieving its purpose?

## 2.5 TRIBAL NICKNAMES

We are all familiar with the legend of King Arthur and the Knights of the Round Table. But which version do you believe? Historians, storytellers and film-makers have favoured several different versions of the story, some of which have been set centuries apart. So, despite the story being well known to us, none of those versions of it may be true. There is a real possibility that King Arthur and his Knights of the Round Table are an entirely fictional set of characters. More likely, they are an amalgam of several real characters rolled into one legend, with added embellishment through generations of oral storytelling. Regardless of the truth, the myth has lasted through the centuries due in some part to the nickname attributed to Arthur and his tribe.

The Knights of the Round Table were fearsome and brave. They are said to have protected England, supported the vulnerable and kept law and order. Why were they given this nickname? According to the legend, before King Arthur tables were long and hierarchical with the most important person sitting at the head of the table. That approach gave certainty, but it also kept people firmly stuck in their place. Social mobility was exceptionally rare.

Everyone knew that Arthur was King; and Arthur didn't feel the need to constantly remind his subjects of that. So, King Arthur decided to sit amongst his fellow knights as an equal. As round table has no head, each person sitting around it becomes as important as everyone else. In one gesture, King Arthur was expressing "I am one of you" and "I value your contribution". That humility allowed the Knights to shape their rules, values and actions.

## Nicknames can last the test of time

The Knights of the Round Table is a tale which therefore supports the values of unity, teamwork, equality and humility. Those values still feel like ideals worth aiming for, so they resonate well even today. That's why the story has been told so often that it's stuck in our consciousness. The "Knights of the Round Table" nickname links directly back to those values. That nickname has lasted the test of time. Businesses could do worse than learn the round table lesson.

~ ~ ~ ~ ~

Robin Hood is another World-famous English historical character who may not have existed. There are several theories about who Robin Hood was, if he ever lived at all. Robin of Locksley and Robert Earl of Huntington are two of the real names in the frame. Another is William Le Fevre, who was part of criminal gang and became a fugitive known as William Robehod. These aren't the only names that people have tried to claim was the real Robin Hood. The earliest reference is probably a 1226 court reference to a "fugitive" called Robin Hood from Yorkshire[35].

---

[35] Reported by National Geographic History in January/February 2019.

There isn't just uncertainty about his real name. There is also a dispute about where Robin Hood lived. The perceived wisdom is that he lived in Sherwood Forest, Nottingham. But some historians claim it was Barnsdale Forest in South Yorkshire and not Nottinghamshire. Both areas were heavily forested at the time, which helps to feed the debate. The Great Oak tree, which Robin Hood allegedly lived inside, is a real tree within Sherwood Forest, which points to Nottingham, but that tree is said to be too young for Robin Hood and would have been a mere sapling at the time.

Just like the mystery of King Arthur, the truth is probably lost to us. Just like King Arthur, Robin Hood is most likely an amalgam of several real historical figures, enhanced by generations of good storytelling.

But, just like King Arthur's and his Knights, in a way the truth doesn't matter. Robin Hood stands for something we like. He hates injustice and oppression. So, when the poor are over-taxed by King John and the Sheriff of Nottingham, Robin Hood takes the money back and gives it to the poor. Robin Hood and his merry men are vigilantes, administering the justice that has gone missing from England. It's a powerful story, designed to keep royalty and politicians in check, acting as a reminder never to tax the people too hard. It's a tale worth keeping alive.

If your tribe is focused on reducing inequality and helping the poor, then telling stories about a modern-day Robin Hood could form part of your tribal folklore. Robin Hood and his Merry Men is a nickname that has lasted the test of time. A modern more inclusive version of it may be a good name or story for your tribe to adopt.

~ ~ ~ ~ ~

Together with colours and badges, tribal behaviour in sport also includes team nicknames. The mere mention of a sporting nickname conjures up the tribe's playing history and pride. In Rugby Union's Premiership, there are teams known as Wasps (who play in Coventry) and Harlequins (who play in London).

Harlequins rugby team began in 1867, originally formed as part of Hampstead Football Club. In 1870 Hampstead changed its name to the Harlequin Football Club when the club began to take in members from further afield than just Hampstead. They chose the now famous four coloured quarters for their shirts.

But some players and coaches were unhappy with this. They wanted to carry on using the same HFC (Hampstead) logo and Latin motto. They felt their tribe was being lost to them. So, some of those other players and coaches left. They adopted the Hampstead playing colours of black and gold and they gave themselves the nickname Wasps. The rest is history.

~~~~~

When English rugby league supporters talk about the Tigers, they are almost certainly talking about Castleford because no competitor in Superleague has the same nickname. But in Leicester, or amongst rugby union fans, the Tigers means Leicester Tigers. In Australia, the Tigers means Wests Tigers, which is another rugby league team. In English football, Hull City is also known as the Tigers, as are Detroit's major league baseball team amongst other professional sports clubs. American Football team Cincinnati Bengals is yet another version of Tigers.

## Nicknames should be rare if not unique

Nicknames need to be descriptive and distinctive. Animal names can be very descriptive especially in sport. They are even better if they are unique. Having a unique name or brand image helps a tribe to promote itself. Having a common or duplicate name can water that promotional effect down. If someone mentioned the Tigers in a sporting context, would you think of Castleford, Detroit, Hull, Leicester, Wests or someone else completely? With several other teams sharing similar imagery, Tigers is a descriptive and distinctive nickname, but it's by no means unique.

The nickname Saints isn't exclusive either. It can mean Southampton FC (English football), St. Helens (English rugby league), St. George-

Illawarra (Australian rugby league), or New Orleans Saints (American Football) amongst others, depending on which sport and which country you're talking about.

The best nicknames use a familiar word which links directly to the organisation's values. Sports teams have concentrated around a limited number of areas for inspiration. Even within those limits there are still plenty of examples such as:

## ANIMALS AND BIRDS:
*including* **Wolves, Rhinos, Bulls, Bears, Bucks, Rams, Tigers, Dolphins, Bulldogs, Panthers, Jaguars, Broncos, Hawks, Eagles, Falcons, Jays, Ravens, Colts and Cougars.**

## MYTHS AND LEGENDS:
*including* **Angels, Giants, Dragons, Devils, Magic, Titans and Wizards.**

## WARRIOR GROUPS:
*including* **Centurions, Vikings, Knights, Chiefs, Chargers, Warriors, Patriots, Raiders, Rangers, Rovers, Outlaws, Cowboys, Pirates, Saracens, Redskins, Buccaneers, Cavaliers and Crusaders.**

## WEATHER:
*including* **Storm, Suns, Heat, Thunder, Lightning and Heat.**

## ROYAL CONNECTIONS:
*including* **Kings, Queens, Palace, Royals and Harlequins.**

## INSECTS:
*including* **Wasps, Bees, Scorpions and Hornets.**

## COLOURS:
*including* **Reds, Browns, Red Sox, White Sox, Blue Jays and All Blacks.**

## POWER AND MIGHT:
*including* **Pistons, Dynamos, Rockets, Raptors, Jets, Spitfires.**

## VALUABLES:
*including* **Nuggets and All Golds.**

## NATURE AND GEOGRAPHY:
*including* **Albion, Rockies, Forest and Vale.**

There are other miscellaneous examples including: Hotspur (named after medieval nobleman Sir Henry Percy who held that nickname and owned land in modern day Tottenham) Celtics, Wednesday (because the team first played on Wednesdays), Trail Blazers, 76ers (after the signing of the Declaration of Independence in Philadelphia in 1776) Jazz, Knicks (after knickerbocker shorts worn by Dutch settlers), Moors, Trinity (after the Holy Trinity Church where the founders came from) and Athletic.

The fewer teams that share your tribe's nickname the more distinctive it is. Unique is best of all. Just make sure it's descriptive, distinctive and inclusive enough to attract followers now and in the future.

~~~~~

In English football most teams are named by taking the place name and adding a suffix such as United. Some of those suffixes are unique; and some are used by several teams despite the potential confusion.

## THE LIST OF SUFFIXES *includes:* **Albion, Alexandra, Argyle, Athletic, City, County, Dons, Forrest, Hotspur, North End, Orient, Palace, Rovers, Stanley, Town, United, Vale, Villa, Wanderers and Wednesday.**

If a football fan talks about Orient, then there is only one team he or she can be talking about. But if it's 'United' then it could be Manchester, Leeds, Newcastle, West Ham, Rotherham or a very large number of other clubs.

Sports teams in the same local area tend to have different club names, home grounds and different colours so their tribes remain distinct. The city of Nottingham is a case in point. It has two professional football clubs. Nottingham Forrest play at the County Ground and wear red and white. Notts County wear black and white stripes and play across the city at Meadow Lane. Other than football and their shared city's name, Forest and County have almost nothing in common.

~~~~~

Businesses use names to describe their divisions, teams and units. Those names tend to be functional descriptions, like Accounts, Distribution and Sales. Apart from informing other people what work they do, the terms don't add much to the culture of the organisation. The team could be part of absolutely any organisation.

An alternative would be to use a call to action that supports the tribal purpose, or a word that reflects the tribal values required. The more invested in the wider purpose that a team is, the better it will perform.

The nicknames that you give your divisions, teams and units should inspire and fit within your VPV. So, your set of names could be unique. The following are just a few thoughts.

- **If your purpose is to invent and innovate, then your Research and Development team could become known as The Innovation Lab, Transformers, World of Wonders, Field of Dreams or the Revolutionaries to help encourage very creative products and services.**

- **If you are a manufacturing business, then Production could be re-named the Forge, Thunder and Lightning or the Engine Room to encourage a big collective effort. Or it could be called Creating Dreams or Changing Lives to emphasise the positive impact of all that effort.**

- Sales could be Trailblazers, Gold Rush, the Missionaries or Story-makers to help create an evangelical fervour about selling the organisation's products or services.

- Distribution could be called Delivering Dreams, the Storks or Santa's Elves to emphasise the value and importance of how products and services are delivered to customers.

- Information Technology could be the Tech Titans or the Data Gurus to encourage a creative, problem-solving attitude.

- Accounts could be nicknamed the Investors, the Treasury, or Pennies and Pounds as a reminder that the finances empower the organisation.

- Human Resources could become one of a number of different alternatives, depending on the approach you want to take. HR could become the Teachers, Tissues and Hugs, or Baywatch to indicate the training, emotional and practical support and on offer.

Only your own nicknames will make sense to you and your tribe. None of these examples might work for you. Each tribe needs to find its own way of building engagement and pulling the power of its people together. When you're looking for a new job, would you rather join a research and development team, or join the Field of Dreams?

~~~~~

As well having team and organisation nicknames, tribes tend to allocate individual names for their members. They include giving personal names (family tribes), job titles (employers) or nicknames (friends or sports teams) for every tribal member. Having a unique name that positively links you to your tribe can bond you even tighter to it. But it's also true that if a name, title or nickname is patronising, offensive, demeaning or belittling it will have the diametrically opposite effect, driving a wedge between tribal members.

Sir David Attenborough opens BBC1's Dynasties series with the words "The family is one of the most powerful forces in nature." It could also be said that families are the most powerful human tribes. As most people's first proper tribe, our families normally name us. The parents typically choose the personal names of their children. As a result, we live our whole lives answering to the family names we were given at birth. Some children get two or more personal names to go with their family surname. That way the child can choose to use a second or even third personal name if they prefer it. Some parents give their children nicknames. Some of them stick and carry on into adulthood. Family based nicknames can spread out to friends and even work. Whichever name is commonly used for a family member, it is part of the web of connections that ties that family together.

## Our titles influence how we behave

In a business with a pyramid hierarchy, job titles are used to denote the importance of each tribe member. But those titles are often impersonal and arbitrary. Our titles affect how we behave. They give us our permissions, but they can restrain our actions. Being allocated a limited role or precise set of responsibilities can limit our creativity. So, job titles shouldn't be too narrow. Rigid roles and hierarchies can stifle mission-critical decision-making. They also create gaps between them that no one is responsible for filling.

Typically in a pyramid structure, the further away from the top you are, the less engaged and invested you feel. In flatter, more inclusive structures titles tend to matter less than the relationships themselves. Either way it's very important that everyone know who is responsible for what.

~~~~~

Using titles and nicknames that make people proud to be associated with the tribe can have a unifying effect. Generic terms like partner and associate can be used to make people feel an important part of the tribe. As long as those roles are meaningful and beneficial, they can help to pull a group together.

Ideally names that value each person individually and simultaneously support the tribe's purpose provide a dual purpose. That's why the combination of individual personal names and a collective surname works so well for family groups. Businesses should try to make job titles unique and relevant to the tribal purpose. If everyone's role really does matter to an organisation then why isn't each job given its own unique title? A simple example would be for a group of litter pickers to give each other Womble names like Orinoco and Madame Cholet.

If you have a big team that's doing the same job, it might be difficult to create enough individual job titles. If everyone likes sport, you could allow them to use their rugby or football team, to help differentiate Man City Pete from Saracens Pete. This would allow staff to bring another tribe into work and bond them together, indirectly strengthening their attachment to work. If sport doesn't work well enough then allowing every employee to pick a favourite film or band could work. Or if you want to take a bigger step towards a tribal approach, you could create a theme that reflects your tribe's purpose and the character of the team you want to create. So if you have an eight person manufacturing team, you could nickname them Storm, Thunder, Tempest, Hurricane, Cyclone, Gale, Typhoon and Lightning.

Or instead of imposing a theme, you could allow your employees to be known by a nickname of their choice (subject to an organisational veto).

~~~~~

In your organisation:

- **How does your tribe use names and titles?**
- **Do the titles support the tribe's purpose?**
- **Are they unique?**
- **Is everyone comfortable with what they're called?**
- **Is everyone motivated by what they're called?**
- **Do your names and titles help you to build your tribe?**

# 2.6 TRIBAL VALUES

The World around us is volatile, complex, uncertain and ambiguous (VUCA) which creates a moving horizon for tribes to continually adjust to. To enable a tribe to stick together whilst the World challenges it at every turn, it needs a set of core principles that govern a tribe's decisions and behaviours. These are its real values. Agreeing a set of tribal values, placing sufficient emphasis on them and applying them fairly can help to hold a tribe together whilst it achieves its purpose.

Skills can be taught and learned. Values are inherent. Without a clear set of agreed values an organisation cannot operate as one. Tribal power comes from every tribe member behaving in the same way as every other one. That creates a tribal flow. Tribes need an agreed set of values in order to establish acceptable and unacceptable behaviours.

Trees take the moisture and nutrients they need from the earth around them. They do it through a root system that both connects them and feeds them. Tree roots provide for growth and sustainability. As people, the values that matter to us are own form of roots. Without them we lose our connections and our fuel for personal growth and development. Without agreed values, tribes can't operate properly as tribes.

Every tribe has a different combination of:

1. **Values (which ones have been chosen or allowed to take hold?)**

2.  **Emphasis (what focus and emphasis is placed on each value?)**

3.  **Application (how and in what ways is a value applied?)**

No other tribe has exactly the same combination as any other because the VPV, people and circumstances within each tribe are unique.

~~~~~

Rather than just being corporate wallpaper, business values should be agreed, instructional and relevant. Organisations should aim for a collection of values that is meaningful but short enough to remember. Any more than perhaps five or six values will be too challenging to remember.

Ideally, the first initials of every value will make an acronym that's a common word in its own right. That will help everyone remember all the values. It would be even better if that common word is also a value in its own right and relevant to the other values. One example is the use of the value and common word "TRIBAL" as the acronym, based on a combination of say Team worker, Resourceful, Innovative, Bold, Authentic and Loyal.

Using relevant acronyms for your values can help to promote those values and keep them in mind. WAR is an example of an emotive word which can be used as acronym in several different ways. One version uses W for Work, A for Attitude and R for Responsibility. WAR can also be used for motivational messages such as We Are Ready, We Are Right, Willing Able and Ready, We Are Relentless, We Are Resilient, Within Arms Reach; or We All Ride. You can use the same acronym to relay and promote different messages. Where it fits with your values and vision, you could "Go to WAR" where WAR stands for Working Against Racism for example.

However that acronym won't suit every organisation for obvious reasons. There are endless possibilities for acronyms. For example PEACE can also be used to stand for People Everywhere Are Created Equally, or Positive Empowerment Adds Creative Energy. GOOD could be used in sport to mean Great Defence, Outstanding Offense.

## *All stakeholders should help to choose the values*

Organisations need to find their own values from carrying-out a process of self-analysis. That exercise needs to be inclusive and involve all of the tribe's stakeholders. The chosen values have to actively support the tribe's purpose and vision. By matching values and purpose, those values can help to unleash the tribal power that gets big things done. Strong and inclusive values provide the reassurance for people to put their organisation first. That draws everyone together in the same purpose.

There is no harm borrowing ideas from other organisations, but unless they are genuinely relevant and agreed they won't add the tribal power they should.

~~~~~

In England there is no constitution. The closest thing we have is a Bill of Rights which was passed in 1688, twenty-two years after the Great Fire of London. The Bill of Rights was designed to re-establish the authority of Parliament that King James II had subverted. The Bill of Rights included rights establishing free elections of MPs, free speech in Parliament, bail should not be excessive, juries should be "duely impaneled and returned" and there's shouldn't be any fines, forfeits or punishments before conviction. These principles underpin the laws we have in this country. They act as a set of national values. The UK's Bills of Rights is not as extensive or as current as the Constitution of the United States of America. It is not as well embedded or protected either.

There has been a written Constitution in the United States of America since 1789. The Constitution is made up of the initial Bill of Rights and the twenty seven Amendments passed since then. The Constitution acts as the values control-valve in America. The Constitution has stood the test of time precisely because it has been debated and amended over the years. It is fairly rigid, but with enough support Congress can amend it. Examples of key amendments that have been passed include: the Second Amendment in 1791 (giving individuals the right to bear arms), the Sixth Amendment in 1791 (giving the right to a fair and speedy trial, by jury, in public), the Thirteenth Amendment in 1865 (abolishing slavery), the Nineteenth Amendment in 1920 (giving women the right to vote in all States); and the Twenty-Sixth Amendments in 1971 (giving US citizens the right to vote at the age of 18).

The deeper an organisation's values are embedded in its rules and regulations, the more likely they are to last.

~~~~~

What did the Ancient Romans ever do for us? The answer, as we know, is that the Romans gave us many things including: straight roads, sanitation, welfare programmes for the poor, public health initiatives, religious tolerance (of Christianity), the presumption of innocence until proven guilty, shoes and socks, wedding rings, concrete and the basis of our modern calendar (including leap years and the month of July, which Julius Caesar named after himself[36]). But arguably the most powerful part of their legacy is a value system.

A surprising number of those Ancient Roman values are still used today. Whilst not every Roman citizen followed them religiously, they were repeated as mantra and regularly enforced. There were real consequences of not abiding by the core values. Poverty, banishment or death loomed over every free Roman if he or she behaved inappropriately or disrespected the Gods.

## Values form a key part of legacy

Each value was distilled into a single word. Many of them are familiar: Auctoritas (spiritual authority), Clementia (clemency/mercy), Dignitas (dignity), Firmitas (tenacity), Frugalitas (being frugal/economical), Gravitas (responsibility), Honestas (honesty and respectability), Humanitas (humanity), Industria

---

[36] His adopted son Augustus Caesar is said to have then named August after himself. As it only had 30 days compared to 31 for his father's July, he took a day from February.

(industriousness), Pietas (piety and dutifulness), Prudentia (prudence), Salubritas (being salubrious and wholesome), Severitas (severity/sternness) and Veritas (truthfulness).

Those values were deeply ingrained in Roman society. Without a belief and respect for those core values, the Roman Empire would not have lasted over two thousand years or stretched over five million square kilometres (2.2 million square miles). As if these values weren't strong enough, there was also the ultimate conformation statement just to keep everyone in line "When in Rome do as the Roman's do."

The Romans were a historical super-tribe. They didn't bring barbarism, they brought civilisation. The Romans imposed their values, traditions and customs to an estimated fifty-one tribes across Italy, England and Wales (then known as Britannia), Spain, France (Gaul), Greece, the Middle East (Judea) and the North African coast.

To ensure as much integration as possible, Rome cleverly taught Latin wherever its armies went. To ensure economic improvement, Rome also integrated every tribe into its trading routes, building over 50,000 miles of roads to move its troops and goods across the Empire. This brought greater prosperity to every part of the Empire and raised taxes for the glory of Rome. To create greater loyalty and fealty to Rome, the Roman Army recruited soldiers from every conquered tribe. This was unifying act and a necessary one, as there simply weren't enough soldiers in Italy to conquer such a vast area. The impact of the Roman super-tribe is still being felt in our modern words and values today.

~ ~ ~ ~ ~

As James Kerr wrote in the inspirational 'Legacy' the New Zealand All Blacks also have clear values which include Humility, No dickheads, Champions do extra and Better people make better All Blacks.

Every All Black is challenged to leave their playing shirt number in a better place than when they received it. They are expected to be a better person and a better player than every past All Black who wore the same number and every All Black who will wear it in the future. To aim so high creates an extraordinary pressure. But by taking that challenge head-on and giving their very best, every all Black can become the best person and the best player that they can possibly be.

~~~~~

The Teton Sioux had eight core values. They were of their time and arguably ahead of ours. The eight values were: praying to Mother Earth; honouring and respecting all life; showing compassion to everyone as everyone is part of the circle of life; honesty and truthfulness; generosity and caring, taking only what you need; humility and living to the laws of nature; the value of wisdom; and protecting Mother Earth.

With values like these, how could the Sioux have been labelled savages?

~~~~~

The UK Labour Party appears to promote itself as a values-based political party, standing for social justice, equality and workers' rights. Labour focuses on the individual and openly claims to be the people's party. Basing its philosophy on the premise that workers create wealth, the Labour Party advocates and supports the rights of those workers. Labour likes there to be a strong and substantial state to hold royalty, business and the wealthy in check.

Historically criticised for spending what the country cannot afford, Labour would argue that it is doing public good by supporting the poor and vulnerable; as well as providing equality and fairness for everyone. So a Labour Government typically spends more money on the NHS, Housing, Transport and Education than a Conservative administration, who by contrast wants to have a smaller state that demands a lower tax burden.

Although the advent of Tony Blair's New Labour briefly took the Labour Party into a more inclusive position in the centre of politics (and into Government) the party's traditional socialist values were then restored under Jeremy Corbyn. Many would say that Labour's 2019 General Election policies were was too far 'left' and even delved into modern Marxism. Labour's day to day policies were clear. That was a strength. They stood up for the disadvantaged and wider society, which was another strength. But the policies being offered seemed unaffordable and desperate which created serious doubt over their delivery. The constraints on business alienated more voters. Rather than leaning-in to a super-tribe across the whole of the electorate, Labour leaned further out.

Any organisation in crisis tends to take on water in several places. Labour's seeming failure to tackle anti-semitism inside the party lost it respect as an advocate of equality, losing voters. If that combination wasn't enough, the party's position on Brexit was anything but clear. Fence-sitting is not a popular policy. No one could be totally sure what the right choice was, but we were all asked to make a decision. That's what voting is. By choosing not to choose, Jeremy Corbyn looked indecisive and weak. He was fatally damaged by not choosing a path. Some say that privately he knew exactly what he wanted, but publicly he hedged his bets. A leader's lack of clarity and conviction is very off-putting. It affects the whole organisation's credibility.

Even when policies are easy to understand, that doesn't them believable. All political parties claim that they stand for a "balanced economy" between workers and businesses, equality and fairness and support for the poor and vulnerable. But what is the reality? What do they stand for? There have been too many lies and half-truths for us to really know anymore. Devastated by the 2019 General Election result, Labour has to re-set itself with a clear opposition programme for Government. What does it stand for?

## What do you stand for?

The more open and purposive that political parties make themselves, the easier it is for them to attract new members and voters. The closer to the centre of politics those principles and values are, the more members and voters are likely to join them. Every organisation needs to be determined to deliver its own vision, but it also needs to have its head up to see if anyone else is bothered.

Creating policies which have a clear, practical focus rather than a philosophical one is much more helpful and attractive to potential members and voters. Providing specific details of policies gives voters the clear choice whether to vote for or against the party. A political party's values should be evident within those policies. As a purely hypothetical example, instead of saying something woolly and imprecise like "We are tough on knife crime" a political party should explain what it plans to do and offer practical solutions. That way people can decide whether they agree or not. Below is an example to illustrate the point:

"There has been a large increase in knife crime in the UK, which we are going to reduce by:

- **Doubling the maximum sentences for crimes which involve the use of a knife.**

- **Giving clear guidance to Judges on how to apply these new sentences so that our streets are safer.**

- **Requiring all shops and online retailers to verify the age of 18 or over of all customers buying knives and keep a record of their details for 12 months after purchase.**

- **Make it illegal to carry a knife or blade of any length in public without good reason.**

- **Confiscating and destroying any knives or blades which are carried in public without good reason.**

- **Requiring a license to be obtained and shown at the point of purchase for all knives with blades that are longer than six inches long.**

- **Confiscating and destroying any knife or blade which is longer than six inches, where the person owning or possessing it doesn't have a licence (whether the knife or blade is in public or not).**

- **Having a knife amnesty for one calendar month to try and remove as many knives off the street as possible."**

This is only a hypothetical example, to illustrate how values can be turned into practical policies. Every organisation needs to turn its values into practical ways of operating. All policies should be values driven.

~~~~~

The Samurai were the highest military class in feudal Japan, reaching their zenith during the Edo period from 1603 to 1867. The strength of the Samurai came from the Bushido Code its members lived by. The nature of that code was revealed in the word Samurai, which means 'to serve' in Japanese. Nitobe[37] summarised the Code in eight core principles.

**Rectitude,** *which meant having a firmness of stature and an unwavering nature.*

**Courage,** *which meant having the courage to live righteously and to do the right thing.*

**Benevolence,** *which meant genuinely caring about other people and showing them mercy. Confucious believed that benevolence was the highest trait of leadership.*

**Politeness,** *which meant respecting and caring about other people. Politeness was a concept beyond merely saying please and thank you, it was the expression of benevolence.*

**Honesty,** *which meant living simply and with sincerity. It was the exercise of abstinence and the rejection of luxury.*

**Honour,** *which meant living with respect and duty, putting others first. The fear of disgrace was very strong for the Samurai.*

---

[37] Inazo Nitobe wrote Bushido: The Soul of Japan. It was published in 1900. The book explores the Samurai way of life.

**Loyalty,** *which means a sense of commitment to fellow Samurai and the Bushido Code; and the duty of serving the people.*

**Character and self-control,** *which meant living by the moral standards required and not being intolerant or short-tempered.*

Despite being best known for the Samurai sword, the Samurai in fact valued compassion higher than confrontation and benevolence higher than belligerence.

~~~~~

Charities tend to be focused around a clear purpose and vision of the future. The wider their purpose, the easier they can gain new supporters and volunteers. Charities tend to have purposes which are strongly values based.

Amnesty International is a global human rights movement which is entirely values driven. It investigates and uncovers abuses and injustices. Amnesty's purpose is stated as being to help "where justice, freedom, truth and dignity are denied". Amnesty claims to be able to galvanise over seven million followers across the World to support its work. It reaches out to a network of committed volunteers, making Amnesty a tribal movement with a clear purpose. The values it stands for are the very values that it protects. Those stated values include being audacious and rigourous. The fact that it operates across the World means that a tribal movement has been created around those values.

~~~~~

The Government has a Communities Secretary [38] which is a vitally important role. But resolving the UK's community and equality issues requires far more focus and investment. The fabric of society has to be maintained and repaired. Homelessness is rising by an estimated 36 people per day in Britain. That perhaps doesn't sound too many but according to Shelter there are now over 320,000 people sleeping

---

[38] One Communities Secretary has been James Brokenshire, which is a name that you just couldn't make up.

rough, in hostels or in other temporary accommodation. There are more homeless people still who have no contact with local authorities or hostels (and whose data is therefore not recorded). Crisis at Christmas is a national charity which seeks to get people out of homelessness for good. It does it through a process of integrated education and training, providing support with housing, employment and health. The charity has a tribal and values driven strap-line "Together we will end homelessness". National homeless charity Shelter makes a similar appeal "Help us make sure no one has to fight bad housing or homelessness on their own." These strap-lines are truthful and realistic. On its own it cannot end homelessness, but together we could.

~~~~~

Oxfam is a global charity which responds to emergencies, saving lives and helping victims come back stronger afterwards. Oxfam describes itself in tribal terms, as a "global movement of millions of people who share the belief that, in a world rich in resources, poverty isn't inevitable."

Save the Children is another global charity with a clear purpose and values. It aims to protect children, give them a healthy start and give them the chance to learn. It too describes what it does in simple terms "We save children's lives and build better futures." It is easy to align the organisation's values with such a clear purpose. They are Accountability, Ambition, Collaboration, Creativity and Integrity. The first one Accountability has the description "We take personal responsibility for using our resources efficiently, achieving measurable results, and being accountable to supporters, partners and, most of all, children." Save the Children is a values driven organisation.

The Child Poverty Action Group aims to end poverty for children. It contends that one in four children in the UK grows up affected by poverty; and those children do less well at school and earn less as adults. The following is offered as a statistic which shows the extent of the problem. "By GCSE, there is a 28 per cent gap between children receiving free school meals and their wealthier peers in terms of the number achieving at least 5 A*-C GCSE grades." The Child Poverty Action Group has a clear purpose, which is to try and eradicate child poverty. Its vision is of a world where no children are affected by poverty. Its values are geared around its central purpose, putting children in poverty first. The Child Poverty Action Group recognises that there needs to be cultural change before poverty can be eradicated. In other words, society's values need to be changed. The Child Poverty Action Group is trying to do just that, by instilling own vision, purpose and values wider and deeper into society.

## Try to sing from the same hymn sheet

Rotary International is a global network intent on making a positive, lasting change in communities around the World. Rotary's purpose focuses on six core areas: promoting peace, fighting disease, providing clean water sanitation and hygiene, saving mothers and children, supporting education; and growing local economies. Its motto is Service Above Self and its five core values are: service, fellowship, diversity, integrity and leadership. Rotary claims a network of 1.2 million "neighbours, friends, leaders and problem-solvers" to help it deliver its Vision. With a tribe of that size and values that are focused on achieving its purpose Rotary can do an enormous amount of good. The alignment of an organisation's values to its purpose and vision cannot be under-estimated. Generating tribal power is only possible when all three sing from the same hymn sheet.

Charities must always protect the people they are helping and never take advantage of the vulnerable. Where an employer or volunteer's values are inappropriate or at odds with the organisation's values, that cannot be continue. The abuse carried out by the actions of a small minority of charity workers and volunteers has to be rooted out, so that the enormous good work done by charities' can still be done.

~~~~~

Our intrinsic values dictate how we tick. The same is true of organisations. Values which cannot be ignored, overridden or abandoned are strong and powerful. The more sacred its values are, the stronger a tribe is likely to be. Writing them on the walls inside your reception area, won't be enough to persuade anyone to adopt them. Values don't add value unless they support the vision and purpose. Where values and ideals are powerful enough to defeat any competing influences, they will be positive drivers and defenders. If in reality those values are subservient to the importance of making money, they will not strong enough to hold the tribe together.

A tribe can generate more external interest and support for its purpose by promoting its values at the same time. That means explaining both what you do and how you do it. Leading with your values makes people listen. The Body Shop does precisely that through the positioning statements "Nature Inspired Beauty. Never tested on animals" and "Cruelty-free make-up, skincare, and hair care products".

Innocent Smoothies does the same with a positioning statement that says "hello, we're innocent and we're here to make it easy for people to do themselves some good (whilst making it taste nice too). Since then we've started making coconut water, juice and kids' stuff, in our quest to make natural, delicious, healthy drinks that help people live well and die old."

Internally, a tribe will achieve more consistency and alignment by underpinning its actions and omissions with values based decision-making. If a set of values really matters it should dictate the method and pace of travel. Making decisions that don't have a values base means a tribe can lunge from one approach and one principle to another. That is unsettling for members and potential members alike. Uncertainty inside an organisation usually leads to frustration, disagreement and people leaving. Whereas clarity and consistency pull like-minded people closer together.

Values need to be used or they wither and die. Tribe members have to live them and defend them. Every tribe member needs to call-out opposing and inconsistent behaviours. It's their duty to protect the tribe's values in practice as well as in theory. Many people don't want to ruffle feathers, but unless tribe members act in the present they will lose their future. Speaking up should always be constructive and done within the tribe's values. Otherwise it's bad values following bad values.

## *Values have to be valued*

Externally, tribes can sustain and promote themselves by calling-out opposing behaviours and values of other tribes. But that is not without risk. Tribes can also gain kudos points by refusing to be drawn into a slanging match. Sir Richard Branson tries to take the latter approach. "Rather than attempting to deride our rivals, we will continue focusing upon ensuring our customers get the best service and experience in the skies. I feel sorry for anybody who revels in negativity."

~~~~~

Employees, customers, investors and potential business purchasers will be more attracted to businesses that avoid controversy. They will have values by association. Bad values cost money. Some will have blanket bans on organisations and links which might include: weapons, dirty energy, worker exploitation, poor human rights, tobacco and alcohol. Others might use a maximum threshold, where no organisation they're involved with has a turnover of more than say 10% with a controversial product or service.

~~~~~

For several years I judged the Business Personality of the Year category at a set of regional Business Awards. Trying to find a winner was always tough. Each year I interviewed over thirty people in person. One year was particularly difficult. During his interview a candidate told me a great story about values and relationships with customers which I want to share. The fact that he wasn't the eventual winner shows how difficult a category it was to judge that year.

The person in question ran a business that sold windows and doors. They had a good reputation and I wanted to know why. So I asked for story to illustrate their customer service. After a few fairly good but fairly bland examples, the business leader told a slightly different story.

One Summer's day a fitting team went out and fitted new windows and doors on a local house. The team finished for the day and went home. Sitting in his office at work the business leader received two phone calls. One was from the house that was expecting brand new windows and doors. The other was from a neighbouring property, which now had unfamiliar windows and a brand new front door. On finding his company's card on their doormat they had immediately telephoned to find out what was going on.

The business leader promised each couple that he would explain in person and set off for the street in question. On his way he had to decide what to do. Who should he visit first? What on earth could he say? He knew that his business would be judged by how it dealt with both families. What did his company want to be famous for?

Mortified and genuinely upset about the mistake, this business leader knocked on the brand new front door of the wrong house. He has chosen the values he wanted his company to be famous for. He was immediately apologetic. Visibly shocked the couple invited him in. The business leader made them an offer. They could choose between three options. They could have their old windows and doors re-installed, or they could keep their new windows and front door for free, or if they preferred they could even choose any other windows and door from the catalogue and have them fitted for free. It was a generous offer. The couple began to calm down and started weighing up the options. They couldn't really lose. But the company could.

The three-way offer was a risky one. Two of those options would cost the company twice. The old windows and door would not have gone back on properly. So if they couple chose this option the company would have had to somehow try and match those old windows and door with a second set of new ones. Similarly if the couple chose a new set of windows and door from the catalogue then the new ones would have had to come out. They too would have been unusable.

*Trust in your values*

30

There was only one good answer out of the three. Even so, the business leader felt that the company had to do the right thing. It was the company's error and its responsibility to put things right as best it could. Putting values before profits, produces more value and more profit.

The couple went out side and had another look at their new windows and door. They were still a bit shocked, but the business leader's quick actions and generous offer had gone a long way to placate them. In fact they quite liked the new windows and door. So they decided to keep them. They thanked the business leader for being so good about the mistake.

Moving along to the road, he then spoke to the original couple. They had come home from work to see their new windows and door only to find that nothing had been done. They were very disappointed. They felt that he'd let them down. They were angry. After apologising profusely for making a mistake with their order he offered them a 50% discount if they'd let him re-order the door and windows and fit them a few days later. They thought about the offer. They didn't really need the windows fitted immediately and the 50% reduction would save them a lot of money. Sticking with the company saved them re-choosing and re-ordering with someone else. They were pleased with his offer and accepted it.

Then the business leader paused. He told me that he'd learned a lot from the experience. As a result of what happened, the company had changed the way its teams operated. They now reported back from site to double-check a job before they started. That mistake shouldn't happen again.

Then he told me that he had been very lucky. I asked him why. He replied that over the following months both couples had referred him multiple new customers each. One couple had referred over ten new customers. The profit from those additional sales had not only covered the loss from the company's mistake, but it had left the company well ahead. His values had paid off.

How you deal with your mistakes says more about you than how you deal with the jobs that go well.

~~~~~

In May 2019, the BBC reported that an agency called Two Circles had broken-down the UK sports sponsorship market into sectors. According to the report, the biggest sponsorship came from Financial Services at 19%. Together with Automotive 14%, Airline 13%, Gambling 12%, Alcohol 9%, and Soft drinks 7%, these six sectors make-up 74% of sports sponsorship between them.

The missing 26% is "Other." This category seems likely to increase as a percentage of the total in coming years because of the commercial, political and moral threats to existing sectors. Over the years the appropriateness of advertising for certain types of brands has been challenged. Smoking brands were banned from television in 1965 in the UK and smoking brands pulled out of sport as part of a self-regulatory agreement. Alcohol and Gambling have been heavily challenged too. Sponsorship from both seems likely to reduce over time. Gambling is under particular regulatory pressure. The Gambling Commission is focused on preventing, educating, treating and supporting problem gamblers. This new 'climate' around the dangers of gambling and the drop in profits from Fixed Odds Betting Terminals have together created a head-wind against gambling sponsorship. GVC Holdings, which owns Gala, Ladbrokes and Coral decided individually to stop all football shirt sponsorship, as well as stopping perimeter advertising at football matches.

With increasing concern over climate change, from groups such as the Airline sector is likely to come under moral pressure. Will an Airline be as attractive a brand partner in coming years? With increasing concern over obesity and healthy eating, the Soft Drinks sector is likely to come under pressure too. The same goes for Fast-Food brands.

The cost may make it prohibitive for other sectors to get involved at today's prices, but sports teams should align their sponsorships with public and tribal values as well as how much money a potential sponsor can offer. Every tribe should look to partner with brands that support its values and the values of its supporters. How often does that happen?

If the brands with the most money reduce their profiles in sport (as seems possible) more sponsorship will have to come from the morally acceptable elements within "Other." Building those partnerships now seems a prudent step for sports teams to consider.

~~~~~

In June 2019, drinks giant Diageo ended its thirty year relationship and latest sponsorship deal with the London Irish rugby team over the club's signing of former Ulster player Paddy Jackson. Until Jackson's signing, the London Irish rugby brand and Diageo's Guinness had become almost synonymous.

Recruiting Jackson was always going to be contentious. His contract had been revoked by the Irish Rugby Football Union (IRFU). Some will say that as he was found not guilty of rape or sexual assault in 2018, London Irish should have been morally free to sign him. But others will say that the jury got it wrong. Regardless of the verdicts, the IRFU took a moralistic view, in line with its values.

His former club Ulster has since introduced behavioural classes which include discussions on alcohol, sexual consent and social media use for all professional and academy players. The training is being delivered throughout the season by trainers from Women's Aid Northern Ireland.

Since withdrawing its sponsorship, a spokesperson for Diageo said they met with the club to express concerns. But it seems that the decision had already been taken. "Their recent decision is not consistent with our values and so we have ended our sponsorship."

In reply, London Irish informed the BBC that the club was "understandably disappointed" with Diageo's decision. Would the club have signed Jackson if it had sought out Diageo's views first?

Unless an organisation works closely with all of its stakeholders, it risks severely weakening its tribal power.

~~~~~

Other than a sense of purpose, a tribe's values are its most important element. A tribe's purpose is that tribe's 'what' and its values are its 'how'. Any time spent by a tribe and its stakeholders agreeing, living, monitoring and reiterating the tribe's values is time well spent.

Are your tribe's values clear and engrained? Do your brand partners have similar values?

## 2.7 SPIRITUAL HOMELAND

Jealousy is envying what isn't yours. Greed is wanting ever more when you already have enough. Many wars have been fought over land, fuelled by jealousy and greed.

By contrast, being territorial is about protecting what's already yours. Tribes are typically highly territorial. They are naturally protective of their safe and sacred places, especially their land and homes.

### *Tribes are highly territorial*

Tribes have traditionally had a strong connection with the land they live on. The Sioux were a plains people and their relationship with the land was full of love and respect. Although they were nomadic and regularly moved from one place to another, it was always within their own tribal lands. The land was vital to their way of life. It was spiritual and sacred.

When the Sioux lands were being forcibly taken from them, Sitting Bull reacted by saying "Is it wrong for me to love my own? Is it wicked for me because my skin is red? Because I am Sioux? Because I was born where my father lived? Because I would die for my people and my country?"

Tribes without a spiritual homeland will struggle to stay together. In modern times, a spiritual homeland might not a physical place. It might be a virtual one like WhatsApp or Facebook.

~~~~~

Football wasn't always an exclusively feet only game. In the Middle Ages, there were various antecedent forms of football, typically classified as mob football. They sometimes involved the use of hands and sticks, as well as feet. Matches were played between neighbouring towns and villages. They often involved an unlimited number of players on opposing teams, which created a heaving mass of humanity trying to kick, push, lift or drag an inflated pig's bladder towards the markers at the other end of a town. There were often brawls. Local rivalries were very strong. It seems that the concept of home and away matches began during this period.

Although football may have been first played in China in 300 BC, modern football first took hold in England. The earliest competitive match which was exclusively foot-ball seems to have taken place in Cawston, Nottinghamshire, some time between 1481 and 1500. After that the game grew in popularity. In 1526 Henry VIII ordered 45 pairs of velvet boots and "a leather pair for football". The game finally became professional in 1885. Ever since, football's influence has spread far and wide. At any time of day or night, there will be teams playing football somewhere in the World, using footballs, pig's bladders, tennis balls, tin cans or anything else they can kick towards a goal. Whatever the truth about its origins, England is accepted as the spiritual home of football and it is now part of the British DNA.

Football is now the World's most popular sport. It is played in virtually every country. A pitch can be created almost anywhere. All you need to start a game is a ball and "jumpers" for goalposts.

Professional football is a business. Many English football clubs have long histories. Every professional team plays half of its matches at its home stadium. That's where its loyal fans turn up in numbers to support it. A football team's home ground is its tribal centre, or in other words its spiritual homeland. Unless you have become a global brand, the further away you are from the epicentre of events the fewer people belong to a football tribe. So every club tends to have a high percentage of its supporters living within an hour's drive of its ground.

Sports clubs and their local communities share strong ties. As Jock Stein once said "Without fans who pay at the turnstile, football is nothing. Sometimes we are inclined to forget that." The connection between a sports team and its local community often seems unbreakable, but not every football club started out where it is based today.

~~~~~

Although Arsenal FC is famous for its North London location and its local derbies with Tottenham Hotspur, it was originally a South London based club. The team was originally formed in 1886 as Dial Square by the Royal Arsenal, Dial Square workshop employees who created the team[39]. The name became Woolwich Arsenal after the London Borough the team played in. The club's first badge mirrored the Woolwich Borough coat of arms which includes three cannons with lions' heads at their loading ends. In 1913 Arsenal re-located north of the River Thames and changed its name to The Arsenal the year afterwards. The single cannon logo remains to this day. Remarkably that move across the city stuck and over one hundred years later Arsenal is one of World's leading football teams.

Interestingly as I write this, I have just seen an Arsenal and Adidas video on You Tube promoting the new playing kit for the 2019/20

---

[39] Confirmed in The Beautiful Badge by Martyn Routledge and Elspeth Wills.

season. Ian "Wrighty" Wright fronts it. What's the theme? "This is home." With phrases like "North London is home" and "And remember we run North London" Arsenal is well and truly embedded in North London.

## "This is home"

I wonder how many Arsenal fans would stop supporting the club if it was transported South across the river today? With all the money in football, a club like Arsenal could probably survive that sort of relocation, if the club stayed in the Premier League. But would it?

Not every relocation has gone as well as the Arsenal one. When Wimbledon FC transferred to Milton Keynes in 2003 it created a fundamental identity problem for two clubs. The move was forced on the fans by the club's ownership. Many of those fans felt a strong anger, because of a compelling sense of attachment to the club's spiritual home in Wimbledon. They passionately resisted the move. The decision to relocate the club was so divisive that a group of those fans splintered off and created a whole new football club. So as Wimbledon FC began its new life as MK Dons in Milton Keynes, a brand new football club called AFC Wimbledon began to play matches in Wimbledon.

The owners of MK Dons bought Wimbledon F.C.'s name, players and place in the league structure. The new Wimbledon club called AFC Wimbledon had to start life from scratch in the Premier Division of the Combined Counties League (the ninth tier of English football). After series of hard-won promotions, the 2017/2018 season saw the two clubs finally face each other in League One, the third tier of English football. In September 2017, Wimbledon hosted MK Dons in Wimbledon. AFC Wimbledon could have taken the moral high-ground and welcomed them back "home." Instead the hosts chose not to mention the visitors in its match-day programme and only referred to the team as MK on its electronic scoreboard. Feelings were still raw.

AFC Wimbledon now sits in League One, the same league as MK Dons. It's rise from the ashes powered by the passion of the club's loyal fans and a sense of belonging in Wimbledon.[40]

~~~~~

Former Liverpool player and BBC pundit Mark Lawrenson won five league titles, one European Cup and three League Cups in seven seasons at the club, playing his home matches at the club's World famous Anfield ground. After Liverpool's historic win over Barcelona in the second leg of the 2019 Champions League semi-final, Mark wrote an article for the BBC about the Anfield effect.

"As a Liverpool player, I learnt for myself what a difference that support makes - I would describe it as a feeling of 'whoosh', and 'wow'. You might think you are tired, but then you run and chase the ball and make a tackle and the place goes mad. You are thinking 'how good is this' and you want some more of it. For the opposition, the opposite is true. The crowd unsettles and unnerves them, as much as it lifts and inspires the Liverpool players. I have seen plenty of times, where world class players are made to look ordinary because the atmosphere is so intense they barely get a chance to breathe, let alone think. That was exactly what happened on Tuesday. The Liverpool fans were incredible right from the start and just kept going. By the end of the night, Barca were totally shot to pieces. The longer the game went on, the more ordinary they looked, and that is the effect that Anfield can have on you." If that match had been played anywhere else the Anfield effect would have been nullified.

## *"The crowd unsettles and unnerves them"*

Our working and living environments have a massive effect on us. Where you live can even have an effect on your physicality. Being born into the Kalenjin Kenya would give you the genetics, physicality, diet, climate and lifestyle to be a long-distance runner. That's because all these forces make the Kalenjin Kenya slim, with small calves and ankles. If the Kalenjin didn't live together in the same location then

---

[40] The 2018/2019 season looks like the teams may reverse places.

their genetics, diet, climate and lifestyle would all change. Over time so would their physicality.

Similarly, the Sherpas have been living on the Himalayas for over 6,000 years, which allows their bodies to adapt to the extremely cold temperatures and low oxygen levels. If they didn't live there then future generations wouldn't be as adapt as climbing as they are.

The people of Okinawa, Japan have the largest concentration of centenarians in the world. Their exceptional long life has been put down to the healthy diet they have all been eating. Their collective good habits have been passed down from one generation to another. The Okinawan diet of vegetables, grains, soy, tofu, fish, squid and octopus has kept its people very healthy. But sadly for Okinawa, there has been a rise is the number of health issues in recent years. This has been traced back to the plethora of fast food outlets which arrived after a US Military base was opened in the area.

What contribution is your location and working environment making to your people's genetics, diet, climate, lifestyle and physicality?

~ ~ ~ ~ ~

Relocating your business premises can improve and lift your organisation's working environment. An office move can improve the available facilities, add free on site car parking, offer better access to local shops and even improve workplace culture. Or it could bring about a change for the worse, if the move has the reverse effects. Even if the end result will be positive, the process of moving sites comes with temporary down time, infra-structure costs, staff unhappiness and departing customers. Relocating business premises also risks breaking all of the community links that the Company has built and developed.

Transferring to a new modern building can transfer a business into a different geographical, social and economic space. There is no doubt that employers can substantially increase employee engagement and business performance by making improvements to their working environment. But making everything new is not always best. Employers need to try and re-create their tribe's homeland in a way that's fit and reflective of its past, as well as making it fit for the future.

## *Relocating offices can break all your community links*

Taking symbols of the past along with you and giving them a place in the present can keep a tribe's heritage alive for its descendants. But what's being left behind for good reason should not have to come along for the sake of it. Heritage should always have a value or it's not worth that label.

~ ~ ~ ~ ~

West Ham United is one of a number of London based football teams. Local rivalries are as intense in London as they are in Manchester, Liverpool and Sheffield, but in London there are multiple local rivalries within the same city.

West Ham plays its football in the London Stadium, inside the district of Stratford. The stadium was previously the main venue for the 2012 Olympic Games. The club hasn't always played in that part of London. West Ham's first ground was on Hermit Road in Canning Town. Then the club moved to Browning Road in East Ham, followed by a shift to the Memorial Grounds in 1897. The only reason the club isn't called East Ham United was because they were already called Thames Ironworks FC at the time. These associations have led to the club's nicknames the Hammers and the Irons.

The team became West Ham United in 1900 and carried on playing in the Memorial Grounds until 1904, when the club moved to its spiritual home, the Boleyn Ground in Upton Park. There the club found stability, spirituality and over 100 years of its history. It was there that the club moulded its identity and where the likes of Sir Bobby Moore (England's 1996 World Cup Winning Captain with 108 caps), Sir Geoff Hurst (England's 1966 World Cup hat-trick hero) and

Sir Trevor Brooking CBE (647 club appearances and 47 for England) all graced the turf.

Controversially, the club's owners relocated the team to the London Stadium for the start of the 2016-2017 Premier League season. The background to the move was huge debt and an increasing pressure to become more competitive. All of the club's main rivals had state of the art, purpose-built football stadia to build their tribes around. Upton Park was ageing and half their size with a 35,000 capacity. The London Stadium was available. As a semi-converted athletics stadium it had 66,000 seats.

Rather than sitting as close as ten yards away at Upton Park, supporters now sit between twenty and ninety yards away from the action. The raw and rowdy atmosphere was part of the appeal. Upton Park was a stirring place to visit as a visiting player or supporter. Once the yell of "Bubbles" went up, a huge chorus of "I'm forever blowing bubbles" immediately followed. It punched through the air and swirled its way around the old ground, gathering the spirit of every past player and supporter for the cause. The hairs on the back of your neck stood on end. Upton Park was a very tribal homeland.

The relocation across London has undoubtedly had some positive financial benefits. Match day income is now much larger and the sale of Upton Park has helped to wipe out the club owners' multi-million pound debt. Transferring has helped to secure the club's commercial future. But had the great spirit of West Ham been lost in the process? Had its bubble burst?[41]

The first season in the new London Stadium was fraught with problems, including the controversial decision to seat tourists and occasional fans in a prime place behind one goal. The London Stadium is spacious and modern with good facilities, but it is soulless by comparison to Upton Park. The community spirit around the new ground doesn't exist anymore, except briefly from merchandise sellers on match days. Home advantage is no longer the same.

---

[41] "I'm forever blowing bubbles, Pretty bubbles in the air, They fly so high, nearly reach the sky, Then like my dreams they fade and die. Fortune's always hiding, I've looked everywhere, I'm forever blowing bubbles, Pretty bubbles in the air."

The club is learning the lessons and in time, the ground will redeveloped exclusively for football. In the short-term, steps are being taken to try and restore a home feel, including adding more bubble-making machines. After an incident where fans got onto the pitch and gathered around the Directors' Box, it seemed that much more was still needed to placate the fans and turn Stratford into the new spiritual home of West Ham United. The club needed to re-establish links with its heritage.

## Home advantage is no longer the same

So in 2019 the club wisely named a third stand at the London Stadium after a West Ham legend. Now the East Stand of the London Stadium has become the Billy Bonds Stand. As the player who holds the club's appearance record, Billy Bonds was a great choice. He joins Bobby Moore and Sir Trevor Brooking as being immortalised in a stand.

Every tribe needs to connect with its past, present and future simultaneously. West Ham is working hard to connect all three and find its fortune. With the huge additional revenue from the London Stadium, West Ham's dreams look healthier than they have in decades. They won't fade and die.

~~~~~

The inside of a tank provides a form of mobile homeland for its crew. Cramped inside a stifling, deafening metal box tank crews operate cheek by jowl under oppressive conditions. Out in the theatre of war, a crew's tank is its base.

The Tank Museum at Bovington has many examples of modern and historical tanks. It also tells the real life stories of the men who risked their lives to fight in them. The museum includes a 2006 quote from Paul Rollins who served in the 49th Royal Tank Regiment. "I loved my crew. We were just like brothers. It is a type of comradeship you don't get in ordinary life. It takes something like a war to make you appreciate the spirit they showed."

Crushed in together, there was a heightened sense of reliance on each other. It is the exact opposite of "every man for himself". Through working, eating and sleeping as a group, they must get to know each other better than their own families do. Each crew develops an interdependence and a camaraderie that is essential. It is tribal.

*"I loved my crew. We were just like brothers."*

The Armed Forces and other teams that face adversity together (such as fire crews) bond in a way that ordinary jobs on civvy street can't easily achieve. Although businesses can't replicate that level of intensity, they can create a unifying sense of purpose and a working environment for a tribe to develop in. That process of tribe-building can be accelerated and enhanced through the intensity of shared challenges and the safety of a spiritual homeland.

~~~~~

Whilst there tends to be a strong local following for the likes Everton and Aston Villa from their immediate communities and through birth, it is much harder for those teams to build wider support. That may be because it may difficult to market your sports team to a wider audience if it doesn't share its name with a major town or city. People who don't live in the local area can't quickly put it in its geographical context. A few teams in England have transcended that limitation and have a worldwide following but they are the big London teams of Arsenal, Chelsea and Tottenham Hotspur.

A sports team's spiritual homeland ideally links the ground, club name and geography together. The city of Southampton offers one single professional football team, with a very clear sense of its origins. At St. Mary's Stadium in Southampton, the Southampton FC fans sing their anthem "Oh when the Saints go marching in". Southampton FC is nicknamed the Saints and its supporters are known as Saints fans. Southampton and Saints are interchangeable names for the same tribe. The club started out as a St. Mary's church team. Its nickname, its hallmark song and the name of its ground are completely aligned and include a direct reference to the club's origins. This clarity helps to sustain the tribe and it sends clear messages to attract the next generation of supporters.

The more an organisation connects with its spiritual homeland and local community, the more tribal it can be. This can be shown through a period of absence too. Tottenham's crowds declined after its temporary move to Wembley while its new ground was being built. Playing at Wembley must be a wonderful experience, but it is a neutral venue. The Spurs fans were homesick for their beloved White Hart Lane. Moving back to the same location, with the same match day rituals is coming home.

~~~~~

The sport of rugby league was born in Huddersfield in 1895 when a group of Northern clubs broke away from rugby union. As a result the sport's UK heartlands are in Yorkshire, Lancashire and Cumbria. Over the last hundred and twenty years the sport has developed within the Southern Hemisphere, in Australia (largely limited to New South Wales and Victoria), New Zealand, Tonga, Samoa and Papua New Guinea. But it has proven very develop it further in the Northern Hemisphere. The decades of history and heritage needed to build generations of supporters, doesn't naturally exist in other geographical parts of the UK and overseas. Unlike football, rugby league isn't a global sport.

Currently Catalans Dragons, Toulouse Olympique and Toronto Wolfpack are trying to buck the past trend of "Grand launch and steady decline". Clubs can be funded by rich benefactors, but unless a fan base and juniors system can be developed a club cannot sustain itself. Every sporting club needs a strong link with its local community. Those links take decades to develop. Like roots, clubs need to grow their community connections as widely and as deeply as possible. Toronto Wolfpack's marquee signing of Sonny Bill Williams needs to be used to promote an extensive junior player programme and community development, or it will be a wasted opportunity.

A sporting club effectively pulls up its own roots every time it moves its stadium. If a fledgling club is forced to move during its development years it can be very damaging. Relocating a tribe's homeland puts its whole future at risk. Doing that with a well established club would be highly questionable. In rugby league, doing it if you're a club outside of the Northern heartlands is surely asking for disaster.

The London Broncos rugby league club has played at far too many different grounds during its relatively short history since 1981. The club's spiritual home has changed at least thirteen times during its history. Those grounds include Craven Cottage (the home of Fulham FC), Crystal Palace National Sports Ground, Chiswick Polytechnic Sports Ground, Barnet Copthall Arena, Brentford's Griffin Park, Hendon FC's ground, the Valley (Charlton Athletic's ground), Barnet FC's stadium called the Hive, the Stoop Memorial Ground (home of Harlequins rugby union club) and Ealing Trailfinders' Sports Ground. It has also played a series of one-off games at football grounds around London including Wealdstone, Chelsea, Leyton Orient and Gillingham.

*Like roots, clubs need to grow their community connections as widely and as deeply as possible.*

The club's spiritual home is not the only thing to change for London Broncos. There have been several changes in its ownership and its name as well. The club was originally formed as Fulham. Since then the club has also been known as London Crusaders, London Broncos and Harlequins Rugby League before reverting back to London Broncos. That's five different club names to cheer for, in less than forty years. How is building a sustainable tribe possible under those circumstances? It is quite remarkable that the club is still in existence. But it is no surprise that its crowds are poor and its success has been heavily restricted. After securing promotion back to Superleague in 2018, London Broncos are still in the game. They are a rare exception. A tribe needs a tribal homeland and time to grow its roots very deep.

By contrast, the 2017 Leader Leader's Shield Winners, Castleford Tigers, still play at the same ground that the club began at in 1926. Castleford was originally a Roman camp on the ford of the River Aire. Now it is a small Yorkshire town of approximately 40,000 people. At the heart of the community is the town's rugby league club. During the Superleague season Castleford Tigers predominantly plays clubs from elsewhere in Yorkshire and Lancashire. The Castleford ground is called Wheldon Road and is also known by its nickname, the Jungle. It holds approximately 11,000 supporters who sit and stand close to the pitch. Both the town and the team are known as 'Cas' which helps to maintain its strong community links.

In 2017, Castleford Tigers finished top of the Superleague and became the most consistent rugby league team in England. The club's clear identity has played a core part in achieving that success. With only one name change (adding the Tigers epithet) since the club's formation in 1926, there is a clear, uncomplicated history to refer to. That can be tapped into, to help guide its future. But despite that heritage and solidity, the present has major challenges. As a club, Castleford needs to play in a modern, purpose-built stadium to secure its financial and rugby futures. That brings a pressure to move away from its spiritual home, which would be a great shame. There have been several attempts to build a new stadium and an equal number of false-dawns to go with them.

Despite their amber tinted spectacles Castleford fans know that the club's ground isn't fit for purpose. However emotionally hard it is, the time has come to re-invent Wheldon Road or more locations. But all the club's history is there in that place. Every home game has been in that same ground. The fans are so close to the action that they almost feel part of it. It feels emotional, like it really, really matters. The players can feel that too. Liam Watts plays prop for the Tigers. He was born locally but left for stints with Hull KR and Hull F.C. before returning to Castleford in 2018. In March 2019 he gave an interview to the local paper about his return.[42]

"When the fans get behind you it really does give you a boost. You see Cas fans wearing their shirts with pride everywhere. It's a small community and a real rugby league town. I wasn't at the club then, but I think when Cas got to the Grand Final I think 80 per cent of the town went -- I think there was only me left here! It's good to see. The

---

[42] The Pontefract and Castleford Express.

town needs us and it's a part of people's lives. They do look forward to watching games week in, week out."

The home fans love the 'old girl'; but visitors to the ground have a different view. In the build up to the opening round of the 2019 Superleague season Sam Tompkins of Catalans Dragons was interviewed about playing at Castleford. His response was very revealing.

"We have a tough, tough challenge going to Castleford. Horrible stadium, horrible fans, they get right on your back and that's what makes rugby league so special. Everyone's so territorial about their ground and Castleford is one of the most intense places to play."

From a tribal perspective, Castleford should think long and hard about moving away. Building a new stadium on Wheldon Road would be the best of both Worlds, but may not be practicable. As things stand Castleford's spiritual home is a powerful weapon on match day, unsettling the opposition before a ball has even been kicked.

~~~~~

Fierce local rivals, Wakefield Trinity needs a new stadium too. There is a constant underlying pressure on both clubs to pool their resources and share a new community stadium. But neither club wants that, as it is the first step down a slippery slope towards a merged club. Neither set of fans wants a shared stadium either, because each club is a separate tribe with its own distinct history, traditions and rituals. The rivalry between these two clubs is part of their essence, part of their reason for existing.

## Calderford Trinity anyone?

The whole Wakefield district is a rugby league hotbed. The sport of rugby league needs both Castleford and Wakefield to be healthy and prosperous. The clubs are close together and the area is not as economically affluent as others, which probably means the governing bodies (Superleague and the Rugby Football League) would like to see one merged club. The game's hierarchy probably sees one plus one equalling more than two, through pooling the resources of both clubs. However, they may be wrong to assume that would provide a super-tribe with a bigger financial footing. In economic terms a merger may seem logical, but instead of three, a merger might end up equalling minus two. Each club has its own spiritual homeland. The location for a merged community stadium would by default end up nearer to one club than the other, immediately alienating the other set of fans. A neutral compromise could end up somewhere meaningless to both sets of supporters. The name of a merged club would start with 'Cas' or 'Wake', immediately alienating one set of fans. Or it might start with a new name altogether after the River Calder than runs through both. That sort of perceived compromise would probably alienate both sets of fans simultaneously. Would either set of fans support a club called Calderford Trinity?

A forced marriage between two sporting clubs is unlikely to produce attractive or healthy offspring. The Hull and Gateshead merger reportedly cost the sport of rugby league £1million, before the new merged club effectively de-merged and both Hull and Gateshead ended up back where they started (with Hull having spent £1million the sport couldn't afford).

A new merged club in the Wakefield district could perhaps eventually grow a new base of support, but possibly not until the governing bod y had run out of patience. What both clubs really need is more investment and promotion of the sport by the RFL in the game's heartlands. Instead, what they will get is the RFL trying to expand the game overseas at the expense of looking after its core clubs. The long established Lancashire and Cumbrian clubs could do with exactly the same help, but they won't get it either.

Rugby league needs to protect its heartlands first and foremost. The reality is that the first of Castleford and Wakefield to secure a new stadium is likely to prosper to the other club's detriment. These local tribes are fierce local rivals, both playing in the top English division of the sport. The longer that is the case, the better it is for rugby league.

~ ~ ~ ~ ~

Mergers and acquisitions are both forms of marriage. The more points of difference there are between the two partners, the more risks to a successful marriage there are. Opposites can attract, but similarities tend to be easier to live with. When two tribes are thinking about merging, they need to agree a combined vision, purpose and set of values before they commit themselves to each other. An agreed collaboration has a great chance of one and one making "three".

When one party surrenders to the other it's not a merger, it's a takeover. People leave a merged organisation far less often after a real merger. If two parties can reach genuine agreement over a new joint VPV, they will be able to combine their energies and resources and make a super-tribe. By aligning those fundamentals the merged tribe can set off towards the same destination, travelling together along the same path.

Normally, the larger party imposes its philosophy, management and systems on the smaller party. Reverse takeovers happen too. What's best for the business may mostly come from one of the merging partners and that's fine. It's the act of 'taking over' that's problematic for modern tribes. Every stakeholder in every tribe should actively choose to belong to it. The purpose and merits of a merger should be chosen because they work for everyone. If they don't or they aren't well enough explained, good people will leave.

## *Mergers can combine energies and resources to make a super-tribe*

The negotiations for mergers and acquisitions tend to concentrate are on the financial terms of the deal, pitching the parties against each other. It's not the best way to unify the parties. Working out the coed purpose first makes more sense. The EU appears to have fallen into this trap by insisting on negotiating the UK's Brexit deal before agreeing the relationship going forward. If the both parties' cards are played close to the chest and each tribe's purpose and vision go unsaid, the success of the merger will be down to luck rather than good project management. If the values of the two tribes compliment each other, the shared workplace culture should be positive. If the value sets don't 'fit' there will be conflict and fall-outs.

On any merger or de-merger, negotiating the future relationship first would make the parties feel more aligned from the outset. The merger deal would then be easier to mould collaboratively. The financial deal would probably end up fairer and more balanced.

In addition to these core fundamentals there is also the importance of the spiritual homeland. Where will the combined business be based? Will it be at a new site, where everyone has to re-event the tribe together, or will everyone cram into one of the merging partner's locations. Moving to a brand new site creates issues around the loss of two sets of existing community links, but it also creates a fresh-start and a potentially unifying opportunity.

Moving everyone into one of the party's premises, turns the other party's staff into instant strangers. Will the merged premises bring across signs of the old? Will the existing staff welcome them in with open arms? Will everyone be rewarded as whole, for good co-working? The more these issues are addressed, the more successful the merger will be.

~~~~~

A shared local geography can be a positive reason for coming together, but a shared border marks out tribal lines and can hold people apart. Every border there is inside an organisation can prise a tribe apart. Examples of internal borders include those between owners and workers, between different departments; and between different office locations. In direct contrast, every connection that links back to the centre and the combined VPV can pull a tribe closer together.

All tribes should treat their neighbours as being stakeholders in their tribe. All departments should treat their other colleagues as stakeholders in their department. Good neighbourly relations can really help a tribe to thrive.

~~~~~

The Barbarians is one of the World's most famous rugby union teams. Formed in 1890, from Southern English teams, the team first toured in the North of England. Since then players have travelled from all over the World to play for the Baa-Baas, taking on a mix of international and club teams at their home grounds. Also known as the Baa-Baas, the Barbarians is a permanent touring team, with no ground and no clubhouse. The club's itinerant nature makes the Barbarians the only mainstream rugby team without a spiritual homeland. So, as perhaps the only truly nomadic rugby team, every game is an away game.

Playing for the club is by invitation only. The honour has to be earned through a player's performances for club and country. The Barbarians team for each match only one week's preparation together. At the beginning of the week the players are given the unmistakable black and white hooped tie, adopting them into the Barbarians tribe. Then by running out in the black and white hooped shirt and black shorts, a player is marked out as a Barbarian forever.

The Barbarians playing kit (uniform) has a unique twist. Every player who plays for the Barbarians wears the socks of his regular club. That way the Barbarians team stands as a collective of skills, geographies and backgrounds. It is that heightened environment and collegiate atmosphere that appeals to so many of the World's great players. The Barbarians is a collaborative, itinerant enterprise. It is a super-tribe.

## *Every game is an away game*

With a new combination of players every game, the Barbarians play on instinct. Rather than following the usual playbook of structured moves, each group of Baa Baas set itself a basic structure and learns a basic set of coded calls. Tactics and routines are minimised because there isn't enough time to learn anything more complicated. When the whistle blows, the team plays its rugby with freedom, without fear and for the love of the game. The Barbarians' style is the closet thing to pure rugby and every professional rugby union player wants to experience it. Building new connections on and off the field adds a new set of challenges and brings a stimulating social side. This special combination of elements is what's made Gareth Edwards, Phil Bennett, Jerry Guscott, Jonah Lomu and so many other outstanding players accept the invitation to join the Barbarians' tribe.

On 27 January 1973, the Barbarians played against the All Blacks at Twickenham. During the match the Barbarians scored perhaps the greatest rugby union try of all time, known simply as "That try". The commentary of Cliff Morgan tells its story. With a voice full of excitement and joy, the words alone can still raise the hairs on the back of your neck.

"Phil Bennett covering...chased by Alistair Scown...Brilliant...Oh that's brilliant!...John Williams...Bryan Williams...Pullin...John Dawes...Great dummy...To David, Tom David...The half-way line...Brilliant by Quinnell...This is Gareth Edwards!!!...A dramatic start...What a score...Oh that fellow Edwards...Who can stop a man like that. If the greatest writer of the written word would've written that story no-one would have believed it. That really was something."

For the Barbarians to have survived for so long without a spiritual homeland is truly extraordinary. By bringing their tribal heritage everywhere they go, the Baa Baas make every away match a home game. Wherever the hooped black and white shirts run out is their spiritual homeland. With so many other tribal elements in place, the Barbarians show no sign of stopping their wonderful brand of expansive, free-flowing rugby. Long may it continue.

~~~~~

One of the key themes of Tolkien's work is the importance of home and the pleasure to be gained from travelling far afield and then returning home. Both Bilbo and Frodo Baggins have long and arduous adventures far away from their home in Hobbiton. In the quiet moments during their epic journeys each of them misses home and longs to return to the Shire.

In the second part of film trilogy derived from Tolkien's The Hobbit[43], the King Under the Mountain Thorin Oakenshield leads a group to recover lost Dwarf gold from Smaug the Dragon. Strongly affected by his own greed and the curse of dragon sickness on the gold, Thorin loses sight of what really matters. Driven by the desire to possess it all, Thorin obsesses over the gold and jewels, in particular the most valuable treasure, the Arkenstone. His infatuation these material things causes Thorin to become utterly selfish, break the promises made to others and accuse his closest friends of disloyalty. Challenged over his behaviour by Bilbo, Thorin resists. Eventually as the cloud of his dragon sickness finally lifts, Thorin sees things clearly and says to Bilbo "If more people valued home above gold, this World would be a merrier place."

~ ~ ~ ~

The film Any Given Sunday[44] is about American Football and famously includes the "inches" speech given by Al Pacino's character Tony D'Amato. The movie also includes other pithy guidance from Tony D'Amato when the team is struggling. Tony's motivational focus is on protecting the team's spiritual homeland. His words are simple and to the point.

*"This is where we live. We're not going to let them f\*\*\* with us in own our house are we?"*

This sort of speech appeals to anyone with a sense of attachment to a place. Would you let a competitor waltz in to your organisation and take what's yours? Would you give your biggest competitor your prize account or lose a cup final without a struggle? No. Defending what belongs to your tribe taps into a core motivation and that can lead to a greater and more sustained effort.

~ ~ ~ ~ ~

---

[43] In the final instalment, The Battle of the Five Armies.
[44] The film came out in 1999 and was directed by Oliver Stone.

There are many odes to spiritual homelands in song, literature and poetry. Each one describes the special link between the tribe's people and its spiritual places. This song lyric is just one example.

*"Make our home in this sacred ground.*
*We've been here for years*

*Solid in foundation.*
*The blood, sweat and tears*

*Raise your voice. Stand side by side*

*And we will sing forever*

*We don't have much but*
*we got each other."*[45]

~~~~~

I recently met a man called Sam[46] who lives in London. One evening he was driving along the Embankment when he spotted six or seven men violently kicking another man on the ground. Instinctively he pulled over and got out of his car. Sam felt that he had to help the man on the ground.

On his own Sam knew he couldn't do enough to stop six or seven men. So he waved other passers-by over to help him make the men stop their violence. Together this group of total strangers started engaging with the attackers and moving in to protect the victim. Remarkably they managed to disperse the attackers.

But almost immediately afterwards the same men came back again. According to Sam they had "hate" and "the desire to kill" in their eyes.

---

[45] From 'Got Each Other' by Ska Punk band The Interrupters.
[46] He is happy for me to tell this story.

Sam didn't know if the group of strangers could stop such determined violence a second time, but he was determined to try. The strangers made a circle right around the prostrate victim. By becoming a human shield, waving their hands and pleading with the men to stop, the attackers eventually gave up and left.

The victim of the assault survived. He refused the group's offers of further help and headed off into the night.

## "No I wouldn't have."

After hearing the story, I asked Sam why he'd chosen to stop. I wanted to know why he'd risked his own life, why hadn't just carried on driving. Sam explained that he had been trying to analyse that himself ever since, but he didn't have an answer. So I asked him whether he'd have stopped if the same incident had been in another town or city? Sam thought about it for a moment and said "No, I wouldn't have." His own answer surprised him.

I suggested an explanation. Sam digested it and then he agreed with me.

It wasn't just a random man that was being kicked to death, it was also Sam's city and the way of life that was being assaulted. The man was a local in Sam's own home City, someone he might have known. The attack was taking place in his spiritual homeland, inside his safe area. Sam instinctively knew that if local people didn't stop to help, this sort of thing would become more prevalent. Subconsciously he knew that the fate of his own neighbourhood was at risk. He wasn't just intervening to save a man, he was intervening to save his spiritual homeland.

We need more people like Sam in every town and city across our country. What would you get out of your car for?

~~~~~

On a personal level, we can have more than one spiritual homeland. Where we live, where we were born or brought up and the stadium of our favourite sports team are all likely candidates. Wherever we feel like we're at "home" can be a sacred and important place. We can have multiple heartlands, places that we love and love coming home to. A spiritual homeland should feel familiar, safe and secure. It should house people from our tribes. The more an office, warehouse or factory keeps us safe, sustained and part of something more fulfilling, the more sacred it becomes.

The converse is true as well. If our home is where the hurt is, we need to change it. That may mean changing jobs or getting more from work, more from our wider lives. The more run down we let our workplace become, the less we care about it and the less sacred it becomes.

Where are your tribe's spiritual homelands? Building a strong connection to place gives you and your tribe greater strength. How strong are your tribe's links to its places?

~~~~~

If your working space doesn't allow for many of the following then try to adapt your existing premises if you can. If not, think about moving to somewhere that can be a spiritual homeland and optimise your working space.

- Areas for relaxed group discussions to share ideas and have project meetings - so that discussions are more natural and free flowing.

- Fridges with free drinks and water heaters with constant hot water - so it's easy to get a drink and keep the working momentum going.

- An area to try out new technology (e.g. new phone, laptop or ipad options for the organisation) - so everyone feels involved and can give feedback.

- An area for free fruit and healthy snacks - so energy levels stay high.

- Areas for confidential mentoring - so learning can be passed on.

- Chill out no phones areas for reflection - so that quality thinking can take place without disruption.

- More space around work stations/areas - to allow easier work shadowing.

- Spacious and well maintain buildings - to allow to high quality working and learning.

- Sticking to the brand colours throughout so everywhere feels part of the same organisation – to help promote joint-working and collaboration.

- Really good natural light (supported by artificial light where needed) - to provide high quality working and learning space.

- Really intuitive heating systems - so that no area is too hot or cold, to promote high quality working and learning.

- Really good ventilation and air circulation - to promote high quality working and learning.

- Access to learning programmes on screen at every workstation/laptop – so personal learning is instantly available.

- Really good acoustics - so discussions are easy; and disruption is reduced.

- Screens with national news, the organisation's purpose, vision and values; and project progress throughout the building - so that there's a context to work in.

- Wall space for artwork by workers or their children – so that it links to and feels like home.

- A sign with the person's name, photo and role up by each workstation – so it's easy to find and speak to other people.

- Spare desks built in to work areas - so rotations, secondments, shadow working and project management can easily take place.

- Sound-proofed booths for skyping and face-timing – so calls can be relaxed and focused.

- Excellent security (including in the car park) - so workers feel safe at all times, which will allow them to relax and be happy to work early/late (encouraging more social and joint working).

- Learning and Development area (physical and/or within an intranet) – for people to leave questions and problems for others to help them solve.

- A sound-proofed public speaking area - for people to video themselves practicing a presentation and then watch it back (with space for others to attend and offer feedback).

- Internal teaching sessions during lunchtimes - so knowledge and skills can be passed on. Link them to annual development goals and rewards for the teacher and learner.

- Flexible/standing desks - so workers can choose their preferred way of working.

- Flexible meeting room partitions to allow for an area to hold a town hall meeting to update staff in person - to come together as one tribe.

- Secure and covered cycle racks close outside - to encourage healthy living.

- Multiple bins for recycling - to encourage sustainability and links to the wider World.

- Canteens or kitchen areas - to allow healthy eating, quick catch-ups and non-work conversations to build rapport.

- In/out boards in all areas - so that people can see who's free and feel a sense of connection to the whole. Ideally make them digital and automatically link to your entry fob.

# 2.8 TRIBAL LANGUAGE

As human beings we are able to hear and interpret the sounds around us. We have also taught ourselves how to make precise and coherent sounds with our mouths. Over the centuries human beings have learned to communicate with each other using hundreds of different languages. As well as their own national or indigenous language, tribes also use their own accents, gestures, signals, codes and terminology to communicate with each other. A tribe's chosen words don't have to conform to any standard dictionary or Wikipedia definitions. They just need to be adopted and accepted as the tribe's way of describing things.

Even within the English language some words can be spelled and pronounced differently. I have chosen to use the English spelling of words throughout this book rather than the American versions proposed by spell-checker.

Without a common tongue, a tribe will splinter and die. That's because growing a tribe is about being inclusive, but also being open to new members with the same purpose. There is a point at which a tribe can become too insular for its own good. That happens when a tribe's language is so exclusive that its members and its stakeholders cannot all understand or properly communicate with each other.

There are too many English words, derivatives, duplicates and different spellings to count them all definitively. Some words can be used in multiple ways to convey multiple meanings. So they potentially count more than once. The 2018 Oxford English Dictionary is reported to have added over 4,700 new words during 2018 alone. It's also reported that there are nearly 47,106 obsolete words in the same dictionary. They might be obsolete in general use, but they may still be used by some of our tribes.

## Without a common tongue, a tribe will splinter and die

English is a complex language which is ever growing. Around the World many countries speak English, but they don't speak it the same way or use the same combinations of words, let alone the same accents and emphasis. There an almost infinite number of language variations available. Each tribe has its own version.

The more different a tribe's communication is from other languages, the more distinct and exclusive the tribe becomes. If its neighbours cannot understand it, a tribe will become insular and detached if it doesn't learn another language too. If it does then it can choose whether to communicate or not. For example Welsh speakers also learn to speak English, meaning they can speak to their neighbours if they wish and not if they don't want to. If a tribe has reached out across the World, spreading its language wherever it went, then it can now communicate with people well beyond its own borders. That's because the people of those destinations now speak its language too. This is particularly true of English, Spanish and French.

~~~~~

The harder that your tribe's language is for others to learn, the more of a virtual border there is. Using tribal terms for common words can help to generate a greater sense of the tribe's purpose and develop a siege mentality. If your tribe uses its own language, it will create a close community dynamic and a tight group of tribal members.

If I said "Down right" to you, what would you do? The answer depends on where you are, but if we were inside a theatre I'd be asking you to move downstage to the right. That in itself has layer of buried understanding. Which way is 'downstage'? As it happens it means moving forwards towards the front of the stage.

What about if I ask you "Where's the bible?" Again it depends on the context. It could be the prompt book in a theatre, the White Book to a litigator or an actual bible. Common language brings common sense.

~~~~~

The more exclusive the common vocabulary is the more likely it will fall into disuse. Focusing on its key words only can help to establish a tribal language that supplements and works with the national language. On a basic level it may be as simple as everyone using one common word for the tribe's core terms. For unity and simplicity, businesses need to use one common term for the group of people that it sells its goods or services to. If it nominates the word "customer" then every tribe member should use that instead of a mix of customer, client, buyer, shopper, purchaser or punter. If you choose to use uncommon words or TLA's (Three Letter Acronyms) they all need to be listed within your tribal dictionary. They could also contain any prayers, hymns or poems adopted by your tribe. Keeping a central record of the tribal language will make it easier to clarify and learn.

Your tribe's language should always support its vision, purpose and particularly its values. No terms should be used at work that conflict with the tribe's core values. Each tribe should therefore have a clear idea of what words and language are not to be used.

Language is a potential barrier to good neighbourly relations. So your tribe needs to learn the signs and languages of your neighbours, so that it can speak fluently with them. That connection helps enormously to steer the best path towards your tribe's vision. Holding back your own tribe's language for communicating with your fellow tribe members helps to keep it exclusive.

~~~~~

Cockney rhyming slang originated in the East End of London, probably during the nineteenth century. To avoid being understood, market traders and criminal gangs wanted to conceal the meaning of the words they were using. So they applied two word phrases for each word that they wanted to hide. The second word had to rhyme with the original word. The first word was deliberately non-rhyming and unrelated. Using the second word on its own was too obvious because it rhymed with the real word, but when the first word was used on its own, the speaker's intentions were suddenly hidden.

For example, the word stairs became rhymed with "apples and pears" and became known as "apples". When a trader or gang member wanted to say stairs, they would simply say "apples" instead. If they'd said "pears" the rhyming link could have given it away too easily. Other examples are "rabbit" which comes came from Rabbit and Pork (Talk), "scarper" which comes from Scarpa Flow (Go), "Barney" which comes from Barney Rubble (Trouble); and "bread" which comes from Bread and Honey (Money). Unless an observer knows the two word phrase and the context, it is extremely difficult to understand what's being said. When used together to make sentences, it is almost impossible to keep up until you're familiar with all the terms.

Layering of rhyming phrases on top of each other makes them even more difficult to comprehend. For example, "Aris" is used to mean bottom. But why? Is that because the words sounds like Arse? Ironically no, not directly. Aris is short for Aristotle. Aristotle is rhyming slang for Glass Bottle. Bottle and Glass is rhyming slang for Arse. Over time 'Aris' has become rhyming slang for bottom and 'bottle' is used to mean having no arse (i.e. bravery) to do something.

## Use a tribal dictionary

Putting that all together, if some one said "He's all rabbit, no bottle. First sign of Barney and he'll scarper" it would translate as meaning "He's all talk and lacks courage. The first sign of trouble and he'll go."

A number of rhyming phrases are used in modern conversation. Every noun can be turned into a form of rhyming slang. A Porky is a lie, after Porky-pie. If something goes Pete Tong, it means it goes wrong. The insult Berk is short for Berkley Hunt, a famous fox hunt. Its real, hidden meaning is much more offensive. Politician Jeremy Hunt's name has also been used to rhyme the same offensive term. Charlie Hunt does the same thing. So calling someone a "right Charlie" or a "Jeremy" means you really don't like them very much.

Rhyming slang can still be an effective way of hiding the meaning of your conversation. Your tribe can create its own unique two word phrases. Rhyming slang can be passing secret messages or conducting confidential negotiations.

~~~~~

Morse Code and the Phonetic Alphabet are two well-established ways of transmitting and disguising language. If you know and understand either, you can quickly and effectively pass messages on, whilst leaving other people struggling to keep up.

In Morse Code the word Secret translates into the following combination of short and long sounds. If you learn Morse Code, you can understand this message ... . -.-..-. . -   It means secret. If don't understand Morse Code, then it just sounds like a tapping noise.

In the Phonetic Alphabet, the word secret would translate into: Sierra, Echo, Charlie, Romeo, Echo, Tango. That's easy enough if it's spelled out slowly, but the faster you use it the less understandable it becomes.

During the Second World War a Polish woman called Krystyna Skarbek worked as a spy for the British. She used words of poems to signify letters, to make it extremely difficult to decode her messages[47]. Using one French poem that Krystyna used, the word SECRET would translate into the following words: Le, Meridionales, Mes, Ravi, Meridionales, Bonheur

~~~~~

---

[47] History Revealed Issue 49

The British Army unofficially uses its own words and phrases, creating a language all of its own. For example, a sick note can be called a Biff Chit. Brag Rags refers to medals and campaign ribbons. There are also examples of rhyming slang, with the term Colonel Gaddafi being rhyming slang for the NAAFI. The term NAAFI itself is an acronym for Navy, Army and Air Force Institute and refers to the military supermarket on the base. So if a soldier says that he's going to the Colonel, only another soldier will instantly know he means the shop. Most people outside the Army would think he was going to see a senior officer. The British Army is a very tight-knit community. Its unique form of language helps to maintain that.

~~~~~

Rugby teams use code during matches, to stop the opposition understanding their plans. This is especially true of line-out calls in Rugby Union. Using a mixture of numbers, letters, words and sounds a team can disguise its intentions. Line-out calls can simply indicate who the ball is to be thrown to, or they can be more complex and signal a pre-planned and well-practiced move which begins with the lineout.

To help to disguise the operational part of the code (the part that tells you what to do), some additional parts are added to the code as meaningless padding. But how do you know which bits matter? You don't unless you are told. That has to be agreed in advance. So a team might decide that only the second word of a three word code is operative. The other words are added to confuse the opposition. Unless you can solve the code, you are left in the dark and excluded.

## Are you in the know?

When a player joins a new team, he or she needs to quickly learn the new team's on-field calls. Doing that instantly turns that player from an outsider into an insider. Being in the know makes you part of the group that's in the know (and not the group that doesn't).

So if, hypothetically, the hooker wants to throw the ball to a second row called Janet Jones, she might shout "Nine - Bag – Thatcher". The opposition doesn't know if the call is Nine, Bag or Thatcher. Even if they knew which part of the call matters, they can't work out what it actually means. So they have to listen, watch and try and work the calls out during the game. Having more than one call for the same throw is vital. "Seven – Bones – Corbyn" would do the same thing. Confused? How does that mean that the ball is being thrown to Janet Jones? It's because "Bag of Bones" is being used as rhyming slang for Janet Jones. "Grumbles and moans" or "Traffic cones" could offer the same option. If you're not in the know, then you have no idea. Layering your codes will keep the opposition guessing. Switching your codes will keep the opposition guessing even harder.

~~~~~

There are many different kinds of codes and ciphers in use. Learning your opposition's codes can give you a huge advantage. Some opposition terms and codes involve a few simple rules. Others are deliberately complex. Without knowing the underlying code, you cannot understand the message's hidden meaning. Until you can translate the code, you can't understand the tribe.

During the Second World War the Germans used coded messages for signals traffic in the conflict areas, including for contact with German ships. The messages were being sent by Enigma cipher machines. As they were in code, they could be sent openly across the airwaves. The Allies couldn't decipher them which left them helpless. So the British set up a specialist code-breaking team at Bletchley Park. The team included mathematics experts and chess champions. Alan Turing OBE[48] and his team in Hut 8 worked tirelessly to crack the Enigma Code. Eventually, after nearly six months effort, the team created a huge electromechanical machine which could intercept and speedily decipher the German Navy messages.

---

[48] Alan Turing is a war hero. He happened to be homosexual. In 1952 he was convicted of gross indecency and had to accept chemical castration in order to avoid a prison sentence. It took until 2013, nearly sixty years after his death, before he was given a posthumous pardon. This action led to retrospective pardons for everyone else who had been convicted of for homosexual acts. The Imitation Game is a 2014 film about the Bletchley Park code-breakers and stars Benedict Cumberbatch and Keira Knightley.

Having cracked the fiendish language of the Enigma Code, the Bletchley Park team was immediately faced with a moral dilemma that tested its values. Every member of the team wanted to save every Allied life that they could. But they knew the crushing truth that the more lives they saved the more likely the Germans would realise that Enigma had been cracked. If that happened the Germans would simply change the code.

## *Until you can break its codes, you can't understand a tribe*

There was no doubt that the war had to be won and to win it, he Allies needed the insight that their machine was giving them. They could not save everyone. The practical question was how many ships could be saved without the Germans realising that the code had been cracked? That meant allowing some Allied ships to be sunk. Which ones? That sense of responsibility over life and death weighed heavily on the team. What was the tribe's overall purpose? It was to win the war.

Turing's team performed extraordinary acts of both technical genius and human resilience. As a result, the Germans were blissfully unaware the code had been cracked and kept using the same cipher for their messages. The machine in Hut 8 unquestionably helped to turn the tide of the war in the Allies' favour. It is believed that cracking the Enigma code probably shortened the Second World War by two years. Understanding what your competitors are saying, allows you to understand what they are thinking.

~~~~~

The power of language can't be under-estimated. Speaking the same language as other people gives you an instant feeling of belonging. That allows you to make educated decisions. Despite the fact that many people around the World speak English, having multiple language skills within your tribe can give you a big communications advantage.

~~~~

Tribes don't have to use codes or ciphers, but their language should be distinct and used by every tribe member. That distinctiveness can come from using a regional dialect. The UK has many accents and local words that only make sense if you're from the area. As a result we can often recognise locals and strangers from their accents and the words they use.

Research by Bath and Manchester Universities found that people can make premature judgements about other people because of how they sound. It seems that's especially true when words are shortened. Until the 1970s virtually all newscaster and television presents spoke in "received pronunciation" (otherwise know as the Queen's English). That perpetuated the strangeness of regional accents. Now with so many accents across all media that's gradually becoming less of an issue. Steph McGovern is an excellent business presenter on the BBC. Steph's Smoggie (Middlesbrough) accent doesn't seem to have been an impediment to her career. Janoaworramean?[49]

The more utilitarian that a common word is, the more variations of it there tend to be across the different parts of the UK. The word for "food" has many variations across the country. They include Fittle (West Midlands), Scran (Yorkshire/Lancashire), Boos (Cornwall) and Bait (Newcastle) to name but a few. Other slang words like grub and nosh and can also be used to mean food.

*The more universal a language is, the more inclusive it is and the easier a super-tribe can form*

A bread roll is a bread roll, but it's also many other words depending on where you're buying it. As it's a very common item, every UK region has a word for it. The variations include Bap, Barm, Barm Cake, Barn Cake, Batch, Bread Bake, Bin lid, Bread-cake, Bridie, Bun, Buttery, Cob, Lardy Cake, Morning Roll, Muffin, Oggie, Rowie, Stotty, Scuffler, Teacake and Vienna.

---

[49] Do you know what I mean?

Each tribe should actively choose its own terminology for its common words. The more impenetrable a tribal language it is, the more it excludes other people. The more universal a language is, the more inclusive it is and the bigger the tribe can potentially become. By choosing secret methods of communicating, a tribe is deliberately making itself hard to understand and hard to join.

Butchers use back slang, to allow them to speak without customers understanding them. Back-slang essentially reverses the letters in words. It is thought to have originated in London's Smithfield Market around 1850. An obvious example is the word yob, which is back-slang for boy. Money becomes "yenom" in back-slang. That might seem easy enough to understand when it's pointed out to you. But when it's part of a whole sentence in back-slang, spoken at speed, it is a very effective form of code. Over time some words have been shortened or modified and there are rules about plurals and ing word endings to help disguise the meaning even further. Back-slang is intentionally hard to understand, especially when spoken in hushed tones.

~~~~~

Science Fiction has invented a number of imaginary languages, which are spoken by a small number of devoted fans. In Star Trek, the Klingons were the USS Enterprise's most feared and war-like enemy. The show's writers didn't just make up random words or sounds for the Klingon characters to pretend to speak, they created a whole new language. According to an online translator "We come in peace" would translate into Klingon as "roj yI'el maH." Although you won't ever hear them say that in person.

## Agree your tribal terms

Another famous example is J.R.R. Tolkien's creation of Elvish languages for use in his books about Middle Earth, most notably the Lord of the Rings. The main Elvish languages spoken are Sindarin and Quenya, although Tolkien invented other Elvish languages as well. If you want to join the tribe you can go online and use an Elvish translator to turn English into Sindarin and vice versa.

You don't need to go this far, but agreeing clear tribal terms will help with communication. And as communication is the most failing aspect of team working, it is always worth developing a common language. The more that tribe members sound the same and say the same things, the more of a tribe there is. After deciding what really matters to your tribe, you can draw up a shortlist of the key terms that you need a tribal word for.

~~~~~

Overall this is a lot of information about tribal language. Is it that important? The answer is an emphatic yes. Try and get a leading performance level from anyone without good communication. You won't.

Tackle it with existing team embers and all new staff. When new people join your organisation, they should be given a dictionary of your tribe's language, terminology and TLAs to help them get up to speed quickly. The faster that they feel a part of their new tribe, the faster they can help you to achieve your tribe's purpose and vision. Your dictionary can also include words that should not be used because they conflict with the tribe's VPV.

~~~~~

Sometimes the power of silence can be used instead of words. The Silent Walks that took place after the Grenfell Tower disaster were highly emotional and very powerful. No words were needed. The silence resonated with anyone seeing the images. Everyone can understand that kind of language.

~~~~~

Having got to this point in my writing, I discovered Susie Dent's fantastic book[50] on modern tribal languages. Susie, of Countdown fame, has researched the languages of approximately seventy modern British tribes and her book explains how those private

---

[50] Dent's Modern Tribes - The Secret Languages of Britain.

languages work. If you are looking for more insight and inspiration on how to develop your own tribal language, Susie's book is a great read.

Some of my favourite terms are 'canteen medals' (by the military), 'sherbet' (by cabbies), 'ofima' (by golfers) and 'bucket of nails' (by darts players). I won't steal Susie's thunder by telling you what they mean. By deliberately not revealing those meanings I hope I am proving the point that if you don't understand a tribe, you can't be in that tribe.

~~~~~

Which languages, terminology and acronyms do your tribes use? Is there a shared way of communicating, a form of common tongue? If not could you establish a shared set of words? Speaking and sounding like other tribe members helps to unify a tribe.

Does every tribal member say the same things and sound the same? If you want to know how engaged a tribe member is, listen closely to what they say.

## 2.9 TRIBAL STORIES

With our heightened abilities to speak and listen, the communication between us is often verbal. Shared explanations, of how things work, teach all of us to find our way in the World. Using real life examples can really help to bring those explanations to life.

Telling stories about your tribe's history helps to bind its present and past together. Stories can be of any length or style. A few well-chosen words that illustrate and promote the tribe's vision, purpose and values can be just as compelling as an epic saga. Stories don't always have to be about tribal legends doing amazing things. Examples of small tribal actions can be well worth telling too. Successful stories confirm the rightness of your purpose. They highlight the values you believe in. They offer further reassurance about what is important to the tribe.

Work can be uninspiring. No one actively chooses a mindless automaton life. Without inspiration, there is less perspiration. Hearing a tribal story can take people out of the monotony and routine, lifting them up to a higher plain where the tribe's purpose kicks in. Helping people to find a purpose beyond the work itself can generate far more tribal power. Feeling fulfilled can be enormously rewarding and hugely motivating. Feeling empty and unfulfilled doesn't power very much. Without stirring your soul, your life is not being lived.

## What are your tribe's stories?

To take people out of emotional poverty, a tribe has to create a tight connection between its people and the tribe's purpose. Stories have a big part to play in that. Tales of how members have helped each other and lived the tribe's values can resonate wider and deeper than tales of making money or acquiring things. A tribe should tell and re-tell its tribal stories.

At the end of The Commitments[51] manager Jimmy Rabbitte is gutted that his band has fallen apart. The worldly wise Joey "The Lips" Fagan turns to him and says "The success of the band was irrelevant - you raised their expectations of life, you lifted their horizons. Sure we could have been famous and made albums and stuff, but that would have been predictable. This way it's poetry."

~~~~~

---

[51] A 1991 film based on Roddy Doyle's book. The film focuses on the Dublin music scene and has an amazing Soul soundtrack.

Spending your time and money following a sports team is the hallmark of a loyal supporter. Every trip and every game creates new memories. Over time, a bank of stories is created about a team, including tales of its glories, great players and the trophies that it's won. Accounts of the past can rekindle powerful memories and help to inspire the successes of the future. The fans who went to those winning finals or big games still tell stories about them. They will carry on talking about them until their memories have faded or they have all left this mortal coil. Supporters who weren't even born when the team last won something wait impatiently for their turn to go. Those that missed the opportunity to walk up Wembley Way, into Old Trafford or across the Twickenham car park know that they missed something magical. They remain envious for life. It's as if the fans that made the match have a medal that they don't.

Taking a train ride, bus journey or walk amongst fellow supporters on the way to a match feels reassuring. Inside the stadium, sitting or standing amongst a crowd of your team's fans brings a pure tribal pleasure. The tribe's colours, uniform, logo and songs are all on display. Being among of the partisan mass that supports your team means feeling part of the herd. It provides us with social belonging. It adds another set of stories into the mix.

Being a loyal supporter means watching a team in all weathers, even when it isn't winning much. The stories of losing finals and even relegations are powerful too. They are about what might have been. The experience of being beaten and missing out on success can devastate coaches, players and fans alike. But those experiences can also be the fuel that their fire needs to go one better next time. Stories can help to rebuild the desire that's been lost. Stories can re-establish a team's mojo, allowing it to get into another final or back into the division above. The stories of defeat can be as powerful as the tales of victory. Whether your team is successful, mid-table or struggling doesn't matter. Tribes built around sports teams commiserate, speculate and celebrate together through story-telling.

~~~~~

In the 2016 Rio Olympics, Great Britain's Women's Hockey team performed brilliantly and after an unbeaten run they made the final. The team was playing for Gold medals and the right to be called the Olympic champions. The match was against the Netherlands who were the existing World and double Olympic champions.

During a hard-fought game, Great Britain's goalkeeper Maddie Hinch saved a penalty and several short-corners. The whole team survived long periods of pressure. Both finalists were playing fantastic hockey. There was virtually nothing to choose between them. At the end of normal time, the match was a highly tense three-all draw. There had to be a penalty shoot-out to decide the winner.

The Netherlands must have thought that they had the advantage. They had just won their semi-final on a penalty shoot-out. They had a proven big-match mentality as the World and double Olympic champions. Their confidence was high. But British goalkeeper Maddie Hinch had been studying them. She had worked out a plan to counter each one of the Dutch penalty takers. With those plans written down in a little black book, she was tactically prepared. With messages to herself such as "Chill Out" and "Stay Big" written in marker-pen on her water bottle, Maddie was mentally prepared.

Television is perhaps the greatest story-teller, bringing us daily stories from right across the World. As a result, millions of people were watching the 2016 Olympic hockey final on screens around the globe. Tales with high drama can really grip people's attention and an Olympic final with that goes to penalties is a great tale. One of the two finalists would be the Olympic Champions, the other team merely runners-up. Gold medals and a lifetime of joy were at stake.

## *The Maddie Hinch story is inspiring to many*

As each British player stepped up, their teammates were powerless to help them take their penalties. Despite hockey being a team sport, penalty-taking is all about individual nerve and performance. The pressure on the British goalkeeper and penalty-takers must have been immense.

One penalty after another, Maddie Hinch controlled her fears and executed her game-plans, saving all four Netherlands penalties in turn. Every tactical plan she'd made was the right one; and Maddie's mental strength allowed her to execute each plan superbly. Great Britain won the shootout two-nil and with it the Olympic title. The whole team played superbly and Great Britain won because the every player was World class on the night. Amongst their passion, skill and determination as a team, Great Britain had the coolest blue head in the stadium.

Since that final, when young potential hockey players are weighing up whether to play the game, all someone has to say is "One day you could be like Maddie Hinch." That story offers inspiration for anyone. According to the Great Britain Hockey website 10,000 extra players started playing club hockey after that 2016 final.

This compelling story worked brilliantly for hockey. Which stories of past achievements can you tell to inspire the next generation in your organisation?

~~~~~

Many stories are written to positively promote a set of values, such as stories of good battling valiantly against evil. Those stories seek to subconsciously influence the reader or listener into choosing a side. The most obvious examples of good and evil stories are found in the Bible. There are endless others. The genres of Science Fiction and Fantasy have probably created the largest number of stories pitching good against evil. They include Harry Potter, The Lord of the Rings, Percy Jackson, Star Wars, The Lego Movie and The Chronicles of Narnia amongst countless others.

Some stories set out to influence the reader with a fixed set of social and political values and messages like Animal Farm, A Clockwork Orange, Dances with Wolves, 1984, I'm Alright Jack, Dr. Strangelove, Avatar, The Lord of the Flies, The Maze Runner, The Matrix, The Hunger Games and television programmes like Dr. Who. They give one perspective, inviting you to get on board with it.

## Which side are you on?

Other stories are adopted to support an existing set of values. The chosen story is retrospectively interpreted as having hidden meanings, whether or not the story was written with them in mind. The Winnie the Pooh stories written by A.A. Milne form a series of children's books. They have since been interpreted by some as setting a moral compass, with each character representing one of the seven deadly sins or the Christian ideal. Whether or not that was intended, the stories have been analysed in that way. There are different theories as to which character represents which sin, which reveals an instant weakness in the theory. Whilst some of the characters could be attributed to sins, it is a real stretch in other cases. Pooh's gluttony is presumably the starting point for the theory. Christopher Robin is no doubt the Christian ideal. From then on, the argument is less compelling with Pride, Envy, Anger and Sloth to somehow be found in Piglet, Owl, Eeyore, Kanga and Roo.

This Winnie the Pooh theory is not compelling, but it is a good example of people trying to find stories to support their values. People like to hear stories that chime with their own beliefs. Borrowing, adapting or creating stories that reinforce your tribe's vision, purpose and values can offer encouragement and reassurance. Which stories can you use to promote your vision, purpose and values?

~ ~ ~ ~ ~

Stories can be real, fictional or a mixture of both. As long as the themes and messages are the right fit for your tribe, any kind of story can hit the spot.

The 2017 film Wonder Woman [52] has the fictional Goddess Diana Prince as its lead. Motivated by freeing the World from war, Diana leaves the relatively safety of her secret island life with the Amazons and bravely travels to the Allies' trenches of the First World War.

---

[52] A DC comics and Warner Bros. production, directed by Patty Jenkins and starring Gail Gadot.

Desperate to stop the bloodshed and defeat Ares the God of War, Diana heads straight across No Man's Land on her own, capturing an enemy trench. She then liberates the village of Veld, before finally defeating Ares.

With a strong woman lead and a strong anti-war theme, the film actively promotes inclusion and equality. Everyone can be strong, brave, sexy and equal. Everyone can change the World for the better. The storyline obviously hit its mark as it was a critical and box office hit.

~~~~~

Laughing together bonds people and jokes are a form of story. They can be about something silly and inoffensive that everyone can laugh all the way along the spectrum to cruel, heartless bullying. A tribe's humour should fit comfortably within the tribe's values. Banter is never an excuse for harassment. There should be a clear line drawn between appropriate and inappropriate jokes. Tribal members should have clear guidance as to which is which. That can come as part of induction or equal opportunities training.

Without any humour an organisational culture is too austere and uninspiring, but with no controls in place a workplace can become discrimination central.

Can you hear laughter around your office? What does your tribe laugh at? Which subjects are taboo for jokes? What happens if someone makes an inappropriate joke? Every organisation should know its answers.

~~~~~

The way a story is told can heavily influence its impact. The storyteller's chosen tone of voice will have a dramatic effect on how we interpret the story, as will its dialogue, setting, cinematography, sound, casting, costume and lighting.

When filming The Godfather, the decision was taken to light the bad characters from above to shroud their faces in darkness. Characters with a mix of good and bad traits were filmed from the side to leave one side of their faces in shadow. Good characters were lit face on. Movie goers were directed towards a point of view about each character.

When you tell your tribe's stories, how are you leading your audience to reach your point of view?

~~~~~

Good stories come out of overcoming peril, struggle and adversity. A tale of fighting against the odds can offer a positive example for members of the tribe to emulate. Stories can be epic and glorious like Robin Hood, King Arthur, or Hannibal's invasion of Italy from across the Alps. Or they can be gritty like Bath's backs-to-the-wall Heineken Cup win in 1998. Stories can also be about patience and perseverance like Thomas Edison and Sir James Dyson. They can be about keeping a cool head like Maddie Hinch. As long as a story helps to support the tribe's vision, purpose and values it will help to generate tribal power.

*Good stories come from overcoming peril, struggle and adversity*

If a story can be passed down through the generations and transcend time, it can inspire an endless number of tribal members. Without telling and re-telling its stories, a tribe's heritage, values and essence will be lost.

~~~~~

When filling job vacancies there needs to be a meeting of minds and motivations. Asking for stories about each candidate's current working environment and their personal and organisational successes should reveal who they are and how they work. Their values will come alive through story-telling. How much concern and credit do they give to others?

If a candidate is cagey about whom they are, it's probably not a good sign. If after one interview you still don't know them, bring them back, put then at greater ease and ask again. They might be too humble, a little shy or have just had an off day. But if after two interviews you still don't know who they are, move on to another candidate.

Seeing how someone reacts to stories about your organisation is another way to test for suitability. Telling stories about all the support, trust, learning, autonomy and personal development on offer will provide a broad range of appeals. Stories about past candidates who have gone on achieve great things can be motivational. Other inspiring stories can come from the organisation's charitable, environmental and corporate social responsibility initiatives.

All organisations can benefit from having a storybook full of stories for every occasion.

~~~~~

Rather than a business telling stories about itself to make sales, a more successful route is to ask happy customers to give testimonials. Satisfaction is more credible from the mouths of the recipient. Most organisations are alive to this, but most undercook their efforts. Others take the idea head-on. In May 2019 Madza revamped its customer magazine and re-named it Mazda Stories.

~~~~~

Place marketing is when a town, city, county or country sells its best features to attract inward investment. Those 'best' features will include its physical geography, public realm, transport links, technological infrastructure, amenities and employment prospects. Those features will also come from its cultural offering, housing, scenery and people. Creating an overarching place narrative, with core themes, will help to gain some traction.

If that place narrative is co-produced and co-owned by the place's key stakeholders it will gain far more traction. Inclusive thinking on place is critical in developing the creation, marketing and usage of place marketing. Working together as a super-tribe can create many mutual benefits for everyone in that place.

~~~~~

How many stories does your tribe tell? How many are passed down through the generations? Do they support the tribe's purpose? Do they illustrate the righteousness of its values?

# 2.10 TRIBAL ART

Our power of sight allows us to view and appreciate the World around us. Some of the finest imagery comes from nature but some of it is made by human beings. Art comes in many forms, allowing every individual artist to express themselves freely. As a result, art appreciation is very subjective. We like what we like. We don't like what we don't like.

When art is themed or comes from a stable of similar artists, those artworks can be said to be part of an art movement or period, such as Cubism (most notably Pablo Picasso), Surrealism (heavily influenced by Salvador Dahli) and Pop Art (made famous by Andy Warhol).

The Impressionists were arguably the greatest collection of artists in one movement. They included Claude Monet, Pierre-Auguste Renoir,

Edouard Manet, Edgar Degas, Paul Cezanne and Henri Matisse amongst others. Despite their undoubted talent, the Impressionists faced harsh opposition from the conventional art community in France. The term Impressionists was a satirical criticism of the movement, named after Monet's painting Impression soleil levant (An impression of sunrise).

The Impressionists were seen as radical because they didn't paint with neat lines and contours. They defied convention by letting their brushes flow, painting more realistic sky, clouds, water and light. With hindsight they are revered for pushing the established boundaries. Inspired and encouraged by each other's art, they painted themselves into art history. They were a tribe of artists that created their own lasting impression.

~~~~~

Art can help to tell the story of a tribe. Historic tribes produced art in the form of pottery, literature, carving, architecture, sculpture, weaving, photos, painting, design and fashion. Our sense of touch and feel allowed humans to manufacture all kinds of art over time. Many forms of art have been manufactured for daily use whilst others have been created for aesthetic reasons only. Artistic designs have changed and the appreciation of art has developed enormously. Tribes have come and gone, with many leaving traces behind them. Tribal art gives us an insight into the way a tribe operated and what was important to it. Whether it's the Benin [53] bronzes (modern day Nigeria), the Elgin Marbles from Greece, Celtic torcs, Japanese Namban folding screens or something less renown, art can tell a tribal story as well as stimulate our senses.

The Florentine Codex[54] is a record of words and pictures produced by Aztec artists at the behest of Spanish Franciscan friar Bernardino de Sahagún. Ironically as the Aztec tribal images were being recorded on paper, their gold, religion, temples and culture were being pillaged and destroyed by Spanish conquistadors.

---

[53] Actually brass alloy but beautiful none the less.
[54] The best-preserved manuscript of the Historia general de las Cosas de Nueva España, stored in the Laurentian Library in Florence.

## Some art has practical use, some has aesthetic benefits only

The Bayeux Tapestry is an embroidered cloth stretching nearly seventy metres long. It depicts the Norman version of the events leading up to the Norman conquest of England. With images of William Duke of Normandy and King Harold, the tapestry culminates in the 1066 Battle of Hastings. In history it is very often the victorious that get to write the account of what happened.

Lady Elizabeth Southerden Thompson Butler's oil painting of the cavalry charge at the Battle of Waterloo is called "Scotland for Ever!" Hanging in Leeds City Art Gallery, it was painted in 1881 and pictures British cavalry horses charging headlong towards the viewer. The painting is art, tribe and history brought together in a single image, leaving the viewer with a feeling of courage and a sense of belonging.

~~~~~

The Shoreditch Sisters are a modern branch of the Womens' Institute. The Sisters produce cool, hipster knitting as an art-form and a way of making protest. They are proud of knitting a Solidarity Blanket for the women in Yarls Wood Detention Centre; and of sewing a Vulva Quilt to raise awareness of female genital mutilation. The decision may have been contentious but it was peaceful and it clearly worked.

Tribal art can be very thought provoking. Whatever your point of view, telling your tribal stories through art and craft can preserve them for posterity.

~~~~~

Modern tribes use art to stamp themselves on the World. The artwork of business takes many forms.

Photographs and images work well in flyers, online posts and magazine advertisements. Film creates great corporate videos and television advertisements. Symbols can be employed in corporate names and logos. Branding adds the colours and designs used to decorate corporate merchandise. Having a uniform takes ordinary clothes and turns them into corporate fleeces, hats and umbrellas. All these art forms are part of a businesses' art armoury.

## What tribal art does your brand use?

What artwork do you have in your offices, factories, distribution centres and website? Does it reflect and promote your tribe's vision, purpose and values? Are you using art to tell your tribe's stories, confirm the tribe's values and celebrate its achievements?

~~~~~

The Institution of Mechanical Engineers (imeche) has created the symbol of a flame, using a series of thin flame-shaped lines that sit one outside the next. It is part of a national movement to address the shortage of science, technology, engineering and maths (STEM) graduates. imeche is playing its part by trying to increase the number of engineers. Each flame-shaped line stands for a stage in that process. From the inside out, the lines stand for:

- Influence (in terms of having a positive impact on the UK's education policy)

- Understand (in terms of finding out the ways young people learn and develop their attitudes to engineering)

- Transform (in terms of enhancing the practice, skills and knowledge of education professionals)

- Inform (in terms of providing advice and information to potential engineers); and

- Inspire (in terms of igniting an enthusiasm about engineering in young people from an early age).

The campaign has a glossy brochure, with a clear statement of its purpose "We already know that society needs more engineers. It's time to do something about it."

The campaign's imagery embraces the concept of keeping the flame alive. The campaign brochure also has a good call to arms "The time for talk is over. We must lead the change." imeche has used the fire imagery to link to the flames of inspiration and hope. Art can be powerful business tool and influencer.

~ ~ ~ ~ ~

Does your tribe visibly stand out from the competition? How does it use art, images and design to promote itself? Is your tribe maximising all the visible signs available? Does its artwork stir the tribe's members to action?

## 2.11 TRIBAL SONGS AND MUSIC

Music is very powerful. Songs can instantly remind us of who we are and what we stand for. Tribal music can stir your deepest emotions. It's not just songs that have this effect it is music generally. Psalms, anthems, shanties, instrumentals, carols and hymns can all tap into the same emotional well. Music can evoke times and places in our past, linking us to the tribes we shared them with. Hearing songs that remind you of your family or a group of friends transports you straight back to that period of your life, together with the emotions you felt at the time.

~ ~ ~ ~ ~

All kinds of songs and music are capable of creating tribal links. If you are an English rugby union fan, then the familiar hymns Abide with me, Swing Low Sweet Chariot and Jerusalem are stirring tribal songs. They fill the English with instant pride and belonging. Singing Swing Low at Twickenham is a hugely tribal experience.

*Songs can pull a team and its*
*supporters together as one*

However if you are Scottish those three hymns all have negative connotations, precisely because of their association with England. Flower of Scotland has a tribal power for Scots all over the World. Singing it at Murrayfield is a hugely tribal experience. Your reaction depends on which ancestors you have and which national rugby tribe you belong to.

For New Zealand Rugby Union players, the Haka is a sacred war chant that's performed by the whole team before every match. One of the team's most famous players Jonah Lomu described how he approached it "Each Haka has its own interpretation but you have to be in unison with your teammates."

~~~~~

Films tend to make the biggest impression on us when the soundtrack stirs your emotions. Many of the most affecting films have excellent scores and soundtracks. Movies with music at their core can provide powerful social messages and Brassed Off is a very good example of this. Immersive films like Dances with Wolves, the Godfather, Star Wars and Lord of the Rings are all the more excellent because of their soundtracks.

Other films can be lifted up to become good films by virtue of their soundtrack. The background work of strong music can stir the foreground to greater things. The Last of the Mohicans and Local Hero are really good examples of films which were raised up by their exceptional soundtracks.

Perhaps unsurprisingly, all of these films just happen to be tribal stories.

~~~~~

The Labour Party has a party song, called The Red Flag. It is a socialist song which offers solidarity to the Labour movement. The Red Flag is usually sung to the tune of "O Christmas Tree" giving it a familiar tune and rhythm. Traditionally it is sung every year at the end of the Labour Party Conference. Its chorus has the words "So raise the scarlet standard high. Beneath its shade we'll live and die. Though cowards flinch and traitors sneer, we'll keep the red flag flying here."

The Red Flag is a very tribal song, labelling anyone who doesn't stand beneath it as a traitor or a coward. It takes the fixed standpoint that you are either with Labour or you are against it. Forcing people to choose a side will naturally repel some people, but it will also attract other people to the cause.

So far the Labour Party has struggled to win elections with an openly socialist agenda. The Red Flag hasn't as yet proved modern or inclusive enough to bring the majority of voters with it. Without an election victory Labour cannot do the things that it desperately wants to. During the Tony Blair years, the party took a more centrist and all-embracing approach which won New Labour three consecutive General Elections. Tony Blair used the song "Things can only get better" by D:Ream to sell the party's message through music.

With the help of popular and aspirational music, Tony Blair became the longest-serving Labour Party Prime Minister. The challenge for the Labour Party is to stay true to its values, whilst offering a persuasive modern vision for the UK. Jeremy Corbyn failed to achieve that. Then it could win a General Election.

Jeremy Corbyn allegedly left a Labour karaoke night in 2016 after Labour MPs sang that Blairite election song. "Things can only get better" was clearly not the song for Corbyn's Labour regime. The party should think about what other songs would give the modern socialist message that's needed to build a majority across the country. In decades past, adopting Jimmy Barnes' Working Class Man might have been a thought, but it is gender-biased and not inclusive enough.

The more that Labour's chosen music touches voters of all backgrounds and denominations, the more it could help to power an election victory. May be it hasn't been written yet?

~~~~~

Sports teams try to create a strong sense of tribe at their home matches. The singing of the home supporters adds a partisan choir to the club's highly branded stadium, replica shirts, hoodies, fleeces, scarves and coloured flags.

At Anfield, the home of Liverpool FC, the communal singing of "You'll never walk alone" by nearly fifty-thousand Liverpool fans praises the city, the club and the team on the pitch. The song was written and performed by the Liverpool band Gerry and the Pacemakers and has become strongly associated with both the City of Liverpool city and Liverpool football club.

The song "You'll Never Walk Alone" has a rousing tribal chorus that is all about togetherness. Every challenge the City faces can be met with head-on with the lyrics "Walk on, Walk on, With hope in your heart and You'll never walk alone." Liverpool's tribal song is hard to beat.

## 'You'll never walk alone' is as tribal as it gets

The away fans are generally heavily outnumbered at sports fixtures. So they sing as loudly as possible throughout the game to compensate for their lack of numbers. That way the away fans can make themselves heard whenever there is a lull in the home fans' singing. This extra effort and determination helps to show off their tribe inside a foreign territory. Some teams, like Leeds United, are very well supported away from home and sing in chorus to stir their players and defy the home team.

Some of the songs which are aimed to unite one tribe do so by poking fun or showing hostility towards their traditional rivals. The narrow corridor between fun and offence is sometimes crossed. A song which has been sung by Blackburn supporters to one of their near rivals is an example of the humour used to unite a club's home fans. "Your Mum's your Dad, your Dad's your Mum, you're inter-bred you Burnley scum". The song is offensive, but it's also ridiculous, so the humour dominates.

In contrast, songs about the Munich air disaster are an example of the hostile, offensive and humourless. Those kinds of chants and songs are utterly uncalled for. For every fan that thinks it's okay to sing them there are other supporters who think it shames their club and football generally. Some songs divide the members of the tribe singing them, rather than binding that tribe together.

In 2018, Uruguayan football team Nacional was fined $80,000 (£57,500) and their fans were banned for three games after some fans taunted the Brazilian team Chapecoense about the plane crash which killed 19 players and staff. When football songs go too far like this, there should be penalties.

As football is well-policed these days, thankfully the amount of hooliganism and violence in the UK is relatively low. Winning the football and the singing should enough for any tribe.

~~~~~

Music can stir the soul. As a result, corporate advertisers often use music to accompany their brand campaigns. Having a hit song to promote your product can help to sell far more of it.

During the 1990's the advertising team for Levi's needed a song for the new 501's television advertisement. A band called Stiltskin was formed just to perform the chosen song. The resulting single "Inside" topped the UK Singles Chart in 1994. People couldn't get the riff out of their heads. Levi's jeans sold in their millions.

## Using a hit song to promote your product can help you sell more

After the huge success of its debut single, Stiltskin decided to carry on performing together as a band. The follow-up single reached only 34 in the chart. Without another advertising campaign to link to, Stiltskin failed to produce any further chart successes. The jeans fitted the music perfectly. But with its purpose gone, the band found tis music didn't sell.

~~~~~

The song "Tribe" by Kim Viera is openly tribal and includes the lyrics "Way up, way up, like CEO. Way up, way up. I wanna know, are you with me? My tribe, my ladies. My girls, we made it. Make sure they never forget it. Come on, let's get it. My tribe on top. My tribe on top. My tribe on top. My tribe on top." The song includes a clear call to arms with the lyric "Are you with me?"

Contrast this with the Suffragette song 'The March of the Women' which contains the lyrics "March, March many as one. Shoulder to shoulder and friend to friend." Both songs are of their time and both have the same theme of female empowerment at their core.

What do the lyrics of a song say and to whom are they speaking? The easier a song is to relate to the more chance it has of passing on its messages. Togetherness around a purpose will always appeal to people who share that same sense of purpose.

~~~~~

Many sporting songs include a direct or passing reference to the club's tribal homeland. These songs are all part of marking tribal territory. Some of the songs that Castleford Rugby League fans sing at their matches are the same whether the match is at home or away. One such song is "Come on you 'Fords". That song is sung at every match.

But some of the songs change depending on who the opposition team is. If it's a team from Lancashire that's visiting, then the chant of

"Yorkshire, Yorkshire" booms out to remind the visiting supporters that they are in hostile territory. However, when local, big city rivals Leeds Rhinos visit for their derby match, the songs narrow in their geography. Songs of "Cas-tle-ford" and "Clap your hands if you're proud to be a Cas fan" ring out to remind the visitors exactly whose territory it is.

~~~~~

Businesses can use songs, instrumental pieces, theme tunes and jingles and to help to promote their products and services. Songs and music can stir our emotions. Playing music can help to embed a brand in our sub-consciousness. A call to arms within a song can tug on our heart strings. Tribes should use music much more to rally people to their cause.

~~~~~

In 2010 global top four accountancy firm Deloitte started a trend. Fifty-three staff were filmed in a video with songs including 'You're the One I Want' (from Grease) called Deloitte Lipdub 2010. The video is on You Tube. The video made KPMG seem a fun place to go to work.

In 2012 PwC (Price Waterhouse Coopers) raised the bar by launching its own firm song 'Downright Global' (also on You Tube). On one level it is truly terrible. But on a tribal level it works. It explains what they do, gives you an indication of how they see themselves and makes PwC seem more fun than you'd expect accountants to be.

KPMG released 'The KPMG Song' in 2012 selling the benefits of being a KPMG intern. The video (again on You Tube) is fun but its messages could have hit the mark better. It includes the lyrics "It's the friendly smiles and the brown wall aisles and the post-it notes that go for miles and that's why I'm an intern at KPMG". There are surely more compelling reasons that those. The song also includes the lyrics "because our client's a cash cow" which gives a very mercenary impression. The idea was good but the execution was not.

EY (Ernst & Young) followed suit with the EY Anthem in 2014 meaning that all of the top four accountancy firms in the World have used music to help sell themselves as great places to work.

~~~~~

At his concerts Ed Sheeran says that everyone in the audience has something in common as they're all looking at the same stage. In his case they're looking at one man, one guitar and a loop box. Ed Sheeran's greatest strength is perhaps his song writing. Combining the power of his music and lyrics has pulled people from all over the World together to watch him play.

Ed Sheeran is the source of the entertainment. Everyone is looking at him. But standing up there alone, he loves audience participation. Ed describes his audience as his "backing band" and his "choir." He asks the whole crowd to join in saying "Everyone can sing. Not everyone can sing in tune, but everyone can sing."

Having something to say that resonates with other people can give you a purpose. Getting those people to join in with you can build you a tribe.

~~~~~

Does your tribe use songs and music to tell its story and build its brand? What kind of music best fits its purpose? Could a song help you to stand out from the competition? How does your tribe sound? Is it a chorus or a cacophony?

# 2.12 TRIBAL COLOURS/UNIFORM

Tribal colours and uniforms really matter. Being visual, they are often the most immediate signs of a tribe. As with every other aspect of tribe, the choice of a tribe's colours and uniform should be a deliberate decision, not one taken within a cultural vacuum. The active choice of colours and designs should be taken with the tribe's vision, purpose and values firmly in mind. If any business asks a design agency to come up with ideas without giving it any context, it is missing a great opportunity.

Some organisations choose their colours and uniforms in order to match their purpose and values. Sometimes the decision is to be deliberately different to its neighbouring tribes and competitors. On other occasions colours are designed to attract attention and sales or simply to shock.

Colours can also be selected in order to adopt the common perceptions and meanings associated with them. Those perceptions depend on the colour itself, the shade and the context it's used in. Green is the colour of health and growth; and grey is the colour of compromise and calm. They are different colours generating different messages. Different shades of the same colour can completely change its perception. A light brown or natural wood colour offers a down-to-earth warmth and stability. Whereas dark brown is seen to be indicative of an insular and private focus. A colour's traits can also vary when it is used in different contexts. For example, red is the colour of passion, energy and anger. In a situation of war, red sends a strong message of determination and defiance, whereas in peacetime red is more of an inviting, fun-loving colour.

With each tribe's colours making an impact of some kind, that impact should be intentional rather than accidental. Choosing your tribe's colours should be done in context and carefully. As with every other aspect of tribal branding, the wrong messages can have a confusing and detrimental impact.

## Choose you tribe's colours wisely

The England Rugby Union team has for a period worn "England" spelled out in gold-coloured, capital letters on a plain white training top. White is thought to be the colour of completeness and perfection. Gold is the colour of triumph and success. But it is also the colour of affluence and extravagance. The combination might have been chosen because the idea of triumph and perfection seemed like a great combination. But sadly, the look shouts more of affluence and extravagance. Choosing that colour smacks of arrogance. It gives the impression that England thinks it's the better team before the match has even started. That view may be unfair, but wearing those colours gives off an unintended impression. The plain back shirts and humility of the All-Blacks is in sharp contrast. Other teams find it easy enough to motivate themselves against England without any additional encouragement. But they must have been desperate to beat the team with the golden tops and big egos[55].

~~~~~

Uniforms are worn to create an impression. The distinctive look of a bus driver, footballer, nurse or clown helps us to understand what job the person does. Some uniforms are designed to project authority. Police Officers wear a uniform designed to reflect their authority. Judges wear wigs and gowns to create a stern and authoritarian appearance. Other uniforms alert us to help. We are always pleased to see a firefighter, ambulance technician, nurse or a coastguard offering their services. Their presence is reassuring. Their uniform's message is one of helping. School children wear a uniform to teach them to dress smartly and comply with rules. Their uniform's message is one of obedience and following instructions.

---

[55] Whether it's true or not that's a perception.

Uniforms used to send a message as to the worker's social class. Being a butler, porter, maid or lift attendant meant you had to wear a uniform whilst doing your job. The fact you had a uniform typically badged you as working class. Uniforms kept society ordered and set in place. That suited the wealthy and powerful. It didn't suit the workers. Over past decades social mobility has been more prevalent, freeing many people from the uniforms of class. Now more people wear uniforms to be part of something, through choice rather than being forced to.

## *Uniforms should promote togetherness not servitude*

Wearing your own clothes to work is often a sign of control and independence, but not always. Society has moved on and the imposition of civilian uniforms doesn't quite have the same social divide anymore. There are commercial reasons for businesses to use uniforms, especially if they are retailers or services providers. Uniforms can offer messages of familiarity and consistency. McDonald's sells itself as a business offering consistency. Customers know exactly what they are going to get whenever they visit a McDonald's burger wherever that restaurant is located. A uniform approach is reflected perfectly in its uniformed staff. The famous golden arches translate into golden yellow piping on the McDonald's grey uniform.

The uniforms of the emergency services are used to inspire trust and respect. Their uniforms denote their commitment to public duty and their ability to help us.

~~~~~

Military uniforms have long been used to differentiate two opposing sides in battle. They were designed to show friend from foe. The thought was that a bright, bold uniform could strike fear into the enemy. So the more colourful and distinctive the uniform was the better, such as the bright red British Army tunics, or the white mantles of the Knights Templar with red crosses on the shoulders.

Historically, noble families used heraldry to maintain its sense of tribe through the colour and design of its coat of arms. Adopting its banners, armour, helmets and shields was a way of declaring your allegiance to a noble family. Wearing colourful heraldry meant that you were less likely to be accidentally killed in battle by one of your own soldiers.

*Wearing tribal colours helps*
*to show your allegiance*

Despite the perceived advantages of bright uniforms, a key lesson was eventually learned. The brighter your uniform was the more likely you were to be intentionally killed by the enemy. So after the Boer War, operational uniforms are much more practical, hard wearing and camouflaged to blend into the surrounding countryside. To maintain tradition, the dress uniforms for functions remain bright and colourful.

~~~~~

If we find we're dressed similarly to someone else it can make us feel we've got something in common with them. Socially it could be that you're both wearing the same band's t-shirt or the same club's football shirt. When people mirror each other with their choice of branded clothes or uniform, they share an affinity that's tribal. Showing your devotion to a band, or television show is a shout-out to other people who share the same passion. It's an invitation to share a moment of mutual devotion, or even to make a new friend. Wearing a t-shirt with a band's logo on says "I'm really into this music." It asks the implied question "Are you into it as well?" Exchanging smiles or glances with someone wearing the same t-shirt as you is tribal behaviour.

Wearing the same outfit as your favourite film or television character could be just for a one-off fancy dress party. Or it might be because you are part of the tribute tribe that wants to emulate the characters from the band, show or film you're mimicking. Some fans dress up as characters from the television show The Big Bang Theory, who themselves dress up as characters from the DC Comic Universe. Each time you wear your chosen uniform, your allegiance is openly declared.

By advertising your interests on your clothing you are deliberately and publicly revealing your tribal loyalties and connections. By tattooing them on your body, you are making a permanent statement of attachment to your tribe. As people's tastes change and life moves on a tattoo that doesn't reflect a permanent life-long commitment is not necessarily a good idea. "Think before you ink" is a wise suggestion.

~ ~ ~ ~ ~

In 1908 the Suffragettes chose colour a scheme for the movement that would help their supporters stand out and be seen. The three colours selected were Purple (representing dignity), white (representing purity) and green (representing hope for the future). The colour scheme was used for anything that could help to get the message across, including sashes, slippers, cup and saucers, jewellery, chocolates, dresses and even cars. This was a superb branding exercise that feels perfectly at home in 2018.

The words Green, White and Violet provide the acronym GWV, which is said to stand for Give Women Votes. It seems that wasn't the original intention, but it was a helpful coincidence. The deliberate relationship with colour was to signify dignity, purity and hope. All three colours were therefore linked directly to the movement's purpose and values.

~ ~ ~ ~ ~

You only need to go to a football or rugby match to understand how tribes work. The atmosphere is tense, partisan, hostile and good humoured all at the same time. As long as supporters don't cross the line into crime it's a rare and wonderful combination.

The first thing that strikes you is that every club has a colourful playing kit, using its chosen team colours, sponsor and badge. Each combination is intentionally different to other teams, so that you can recognise your team and your fellow supporters. In cities where there are two football teams, the two sets of colours are often starkly different. For example, Liverpool play in red while Everton wear blue. Nottingham Forrest play in red and their city rivals Notts County play in black and white stripes. The contrast is intentional. Colours can come to mean good or bad and friend or foe, depending on the teams you support.

## *Which colours do you most associate with?*

Neighbouring towns and cities use the same colour philosophy to illustrate where their own tribal land begins and ends. Southampton and Portsmouth are close neighbours. In Southampton, supporters wear red and white. In Portsmouth, blue and white dominate instead. There are several towns and villages between Southampton and Portsmouth where there are divided loyalties. A mixture of red and blue shirts can be seen out in public, confirming that neither side holds the territory in its sway.

Once you've picked a sports team you automatically adopt its colours too. So changing a club's colours can break its' fans loyalty. Nicknamed the Bluebirds, Cardiff City football club had played in blue from its beginnings in 1908. When current owner Vincent Tan took over in 2012 he reviewed everything at the club, including the team's playing colours. Based partly on the meanings attached to red (joy) and blue (mourning) in Asia, the club changed its playing colours from blue to red. The club also replaced the club's Bluebird logo with that of a dragon.

Most of the club's fans were deeply affected and furious. They objected and held up blue coloured scarves nineteen minutes and twenty-seven seconds into its matches, to remember the 1927 F.A. Cup win whilst wearing blue. In 2015, after mixed results and two years of fans' clamouring, the tribe's traditional colours and logo were restored. At the club's first home match afterwards, the crowd was the club's biggest of the season. The roar was almost deafening when the team was announced as "Cardiff City, the Bluebirds".

~~~~~

The heavy rock band KISS is famous for songs like "God gave rock and roll to you" and "I was made for lovin' you". But the band is more famous for its stage make-up and live shows, which have featured fire-breathing, blood-spitting, smoking guitars, shooting rockets, levitating drum kits and pyrotechnics. The band's worldwide sales have topped 100 million albums, making them one of the World's best selling bands of all time. But like many other groups, their success was far from instant. The band's first two albums were commercial flops and their record label nearly went bankrupt. It wasn't until a double live album and the publicity about their live shows spread, that the band achieved its first real commercial success.

The original and best-known line-up consisted of Paul Stanley (lead vocals and rhythm guitar), Gene Simmons (vocals and bass guitar), Ace Frehley (lead guitar and vocals) and Peter Criss (drums and vocals). Those four KISS band members took on the personae of comic book style characters, The Starchild (Stanley), The Demon (Simmons), The Spaceman or Space Ace (Frehley) and The Catman (Criss). The band painted their faces with black and white designs which made them distinctive and different from other groups. This unique look persuaded people to try their music.

## *Their painted faces made KISS unmistakable*

The use of face paint by KISS was a masterstroke. It created a form of uniform which helped the band's fame to spread. Merchandise became a substantial source of income for the group. Some of the products released included: Kiss Your Face Makeup kits, pinball machines, dolls, Halloween masks, board games, lunch boxes, trading cards and a pair of comic books issued by Marvel (the first one of which contained ink mixed with actual blood donated by the group) and many other pieces of KISS memorabilia. Devoted fans can therefore buy all of the band's music and all of its merchandise. By wearing the band's t-shirts and make-up, fans can show they are part of the KISS tribe. They can also join the KISS Army, which is the band's official fan club.

In 1980 Peter Criss left the band and in 1982 Ace Frehley followed him out. From 1983 to 1996, KISS played live without make-up. Without their distinctive look, the loyalty of many fans was lost. The first album to feature the band without make-up was called "Lick it Up." The album and associated tour were similar to previous versions but both were less successful than expected. The message was clear. The fans wanted to see their heroes wearing the KISS make-up.

The band's popularity continued to slide until 1996 when the original line-up reunited for a tour, wearing full make-up. Lasting over 11 months, Kiss played 192 shows, earning $43.6 million. It made KISS the World's top concert act of the year. The band's return in full make-up had given the fans exactly what they craved. They turned up in numbers and face paint.

Would KISS have sold over 100 million albums if they had just relied on their music? The answer is almost certainly no. The combined product of music, make-up and live shows yelled out to potential fans. In their heyday, you couldn't fail to notice them. They made a big statement in everything they did. As Ace Frehley put it at the time "People either love us or they hate us, there's no middle ground." Everyone wants to be part of something good.

~~~~~

The heavy rock band AC/DC has its own example of a tribal uniform. Angus Young first wore his old school uniform to a live performance in 1973. The gig went so well that he wore it again. In fact Angus is still wearing a school uniform on stage, over forty years later.

Just like KISS, the band's live shows developed their own rituals, including the thunder of life-sized Napoleonic cannons filled with exploding fireworks. Lead guitarist Angus Young is famous for his wild onstage antics, including running back and forth across the stage, clambering onto Bon Scott's, Brian Johnson's or Axl Rose's shoulders during concerts, mooning, gushing smoke from a satchel on his back, doing his own version of Chuck Berry's duck walk, as well as performing a spasm during which he throws himself to the ground, kicking, shaking, and spinning in circles whilst still playing his guitar. This allegedly came after his brother George advised him that if he ever tripped over his guitar lead he should keep on playing, to make it look like it was part of the act.

By 2015, AC/DC had sold over 200 million records and their worldwide concerts still sell out in minutes. Would AC/DC still be so popular if they had just relied on their music? The answer is almost certainly no. They put on their uniforms and put on a show.

~~~~~

Comedians are paid to make other people laugh. So as well as telling jokes and funny stories, comedians have often tried to make themselves look hilarious too. Historically, jesters with bells in their hats played up for any laugh they could muster. In the Music Hall days [56] comic performers dressed up as toffs (known as Lion comiques), as women (like modern pantomime dames) and as a variety of eccentric performers to suit whichever song or act they were part of. Wearing a funny outfit gives a comedian a comedy uniform.

During the 1970's and 1980's Sir Ken Dodd's wild hair and tickling stick raised a smile before he even started speaking. By advertising that he was a comedian before he even spoke, people were warmed up and ready to laugh. Tommy Cooper's fez did exactly the same thing. Imagine Tommy Cooper without his fez. Would the laughs have come so easily?

By wearing his hats sideways and choosing deliberately undersized glasses, Benny Hill played his uniform for laughs. Then there were comedy props used by ventriloquists, who took the likes of Lord Charles, Emu, Orville and Spit the Dog onto the stage with them. Would Rod Hull have got any laughs standing up there on his own?

---

[56] From approximately 1850 and 1960.

In more recent times comedians have gone for a more casual look. Humour has become more sophisticated. A cheap gag from looking silly doesn't often cut it anymore. The modern tribe of comedians is looking to be taken seriously, as it tries to be anything but. In the era of internet, television and social media comedians don't need to warm the audience up to who they are. Harry Hills' over-sized shirt collars make him an exception rather than the rule.

~~~~~

The 1888 Match Women's Strike arose from wholly unacceptable working conditions at Bryant and May's East End factory at the time. Required to work twelve hour shifts, with little regard for their health and safety match women suffered hand injuries from unsafe equipment and contracted "phossy jaw."[57] Paid appallingly and fined for laughing, the match women were treated as unskilled, cheap labour. Eventually the match women rallied against their oppressive conditions. With no rights and the very real fear of losing their jobs it took enormous collective courage for the 1,400 workers to go on strike.

When analysing why there was such a strong collective spirit and will to act together, the Feather Clubs factor shouldn't be underestimated. With so little money and such awful working conditions the working women were desperate for something to lift their lives outside work. So groups of them had started to buy and share beautiful and extravagant hats. By contributing to a group's kitty you got to wear fabulous and unaffordable hats when you went out courting. For an evening at least, life felt immeasurably better.

## Powered by all the tribes of Feather Clubs

So when the call to strike came, there was already an existing sense of camaraderie that quickly pulled the women together as one. Supported ably by Annie Besant's report about "White Slavery in London" support for the strike grew. Bryant and May had no choice

---

[57] Phossy jaw was a cancer caused by the highly toxic chemical white phosphorous.

but to increase wages, withdraw the system of fines and improve working conditions. The Company also recognised the new Union of Women Match Makers. Powered by all the tribes of Feather Clubs, a 1,400 strong super-tribe changed the world of work for ever.

One year later in 1889 dock workers went on strike and won changes for their working terms. Encouraged by the success of these two strikes, workers in all sectors started forming and joining their own trades unions.

~~~~~

Colour can offer approval and disapproval depending on the colour and how it's used.

According to figures on display at Marwell Zoo's Tropical House, humanity needs to generate 12.5 terawatts of energy. That energy is largely produced by coal, oil, gas and nuclear sources. Yet according to the same figures, there are 30 times that many terawatts available from renewable energy. With climate change being accelerated by generating our energy from other sources, there is a compelling case for producing only renewable energy, otherwise known as 'green energy'.

Calling it green energy legitimises it, because the association labels it nature friendly. Allocating the colour green therefore gives it an unofficial approval rating.

~~~~~

The UK's 'Green Party' is named after the colour association with nature and the environment. According to its 2019 political programme the Green Party has ten political pillars:

- Save the environment
- Green our land
- Protect animal life
- Challenge privilege

- End discrimination
- Champion International friendships
- Liberate our working lives
- Unleash our creative power
- Embed collective kindness in our society
- Deliver quality of life for all

Only three of these ten pillars are overtly 'green' but they are ones the party is best known for. In fact most people only know the Party for the first three pillars. And whilst that is becoming an ever more urgent and necessary political platform, with informal nicknames like "The Tree-huggers" the party needs to gain more parliamentary seats to do its best work. The challenge for the Green Party is therefore to broaden its appeal beyond its green credentials and become known for the other seven pillars as well.

## *Your colour tells a story.*
## *Is it the right one?*

Within the ten pillars, there are powerful messages of collaboration, fairness and community. The word 'Green' alone doesn't convey these tribal themes are strongly as it could. Perhaps a change of name would help, retaining the green elements whilst expanding the party's offering? The ten pillars can stand intact. It's the branding around them that's too narrow. A name like the 'Equality and Environment Party' would explain the party's purposes more clearly.

The party's green colouring should definitely stay, but another complementary colour could be introduced to illustrate the party's interests beyond its environmental principles.

~~~~~

Employers who use colours and uniforms need to think very carefully about which messages they are sending. Employers who don't use uniforms might want to at least consider them. Do your tribe's colours and uniform fit its vision, purpose and values? Do they help you to stand out from the competition, or are your tribe's colours lost in the blur of corporate blues and reds?

## 2.13 TRIBAL CEREMONIES

Getting insight into what makes another organisation tick is always difficult from the outside. The best opportunity for a stranger to get inside a tribe's workings might come from studying its celebrations, remembrances, ceremonies, parades, shows, festivals and processions.

We can learn what really matters to a tribe by analysing its observances. Which occasions and events take place? What are they for? How hierarchical and formal are they? What does the tribe praise and glorify? What sorrow and loss does the tribe mourn? What kind of ceremony is performed when there's a tribal birth, marriage, victory, coronation, retirement or death? Does an organisation have a celebration for a qualification or graduation? Does it have a form of remembrance when someone leaves? What form pilgrimage is sacred?

*We can tell what a tribe stands for*
*when it puts on a show*

All of a tribe's ceremonies should link back to its purpose and values. Partying to celebrate an 'achievement' which takes the tribe away from its core purpose would be self-defeating. Is there a strong enough connection to justify the costs and energy of every ceremony? If not then it can be changed, so that the tribe's public parades, festivals, celebrations and remembrances mark a re-commitment to its purpose, inspire action to achieve its vision; and endorse the tribe's values.

~~~~~

Across Britain there are innumerable ceremonies, parades, shows, festivals, processions, celebrations and remembrances. Each one is celebrated by a different combination of people, because each observance appeals to different people, values and purposes. Not everybody celebrates every occasion. Which ones resonate with you? That depends on which tribes you belong to.

Our many ceremonies, parades, shows, festivals, processions, celebrations and remembrances are too long to list. I am including all the following examples below (even though they are a bit tedious to read) to illustrate how many forms of well-known celebration we are familiar with. How many more are there, that are small, local and private?

Trooping of the Colour, Changing of the Guard, Burns Night, Fireworks Night and Burning the Guy (Fawkes), Easter Sunday, The State Opening of Parliament, Isle of Wight Festival, Diwali, Chinese New Year, The Queen's New Year's Honours, The Edinburgh Military Tattoo, Halloween, St. David's Day, Pancake Day, Father's Day, The F.A. Cup Final, May Day, Hay Festival, Bank Holidays, The Royal Show, Ramadan and Eid al-Fitr, The Proms, Jorvik Viking Festival, Remembrance Sunday, Hogmanay, The Grand National, Harvest Festival, Glastonbury, Henley Regatta, Royal Ascot, Mothering Sunday, Cowes Week, Lent, London Fashion Week, The Cheltenham Festival, Covent Garden May Fayre and Puppet Festival, The National Eisteddfod, Maundy Thursday, The Great Yorkshire Show, The Challenge Cup Final, The Southampton Boat Show, Brass Durham International Festival, The Highland Games, Advent, Wimbledon, St. George's Day, Gold Hill Fair, The Queen's Cup, The Derby, Jack in the Green, Valentine's Day, Movember, The Six Nations, St. Patrick's Day, Notting Hill Carnival, Edinburgh Festival and Fringe, The British Grand Prix, Christmas Day, Twelfth Night/Epiphany, St. Andrew's

Day, The Open, Hanukkah, Boxing Day, Pride, April Fool's Day, Summer and Winter Solstice and the Festival of Lights. The UK is very rich with ceremonies, parades, shows, festivals, processions, celebrations and remembrances.

Tribal people feel positivity about their own tribe's ceremonies, festivals and events. They join a tribe together in celebration or sorrow. Tribal people may also feel negatively about festivals and events which promote other purposes and values. Each tribe's celebration should have a unifying and bonding effect on the tribe. The wider and deeper the tribe flourishes, the further the ceremony's appeal will reach. Sailing is popular all over the World, so Cowes Week and the Southampton Boat Show will appeal to people outside Hampshire and the Isle of Wight.

~~~~~

Native Americans had ceremonies based on their nation's language, songs, stories, colours, dress, rituals and traditions. These were passed on from generation to generation through observation and explanation. One of these ceremonies was called Sundance, which was the annual time for renewal.

The arrival of the Europeans in the 17th Century brought fundamental and permanent change for Native Americans and ended hundreds of years of heritage and culture. Many Native Americans were killed through the force of arms, but many others were forced to live under the white man's rules, which took away their freedom and acts of celebration. The imposition of reservations, schools and Christianity were directly aimed at ending Native American culture and replacing it with white Christian "ideals". The widespread introduction of alcohol caused great harm to the Indian peoples who were not used to it, which further undermined Native American values.

*Carrying on tribal ceremonies*
*keeps the tribe alive*

The Native Americans respected the World around them, so they accepted the white man at his word. They believed that they could share their spiritual homeland in peace. As a result, they were often taken by surprise and outmanoeuvred. Unable to share their experiences fast enough, tribe after tribe fell to the same combination of force and trickery. Native American culture was rendered subservient and important festivals like the Sundance were banned.

Corralled into living a white man's life, generations began to forget their rituals and traditions. Each tribe's way of life blurred and then faded. The proud heritage of many peoples was suffocated and almost died out. But in more recent years the Sundance ceremony has returned. Descendants of the Native Americans, who enjoyed the freedom to participate in the Sundance, have recreated the event for modern times. Native American culture was cynically strangled into submission, but it has refused to die. The act of carrying on tribal ceremonies can keep a tribe alive.

~~~~~

Tribal celebrations and festivals can stay unique to a particular tribe or they can broaden themselves out to a much wider audience, adapting as they do. According to historian and broadcaster David Olusoga [58] "The annual day of the dead festival is a synthesis of the Catholic All Saints day and the rituals inherited from Aztec religion." The festival's core symbol is the caveleras which is the image of a human skull. The festival is very popular in Mexico, Central and South America in particular. The modern festival was highlighted in the opening sequence of the James Bond film Spectre. Adopting and adapting ceremonies that belong to other tribes can produce a new, unique version for your tribe.

~~~~~

Anything that actively helps an organisation to achieve its vision is worthy of praise or reward. But not everything we do needs a festival or parade. There are lots of different forms of thank you and occasions to choose from if we want to mark an event. The method we choose

---

[58] Said during the BBC Television series Civilisations.

16

could include paying a bonus, sending a Happy Birthday card, or holding an award ceremony or church service. Events could be international, national, regional or exclusive to a single tribe. As long as a ceremony supports a tribe's vision, purpose and values it should add to tribal life.

## *What does your organisation celebrate?*

Work related events that could warrant some form of observance include: a new person joining, a promotion, a retirement, winning a new customer, winning a new contract from an existing customer; as well as hitting a team goal or target. When any of these happen, does everyone get to celebrate the good news, or just the person who claims it? How often does a person really achieve anything alone? The more inclusively everyone celebrates a piece of good news together, the better the news it is and more of a sense of tribe there will be.

That's why reward schemes which offer benefits for everyone drive a much greater sense of tribal loyalty than individual bonus schemes. Ideally everyone takes a share of the responsibility for an organisation and everyone shares in the reward that success brings. Whole organisational thinking helps to tie in good people at every level. That allows everyone to celebrate the same success at the same time, providing a greater sense of unity.

~~~~~

What, who and how does your tribe celebrate? Do your tribe's ceremonies link back to its heritage? Do they praise its values? Do they celebrate each step towards achieving its purpose and vision? Do they inspire engagement and loyalty?

# 2.14 TRIBAL BADGES/LOGOS

A logo is a graphic representation or symbol of a company name, brand or trademark. Logos are designed to be easily recognised, acting as a point of affirmation and a form of advertisement for the brand. Any logo that inspires you to take action is having a tribal effect on you.

With so much time and money spent on brand development, many organisations have created a sticky effect on our consciousness. We may think that we control the advertising and branding around us, but each campaign may be having its own tribal effect on us.

~~~~~

The biggest brands in the World have an instantly recognisable logo. Built up over many years of business, a brand's reputation is crystalised its logo. As soon as you see a big brand logo, it makes you imagine the brand's characteristics and brings a related feeling. Seeing a logo for a food or drink brand when you're hungry or thirsty, can create an emotional link which makes you stop and buy that brand's products.

McDonalds' has one of the most recognised symbols in the World with its twin golden arches, which together form an M shape. The brand's logo borrows this symbol, which itself borrows from the original design for the restaurants. That original restaurant design had a yellow arch shape on each side of the building, to make the restaurant more visible from the road. The twin-arches symbol helps to ingrain the McDonalds brand in the minds of every passer-by. Used as the brand's logo it acts as a reassuring reminder to motorists that McDonalds is on hand to deliver fast, consistent and relatively inexpensive food. Does seeing the golden arches make you feel hungry?

<center>~~~~~</center>

According to the Coca-Cola website, Confederate Colonel John Pemberton is credited with inventing the earliest version of the drink. But he didn't invent its unmistakable and distinctive logo. That was created by his friend and business partner Frank Mason Robinson in 1886. Robinson came up with the name and used the logo's distinctive cursive script, known as Spencerian script (which was the dominant form of formal handwriting in the United States at that time). Over 130 years later, Cola-Cola is the number one soft-drink in the World and its logo remains true to that original written form.

## *Logos can inspire emotional reactions*

Changing a long established logo shouldn't be done lightly. Can you imagine McDonalds or Coca-Cola throwing away logos and trying something else? But they would if their logo stopped inspiring brand loyalty, or if it put consumers off purchasing their products. A logo needs to be like Lego. It needs to be a block that your tribe can build on.

<center>~~~~~~</center>

Professional sports teams are constantly trying to grow and expand their fan-base. The selling of club merchandise has a trebling effect that creates a circle of profit. Firstly selling merchandise is a great way to raise funds for the playing side of the operation, which helps to build a team capable of winning more matches. Secondly, every time a supporter wears club merchandise, he or she reaffirms an ongoing commitment to the club. That makes it more likely that he or she will spend more money going to matches or buying more merchandise. Thirdly by adding the club badge and colours to a wide range of merchandise, the club advertises itself through thousands of human billboards. Every time a supporter buys a garment and wears the club's logo in public, the word is spread even wider. If a team is successful and its fans are wearing the club logo in public, someone

2

else might be tempted to start supporting the club. Every time a new supporter buys some club merchandise the whole cycle begins again.

Clubs often sell their merchandise at an inflated price. Without the club's logo emblazoned on it, the product would be generic and expensive. Tribe members will pay the uplifted price because the merchandise proudly displays the club's logo and they know that the profit will go to support the club. To a tribe member it is worth paying an inflated price. Perversely, the more you pay the more loyal you feel.

## We can be human billboards for our tribes

Some people like more than one football team, but they seem to be very much in the minority. Most fans pick one team, either through birth, family connections, friends or watching them play on television. Once you pick a team they are yours and by definition every other team is not. Supporting any sports team comes with thick and thin times, but celebrating and suffering together has the reassurance of being part of a tribe. Choosing a team is the act of committing yourself to one tribe. So a football supporter will have a very positive reaction to seeing his or her own team's logo and colours. But if you switch those logo and colours to those of a rival team, there would be the equivalent negative reaction. You couldn't persuade a Chelsea fan to wear a replica Tottenham Hotspur shirt, let alone persuade them to buy one. In truth you probably couldn't pay them enough to wear the "wrong" shirt.

The more items of your own clothing and merchandise that have your tribe's logo on, the more you are showing off your personal commitment to the tribe. Wearing your club's merchandise makes you a walking advertisement and confirms your tribal loyalty.

Sports teams put their club's logo on absolutely anything that sells, including playing kit, track suits, fashion garments, bedding, clocks, watches, pyjamas, dressing gowns, caps, bags, mugs, flasks, mobile phone cases and games consoles. Any product that can accommodate a logo can be transformed into a tribal symbol and a profit centre.

Buying club branded goods for other people is even better as it helps to grow the tribe. That is particularly important, when you buy a branded gift for the generations below you. Every time a Manchester United or Bath Rugby baby sleep-suit is sold, a new supporter could be about to join that tribe. The influence of branded club goods is strong in childhood. A lifetime of loyalty can be bought through a few baby clothes with logos. Thinking commercially (and cynically) every sports team should heavily subsidise its baby products (if not give them away for free). Ideally, a club should give them all away for free. The more often that people grow up believing they are already in your tribe, the more likely that you will have them for life. When you look back at your baby photos, you get a powerful sense of where you've come from. There is a strong emotional pull to stay true to your roots. If for example there were childhood pictures of you in a Surrey County Cricket bib, Bradford Bulls scarf, or a woolly Newcastle United hat they could create or reinforce a strong and emotive tribal attachment that might last your whole lifetime.

Being taken by your father, mother, grandfather or grandmother to a live match at your team's home ground can have a similar effect. Taking repeated trips to a place smothered in your team's logo builds your loyalty. Seeing the club's sign on the front of the stadium as you arrive instantly reminds you where you are and what you are part of. Bringing home a match programme with more images of that logo embeds its familiarity.

~ ~ ~ ~ ~

The Nottingham Forest F.C. crest was designed in 1973 by a competition winner, after the club discovered that it couldn't copy the Nottingham coat of arms. 855 designs were submitted for judging. The now famous white tree on a red background logo won the competition. An advertising executive praised the design in a publication called Campaign, saying "Above all, it's quick and easy to draw in the bogs at the away end of any grounds you visit."

~ ~ ~ ~ ~

During the Second World War, the 7th Armoured Division of the British Army was fighting in the North African desert, as part of Monty's Western Desert Force. In 1940, the 7th Division decided to take on an additional nickname and emblem of its own, which wasn't normally allowed. The badge depicted a red Jerboa in a white circle, inside a red square. A Jerboa is a desert rodent, which can leap great distances. The 7<sup>th</sup> Division adopted the Jerboa as its logo and adopted its characteristics, becoming known as the Desert Rats.

The Desert Rats took that badge and fearsome reputation with them across North Africa, playing a decisive part in helping to win the war. Together, they drew courage and strength from their badge and nickname. Being the self-named desert rats inspired them. It made them believe that they could do great things. As a result, they did.

*Together, they drew courage and strength*
*from their badge and nickname*

When the 7th Armoured Division struck swiftly at will across the desert their enemy began to believe it too. The Germans feared the men called the Desert Rats and where they would strike next.

Choosing a distinct tribal badge, emblem or symbol can operate as a powerful and inspirational logo which emboldens the tribe and stands out from the crowd.

~~~~~

AC⚡DC's band name and logo came from the Young brothers' sister Margaret seeing it written on a sewing machine. The symbol of a lightning bolt sits between the alternating current (AC) and the direct current (DC) references. The name symbolised raw power and electricity. Adopting it encouraged the band to live up to its name and logo by putting on electrifying live performances. To rock music fans, the AC⚡DC logo is absolutely unmistakable. Can you make your logo unmistakable?

~~~~~

5

If your clothing has a sporting club logo emblazoned on it, your tribal loyalty is proven. That is even more true if it's a permanent tattoo. But it's a bold step to publicly commit yourself to one team. Whilst fellow supporters of your team will like you more, fans of other teams will immediately see you as different and less likeable. The act of declaring yourself to one tribe can drive people in rival tribes away from you.

With the risk of violence at football matches during the 1970's and 1980's many supporters chose to hide their replica shirts and scarves underneath a coat. Other fans left all visible traces of their club affinity back at home. There was a genuine risk of violence if you revealed your affiliation to a team. That was enough to temporarily suppress the long-established practice of showing off your tribal logo and colours.

Nowadays, as things are safer, supporters are happier to wear the signs of the team they support. With a wide range of merchandise available sporting each club's logo, fans can advertise their support by wearing their club's shirt, baseball cap, jacket, hoodie or scarf to matches or around town. Supporters can even have their faces painted, body tattooed or hair dyed. At games supporters can also wave their flags and banners. Afterwards at home they can put on their club pyjamas and crawl underneath their club duvet cover. Every piece of club merchandise will have its logo clearly stamped on it.

~~~~~

Sticking with the same logo is normally good for organisational stability. Re-branding an organisation's logo may lose its heritage value, or it might create a new form of heritage. The Cardiff City re-brand from bluebird to dragon and back to bluebird is an example of where a club's heritage was lost and then re-found.

Castleford Rugby League Football Club had a traditional town based logo from its beginnings in 1926 until the club became known as Castleford Tigers for the start of the 1991/92 season. The original club badge displayed a gold castle on a ford of blue and white waves.

Above it were two white roses of Yorkshire and an eagle holding a miner's lamp. Underneath it was the Latin phrase "Audacter et Sincere", which means boldly and honestly. Under Daryl Van de Velde the club re-branded and its logo was transformed into a tiger's head.

There are obviously no tigers in West Yorkshire, so why would the town's history be discarded for the image of a random animal? The thinking was twofold, to modernise the club and associate it with positive characteristics that could motivate the team and undermine the confidence of its opponents. Tigers are famously fierce and powerful hunters. Those characteristics can fit a contact sports team. Castleford's amber and black colours could be manipulated to match a tiger's colouring. It was an understandable fit.

*There were no tigers in*
*Castleford until 1991*

As many other rugby league clubs were changing their names as well, the new logo was accepted by supporters fairly quickly. Wigan Warriors, Leeds Rhinos and Bradford Bulls were amongst several other clubs to re-brand at a similar time. Nearly thirty years later the Tigers nickname is settled and well accepted now. That said, things might have been very different. At the time Daryl may well have chosen the Cougars nickname if Keighley hadn't taken it shortly before. Having a cougar logo seems unthinkable for Castleford Tigers now.

Finding the right badge that fits your organisation, your stakeholders and your market is very important. Does your organisation's logo fit its purpose? Does it need to be updated? Should you every totally let go of your past? Blending the past, present and future is what super-tribes do best.

~ ~ ~ ~ ~

Fairtrade is an international movement which aims to help producers in developing countries achieve better trading conditions; and it also promotes sustainable farming. Fairtrade's vision is of a World where there are higher profits and better working conditions for growers and exporters. The movement focuses on products like chocolate, cotton, tea, coffee and fruit because they can be sold domestically in producing countries and exported to more developed nations around the World.

Fairtrade certifies any products which meet its exacting standards by adding the distinctive Fairtrade logo to the product's packaging. By publicly stamping approved products, Fairtrade offers consumers a seal of moral approval. As a result of the Fairtrade scheme, producers in developing countries are now achieving better trading conditions.

## *People want to be part of something meaningful*

Buying products marked with the Fairtrade logo, helps you to make a difference and feel better about yourself as you shop. The fact that other people are doing the same means Fairtrade has become creates a tribal movement. Making money for the shareholders isn't something meaningful, even for those shareholders.

The presence of Fairtrade's logo sends out a message to potential purchasers. If you believe in the principle of fair trade, you can choose to buy Fairtrade products. What does your tribe's logo stand for? How is it used?

~~~~~

In nature, animals mark their territory in order to claim and protect their land. Humans have long done the same using different methods. Throughout history, tribes have used natural and man-made fortifications to protect their homeland. The plethora of words we've used to describe them confirms how important they've been. Walls, ramparts, earthen-walls, stockades, hill-forts, redoubts, castles, fences, ditches, moats, trenches, bunkers and barricades are all words to illustrate ways of creating a defensive stronghold.

In the modern age, businesses still mark their territory through their physical buildings. They do it by putting their organisation's logo on the front of their offices. That shows who occupies the office block or factory and it advertises the brand.

Buildings aren't the only place to find corporate logos. They are also added to company uniforms, business cards, umbrellas, email footers and company cars. To spread their reach far and wide, many businesses also use pull-up banners, media advertisements, corporate brochures and A4 flyers to promote their brand. Each one of those brand placements features the organisation's logo in a prominent position.

Many organisations give corporate gifts to their customers and suppliers. With the Bribery Act limiting the scope for client gifts, it is important to make the most of the opportunities that are allowed. Pens, bottle openers, mugs, bags, desk calendars, stress balls, mints, sweets, USB sticks, key rings, mouse mats, sticky notes, travel adaptors and torches and are all commonly branded and given away to existing customers, potential customers and suppliers. There are many other examples of corporate gifts on offer. I have even heard of corporate branded condoms, although I wouldn't normally recommend that you offer them.

## What you give comes with a message

In the light of Extinction Rebellion and a general movement to reduce plastic and waste, what you give away needs to be environmentally friendly. The recipient of any gift needs to feel comfortable accepting it. Maybe offering a donation to a good cause instead, will replace the giving of corporate gifts.

The more practical and useful the gift is the better, as it will be more appreciated and more often used. Giving away high-quality corporate umbrellas is a good way to promote your brand, as umbrellas are on show every time it rains. Not only do they keep your grateful customer or supplier dry, they simultaneously advertise your logo to everyone around them.

~~~~~

Just as we judge other people by looking from the outside in, we can't assess anyone's commitment to the cause by their external appearance alone. Just because a worker is wearing a company fleece outside of work doesn't necessarily show loyalty. It may just be the warmest top they had handy.

Tribes need to regularly remind their own members what they are part of, to maintain a strong collective sense of tribe. Many businesses issue company branded products to their staff as well as to their customers and suppliers. Assuming that the product is worth having, issuing it to staff has a mutual benefit. The tribe's members will feel a greater sense of social belonging; and the gifting of it helps to earn their continued loyalty. Asking workers to pay for their uniforms can increase their connection with it if its value and meaning is already well established. But where it's standard workwear, having to pay for it can remove any sense of engagement with it.

The act of issuing your tribe with a branded jacket, umbrella or fleece can have the mutual benefit mentioned, but it doesn't win their hearts and minds on its own. Tribe members need to be won over by your tribe's vision, purpose and values, not your branded goods. When that happens a worker will choose to wear the fleece because of what it stands for, as well as because of how warm it is. A logo has to represent something meaningful, something worth belonging to.

~~~~~

What actual and virtual items do you brand? How do you distribute them? Which corporate giveaways do you put your logo on? How do you get your brand and logo out there?

# 2.15 TRIBAL SYMBOLS

Tribes can also create and acquire symbols which support their values and vision. Some symbols are distinctive enough to immediately link them with a particular tribe. The tribe's logo might be based on such a symbol. Other symbols can only be understood by the tribe itself. Symbols can be used to tell the stories of a tribe's heritage and values without the need for words.

*Every tribe needs strong
and distinctive symbols*

Symbols are found everywhere. Military medals, Aston Martin car badges and Rolex watches are all symbols of strength, power and wealth. Tattoos, black flags and nose studs are symbols of individuality and defiance. Statues of historic figures are symbols of pride. They are too many types of symbol to name them all. Each one has developed a meaning from its nature and its context. They should reflect and support the tribe's vision, purpose and values. What are your tribe's symbols?

~ ~ ~ ~ ~

Religions use symbols to illustrate the key tenets of their faiths. The symbol of Yin and Yang is the Taoist symbol for the two primal forces in the universe. In Chinese philosophy, Yin (the Moon) is seen as a receptive, passive and cool, female force. Whereas Yang (the Sun) is seen as a warm, active and masculine force. The Yin Yang symbol represents the ideal harmony of these two primary forces, which Taoists believe creates equilibrium in the Universe.

The two-tone design of black (which stands for ignorance) and white (which represents enlightenment), provides a clear and simple contrast between the two opposing forces. By depicting them as flowing around each other, Yin and Yang are both juxtaposed and inter-connected.

The Taoist depiction of Yin and Yang summarises the religion in a symbol. All organisations can illustrate their core purpose and beliefs in a well-chosen symbol.

~~~~~

Symbols can be natural or adopted. As far as we know Wales has never had dragons and yet the dragon is the national symbol of Wales. A bold red dragon sits prominently in the centre of the Welsh national flag, representing Cadwaladr the King of Gwynedd. The link between Wales and a dragon seems to have been first mentioned in Historia Brittonium, which was written in about AD 829.

## A red dragon represents Wales

To some, the dragon is supposed to have been the battle standard of King Arthur and the ancient Celts, giving it a link to Celtic Wales. Evidence from archaeology, literature, and documentary history points towards an earlier Romano-British symbol.

Whatever its original source, the red dragon was successfully adopted by the Welsh and it is now recognisable around the World as a symbol of Wales.

~~~~~

The ways that a tribe uses its symbols affects their impact within a tribe. So do the rules as who can use those symbols.

The Medicine Wheel held a great spiritual significance for the Lakota Sioux. The shape of the wheel represents the circle of life and death, which is constant and never-ending. It also represents the wholeness and unity of the Great Spirit. The Medicine Wheel was a sacred symbol. It was only to be used by a Holy or Medicine Man which perpetuated its holiness.

~~~~~

The Viking Jarls had jewellery of their own, but they liked to wear the spoils of war [59] instead. The Jarls wore neck rings, dress pins, armbands brooches, pendants and finger rings that they had pillaged from their raids overseas. The greater the spoils they wore, the more war-like and successful they were perceived to be. So rather than wearing their own Viking jewellery, the elite Vikings wore the symbols of the peoples they had conquered.

Modern day commercial tribes acquire and merge with other organisations. The new combined version usually adopts the dominant partner's symbols, logo and branding. But unless there is a very good reason, the new business shouldn't immediately ditch the less dominant organisation's symbols. Otherwise it will forfeit some of its own heritage and power.

Too many merged businesses lose the essence of one partner as soon as the signatures are dry. Instead the new combined business should try and harness the symbols of the acquired company and add them into the mix. Establishing a new brand is so much harder than maintaining an established one.

~~~~~

The UK's largest reported hoard of ancient gold was found in a series of discoveries near Snettisham in Norfolk, East Anglia. The site was once a sacred religious place for a famous Iron-Age, pagan tribe called the Iceni (or Eceni).

In 60-61 AD the Iceni Queen Boudicca famously led a revolt against the Roman invaders, in which she and a super-tribe of Britons set fire to London, Colchester and St. Albans. In his writing, the Roman

---

[59] This detail was contained in a March 2017 article in National Geographic March.

Historian Tacitus described Boudicca as wearing a large golden torc around her neck. This was a clear symbol of Boudicca's wealth and power as tribal leader. Necklaces (or torcs) were Iceni symbols of wealth and power. Golden torcs were the greatest symbol of all. Gold is still a symbol of wealth and power today.

## *Boudicca wore a large golden torc*

Modern leaders have job titles, cars and remuneration packages that reflect their power and wealth. They should never be too ostentatious or excessive. In a sustainable tribe, power and wealth should be shared.

~~~~~

Victories in battle create stories and symbols of achievement. Wins in business can do the same. A tribe should tell and re-tell its victory stories and use its symbols of triumph as motivation for achieving even greater feats. The more vivid the symbol and stories about an event, the more value it could add to the tribe.

The history of the Battle of Trafalgar and Lord Horatio Nelson is of one of Britain's most famous victories. In 1805, Nelson led the British Navy at the Battle of Trafalgar. Sailing aboard the defiantly named HMS Victory[60], Nelson sent a message by flags to his twenty-seven ships, with famous line:

## *"England expects every man to do his duty."*

It was absolutely vital that Britain defeated Napoleon at sea. Against the larger French fleet of thirty-three warships, Nelson used an unconventional tactic. Instead of pulling his ships alongside and opening fire, Nelson crashed the English warships into the French line as he'd done successfully in the Battle of Aboukir Bay. Then once the French lines were in disarray, he finally pulled the British ships up

---

[60] HMS Victory is perhaps the greatest symbol of British naval power and can be visited at Portsmouth's Historic Dockyard.

parallel with the enemy. The English took heavy losses before thundering their guns into the French ships and securing a famous military victory.

Lord Nelson was shot and wounded in the melee. He died shortly after hearing that the battle had been won. By leading the British to victory, Lord Horatio Nelson certainly did his duty.

Today a fifty-two metre high monument stands proudly in Trafalgar Square. Nelson's Column is a permanent reminder of our heroic sailor. It is also a defiant symbol of British sea power and military might, positioned so prominently in central London.

~~~~~

Symbols of victory don't have to be permanent structures or designs. There is a myth that before the Battle of Agincourt in 1415, the French threatened to cut off the index and middle fingers of any English archers they captured. So, when Henry V lead the English to victory, the archers stuck up these two fingers to show the French that they still had them, in a "V" shaped sign. Despite its popularity, this myth doesn't appear to have any sound historical evidence to support it. Not least because three fingers are needed to draw the famous English oak longbows.

However the two fingered "V" sign began, it is almost unique to Britain. The gesture of using the index and nearest middle finger has become a British symbol of defiance. Americans don't use the "V" sign, they use the first index finger on its own, which is nicknamed the bird. That single finger gesture is in fact centuries old and internationally used. It can be traced as far back as 423 BC in Ancient Greece, where it gets a mention in Aristophanes' comedy play The Clouds.

In 1940, during Britain's darkest hours, Sir Winston Churchill used an inverted "V" sign, to instil confidence and show defiance. Ever since, the inverted "V" for Victory sign became a national symbol of Britain. Whichever way your two fingers face, using a "V" sign is a very defiant British symbol.

~~~~~

Across the World, historic tribal symbols have included temples, cathedrals, sacred sites of worship, religious artefacts, clothing design, weapons, coins, jewellery, pottery, cave paintings, hillside paintings, carvings, sculptures and musical instruments. Tribal symbols often have a design element to them.

Modern business symbols include the size and styling of an organisation's buildings and signage. A corporate building can act as a powerful symbol of the tribe within it. Each building's features and circumstances are different and so an office's combination of location, age and spaciousness will make a statement about the occupying tribe. Similarly its state of decoration, dilapidation and maintenance makes a statement too. Each of those differentiating factors influences the message being sent to potential workers, lenders, customers and suppliers.

## *What does your building say about your tribe?*

Whether it is accurate or not, the look of an office creates a perception about an organisation. A modern, sky-rise tower-block yells scale and financial clout. A free-standing brick building suggests that the business inside it is solid and independent. A shared modern office space could suggest the organisation is growing and value for money. Whereas a shared older building might suggest that the business is small or in decline.

Anything that doesn't look flashy can symbolise a steady ship that won't get ahead of itself. An office at home implies that the business is lean and cheap to run. In contrast, a huge, glass building by the waterside gives the impression of opulence and success. Inside a marble reception desk or a pond with Koi Carp gives the impression of wealth and influence. On the other hand, modest but functional furniture signifies efficiency and value for money.

Aside from offices, other business symbols include company cars, name badges, website designs, business cards, statues, office artwork, branded goods, email footers and even how members of staff are required to dress. Dress codes vary more now than ever before. Is yours formal or relaxed? For example, does your dress code require men to wear a suit and tie, a branded polo-shirt, or is a t-shirt okay? How much flexibility is there for staff? Some organisations are now allowing their staff to dress appropriately to match their diary for the day.

~~~~~

The first semi-final of the 2019 Women's World Cup found England facing up to the reigning champions and number one ranked team, the USA. England was ranked World number three and was playing with great purpose. Both teams were unbeaten. The match was tense and there was only ever one goal in it.

In the 31st minute, American Alex Morgan scored a goal to take the USA into a 2 v 1 lead. It was a high quality goal and it broke the deadlock. The USA players celebrated wildly. Amongst them all, Alex Morgan's goal celebration was to mimic drinking a cup of tea. After the match she was asked why she had done it. Her answer was "I feel like this team has had so much thrown at them and us. I feel like we didn't take an easy route through this tournament and that's the tea".

If you've never heard that expression, it might be because it masks the more likely reason for that gesture. If you asked an American whether the symbolism of drinking tea meant anything regarding the English, you would get an immediate and rather more tribal answer.

## A tribal symbol of independence

On 16 December 1773 the Sons Of Liberty decided to protest against British rule and in particular against 'taxation without representation'. A tax imposed on the importation of tea from England had led to artificially high prices and then to a crack down on tea smuggling. Historians say that famous Americans John Adams and John Hancock were tea smugglers and members of the Sons of Liberty. The greed of the British East India Company had lead to political pressure and influence on the British Government to make America pay more. The tax on tea was a tax too far. Being controlled by Great Britain, without a voice, was causing increasing frustration.

On the morning of 16 December 1773, the Sons of Liberty decided to make tea the focus of their protest. So later that night hundreds of protesters reportedly disguised themselves as Native Americans and marched into Griffin's Wharf in Boston. The protestors stole onto three ships owned by the British East India Company and dumped three hundred chests of tea straight into the harbour.

The protestors agreed a vow of silence and only one man was ever named and punished. After the single named man was tarred and feathered, no one else gave themselves (or anyone else) up. The British were furious and passed the Intolerable Acts to close the Port of Boston until the tea had been paid for. Benjamin Franklin reportedly offered to pay for the cost of the tea if the port was reopened, but the British refused his offer. That was not a super-tribe decision. Tensions increased across America. History records that The Boston Tea Party was the first revolutionary action in a chain that led directly to the American Independence two and a half years later on 4 July 1776.

When Alex Morgan chose the 'tea' celebration for her goal against England, America knew exactly what Alex Morgan was celebrating. Her act provided a tribal symbol of independence for every USA citizen.

~~~~~

In China, a company called China Merchants New Energy has built a 248 acre solar power plant in Datong which is cleverly shaped to look like a panda from the air. Using the symbol of China's most recognised animal links the initiative to national pride and a support for both 'green' initiatives and preservation. It looks cute too, courting media attention for the brand.

~~~~~

A tribe's symbols should directly relate to its vision, purpose and values. They can act as motivation and inspiration. They should help to tell the tribe's story and attract new tribe members.

What are your tribe's symbols? Where do you use them? How do they promote your tribe?

## 2.16  TRIBAL BRAND

With so much choice and 24/7 access to almost everything you could want, consumers of goods and services now demand instant availability. Living in the modern world means that we have lost much of our natural patience and tolerance.

Unless your brand messages are fresh and compelling they will be lost in the clamour. Unless your products and services are consistent, uniform and reliable you won't get many repeat sales. Unless your website is colourful, beautiful and intuitive, with seamless navigation, you will miss out on the online followers you need to grow. Unless you get your stories and songs into the public consciousness your tribe will stay small. Tribal growth and development requires relentless hard work.

~~~~~

Many tribes come from original ideas, but adopting and adapting other people's ideas can work really well too (as long as you aren't legally passing off).

The Women's Institute (known as the "WI") was formed in 1915 to encourage more women to help with food production during the First World War. The idea was borrowed from Canada.

The WI is now the largest voluntary women's organisation in the UK with nearly a quarter of a million members spread over 6,000 groups. The key to its enduring success is that the WI plays a unique role in providing women with the chance to develop their education and skills, as well campaigning on issues that matter to women. WI campaigns include Link Together to reduce loneliness and Food Matters to reduce food waste.

With a strong brand that's affectionately and unofficially known as "Jam and Jerusalem" the WI offers a positive and collective support group that inspires women and contributes positively to society. The WI is unmistakably a strong tribal brand.

~~~~~

Successful commercial and sporting brands can be identified from its name, logo, symbols and strap-lines. The most successful global brands can be instantly identified by just one of them alone.

*A brand's colours, strap-linesand choice of imagery should promote its purpose*

To become a strong brand an organisation needs to have three elements of supreme clarity:

**1. What the brand stands for (and by the same token what it stands against).** Both relate back to the organisation's brand purpose.

**2. What the brand is trying to achieve.** This is its brand vision. This could be set out in a promise to the market about what it will deliver (which is known as a brand promise).

**3. What behaviours the brand actively promotes and encourages and which behaviours do not fit with the brand.** These are its brand values. These should come out in all the brand positioning, brand personality, brand promises and brand strap-lines.

Clarity and consistency are absolutely critical in growing and maintaining a strong brand. Without a keen sense of why the brand exists it cannot gain the traction it needs to succeed. Losing all sense of clarity and direction will result in a very different brand (if there's one there at all).

A brand's colours, strap-lines and choice of imagery should promote its purpose and help it to achieve its vision. With a clear brand positioning statement and sympathetic imagery and design, a brand can emerge from the pack and grow fast. The styling of a brand should always fit tightly with the organisation's brand vision, purpose and values.

Each brand's styling should be notably different to its competitors to avoid claims of passing-off and to create a point of differentiation. Without creating something new, organisations cannot offer a credible alternative to the existing market.

The positioning of a brand plays a massive role is its success or failure. When a new brand emerges from the pack and starts to become popular, good brand positioning can use that popularity to create even more noise and feed more interest. Leaders should aim to get their tribe to that pivotal tipping point.

~~~~~

To illustrate this, you could take a theoretical campaign that's sustainability based.

The first question to ask is whether there is a clear vision, purpose and set of values on which to base a branding campaign? In this case the answer is yes, as our theoretical campaign has the joint purposes of preserving the countryside and reducing traffic through small towns and villages. Those combined purposes are consistent, clear and easy to understand. Business probably wouldn't like the campaign and not everyone would support it, but a tribe could grow around those purposes.

The vision of the future is a peaceful, green countryside without much traffic noise or pollution. That vision can be easily pictured and described.

The movement's core values might be a love of nature, humility, environmental sustainability and peaceful protest.

So now we know that our theoretical campaign has a consistent and complementary vision, purpose and values. So how could that be branded?

The brand might be called "Traffic Jam and Jerusalem" because:

(i)     Within Hubert Parry's popular hymn Jerusalem there are the lyrics "I will not cease from mental fight, nor shall my sword sleep in my hand, till we have built Jerusalem in England's green and pleasant land."

(ii)    The phrase Jam and Jerusalem is already familiar (from its Women's Institute association) and adding the traffic jam label and mental image sets the scene on the problem we are trying to resolve.

The brand's colour scheme would be natural greens and browns. Jerusalem would be the brand song and background music for any recorded advertisements. The locations of operation would be every person's own street and local community. A tribal symbol might be the image of a pair of green ear-defenders.

## *Traffic Jam and Jerusalem*

Whatever a tribe's purpose, vision and values are, it has to offer a practical solution to the problem it highlights. Its tribal brand has to offer a powerful call to arms and realistic hope of change. A brand could certainly be built around a campaign like this, or any other social, commercial or environmental campaign.

The scale of the challenge would be enormous. Stakeholders to tackle would include countryside communities, the Highways Agency and Local Authorities. The tide of "progress" may be impossible to turn back, but it could be slowed or modified. Without a practical and affordable solution, little would happen. So a campaign like this should concentrate on practical ideas[61]:

(i)     **Initiatives to reduce pollution, such as:**
- lowering maximum vehicle emissions
- automatic congestion charges for travelling through certain areas
- spreading traffic flow more evenly by reduced congestion charges and vehicle tax for night-driving
- automated fine system for exceeding the speed limit
- mass road-side tree and hedge planting programmes
- targeted expansion of rural public transport

(ii)    **Initiatives to reduce traffic noise, such as:**
- better soundproofing in buildings near roads
- requiring reduced sound emissions on vehicles
- using noise cancellation technology in busy areas

This is a theoretical campaign for a real life issue. Real tribes need to find their clarity of vision, purpose and values first. Then they need to apply a fitting branding campaign to reflect those fundamentals.

~~~~~

Global brands Coca Cola and McDonalds have developed loyal customer followings that are worth billions of pounds a year in sales. Food and drink brands like them need to be at least one of tasty, healthy and refreshing. Ideally they will be all three. Potential buyers can be tempted to try products from well-placed advertising and branding, but food and beverage products really have to be tasty, healthy or refreshing for consumers to buy them again. If they are

---

[61] This is an illustration only. There will be more examples of practical steps that could be taken.

also quickly available or relatively cheap, they have a great chance of selling.

Where products have sufficient consumer appeal, one-off customers will choose to repeat the experience. They may transition on to become regular buyers. Happy customers enjoy telling their friends and relatives. They are happy to spread the word. Some become brand disciples and create a buzz about the products they love. Their enthusiasm catches on and it persuades other people to try the same products. Those brand enthusiasts become leaders for the brand's tribe of followers. In a product's early days, buyers who transition from consumers to informal brand ambassadors are worth their weight in gold.

## Customers can become brand disciples

Coca-Cola, nicknamed Coke, isn't everyone's favourite drink[62] but to many millions of people it is tasty and refreshing. Whilst it isn't healthy, two out of the three isn't bad[63]. Stocked in every supermarket and corner shop, Coke is also easy to buy and relatively inexpensive. With stylish glass bottles and feel-good advertisements, the brand personality is young, sociable and cool. Drinking Coke won't make you super-cool on its own, but if you're drinking Coca-Cola you won't look uncool. Coke is tasty, refreshing, youthful and easy to buy.

Coca-Cola's brand promise has persuaded millions of people to try Coke and then carry on drinking it. "Our central promise at The Coca-Cola Company is to refresh the world in mind, body, and spirit, and inspire moments of optimism; to create value and make a difference."

~~~~~

Pepsi Cola has also done astonishingly well in the Cola market. Established in 1898, Pepsi entered the market just over a decade after Coca-Cola.

---

[62] I personally don't like the taste of Pepsi or Coke, but millions of people seem to.
[63] Paraphrasing Jim Steinman's Meatloaf, two out of three is good.

Pepsi has used many brand slogans over the years. In 1947 it used "It's a Great American Custom". In 1958 it used "Be Sociable, Have a Pepsi." In 1979 it used "Catch that Pepsi spirit." Each slogan aimed to catch the prevailing mood of the time.

In the 1980's Pepsi famously linked up with music legend Michael Jackson, to help to advertise it, Pepsi recognised that increasing its brand awareness would lead to increased sales. That started a trend of big name tie-ups for Pepsi which included music stars Lionel Richie, Tina Turner, David Bowie, Britney Spears, One Direction and Beyonce. Then came supermodel Cindy Crawford and sports stars like David Beckham, Lionel Messi and American Football legends Joe Montana and Dan Marino. Success by mutual association has worked very well for Pepsi.

Recent straplines include "Live for now" and "The Joy of Pepsi-Cola." Pepsi has certainly worked its brand identity and brand associations to great effect.

Like Coke, Pepsi is tasty and refreshing. Pepsi appeals to a similar but different group of people to Coke (with some cross-over). Many people prefer the taste of Pepsi to Coke. That's why Pepsi's official and unofficial brand ambassadors are working hard to advocate for Pepsi, day in day out.

## What does your tribe stand for?

Similarly when it comes to food, millions around the globe believe that a McDonalds' burger is tasty and stops you feeling hungry. The food is relatively inexpensive and served fairly quickly. Consumers will sacrifice healthiness in some of their food if it is fast and tasty. With its price point and speed of service McDonalds attracts people who want a quick, cheap meal on the go. McDonald's brand promise fits it's offering well. It is the promise of "simple, easy enjoyment with great service, cleanliness and value."

To top that package off, McDonalds offers Happy Meals for children complete with a toy. What a brilliant brand for a food product. Every parent wants their children to be happy. How easy is it to order a

Happy Meal for your child? And yet now, with climate change protests in every major city, offering plastic toys weakens rather than strengthens the McDonalds brand (unless that stops).

The use of the 'Drive Thru' concept added another benefit to buying from McDonalds. It couldn't be easier or more convenient to buy a meal. You don't even need to leave your car. According to McDonald's own website[64] approximately 70% of the company's U.S. sales in now come from the Drive-Thru windows.

As the fast food market leader, McDonalds has constantly tried to push its offering on to another level of convenience. If imitation is the most sincere form of flattery, then several other fast food chains must really admire McDonalds.

~~~~~

Car salesman Joe Girard[65] was in the Guinness Book of Records for personally selling the most cars in a year. Joe generated over $300,000 in commission from car sales during 1976. That's the equivalent to $1.3 million today. That was just the commission. The total car sales were many millions more. Remarkably, Joe Girard earned that commission from selling cars at one desk in one car showroom.

That sort of success doesn't happen by accident. Joe knew that he needed to reach out from behind his desk. There were too many colleagues in the same showroom for him to do well on walk-ins alone. Joe couldn't afford to sit and wait for business to come to him. So he worked tirelessly to create a huge tribe of customers, prospects and referrers outside of the showroom. In the days before the internet Joe didn't have a Facebook, WhatsApp or Linked In account to stay in touch with everyone. So he manually collected details of the dates people bought their cars and their birthdays. Then he posted cards to celebrate every possible occasion. That way he stayed in the forefront of their minds when it came to cars. Every person that ever he bought anything from became a prospect. Everyone he met was assimilated

---

[64] Newsroom: How Drive-Thru Windows Changed the Way America Orders Food.
[65] Joe Girard's best-selling book "How to sell anything to anyone" explains how Joe became a record salesman.

into his tribe. He was relentless in expanding and contacting his network.

## Use networks of advocates

Amongst Joe's sale techniques, he built and nurtured two networks of advocates for his cars. The first group was his customers, who he looked after so well they told all their friends to come to him. The second group was made up of his referrers who he called his "bird-dogs." Joe wined and dined them and paid them referral fees when they referred customers to him.

Joe Girard built a personal brand that persuaded customers to buy from him ahead of anyone else. But that alone doesn't explain his success. When asked what made him so successful, Joe replied "What made Joe Girard was service, service, service – and I created the greatest advertising in the World, which was word of mouth." Joe Girard created a strong personal brand and it was the tribe he built around it that gave him so many customers.

Every organisation needs to build a tribe of people around its brand. By providing a repeatedly wonderful service a business can create a flow of happy customers. Some of them will naturally recommend you to a friend or family member. But if you can step the relationship up to a higher level and turn them into brand advocates for you, they will recommend many more people to you. You can build a referral network that keeps on forwarding prospects by staying in touch and offering referrers something for themselves. With the restrictions imposed by the Bribery Act 2010 and the Data Protection Act 2018 businesses need to take care with how they manage their networks. But the tools exist to build an extremely productive network if you are as relentless as Joe Girard.

~~~~~

Professional sports clubs survive by building a tribe of supporters that attends their matches and buys their merchandise. Every team needs a loyal group of supporters to be able to pay its bills. Once someone becomes a sports fan they can be hooked for a while, but life happens. Supporters move away, take on conflicting responsibilities, lose their health or interest and every fan ultimately dies. So every team needs to develop a continuous conveyer belt of new fans to replenish the lost ones and that's just to stand still.

It's a big ask to try and persuade anyone to take up watching a new sport, but it is always possible if you properly sell the tribe to potential new supporters. We buy tribal brands.

The influence that a parent has on a child is unquestionable. Amongst many more important aspects of parenting, a child's mother or father can effectively decide which sports teams the child supports. For some families, sport is boring and there is no interest or influence. But where a decision has to be made, choosing which team is tribal. Are you a red or a blue? Are you City or United? The choice does matter.

In some cases a mild form of brainwashing goes on until a child decides to support the club chosen by a parent or another influential relative. From then on, supporting the team links the generations and offers social belonging. Family sporting connections link our events, memories and tribe together. How many of us can remember going to a match with a parent or grandparent? Those memories can be very powerful and evoke strong emotions within us. Ironically it seems that the more a parent or grandparent was pressurised or influenced into choosing a particular sports team themselves, the more vehemently they appear to pass the same obligation on to the next generation.

At a time when schools are trying to help their pupils become independent learners and parents are trying to help their children become independent thinkers, this kind of influencing process is rightly open to question. In a 2016 Benenden survey[66], nearly half (42%) of parents admitted to forcing their children to support the same sports team as them (with 46% of Dad's doing it) and over half (53%) said that they would care if their child went against them and supported a different team.

---

[66] The Power of Parents survey, by Opinion Matters for Benenden

The criticism has even made it into song lyrics. The Proclaimers song New Religion[67] includes the lyrics:

*"Evidence of a new religion, I'll spare you the details, Effluent from a bloated business, with replica shirt sales. Two for the kids, one for the wife, indicating a stunted life. Didn't know gullibility was so rife? Well, you do know now."*

However much undue influence there may be, the act of choosing is ultimately personal. By adopting red or blue, Bath or Gloucester, Tigers or Trinity brings you a new tribe. That process offers instant social belonging. Picking a team is a core part of being a tribal being and if someone has chosen the wrong tribe for you, then chose a different one.

Sport can unite us and help to mend fractured communities. We only need to feel what happens when England do well at a World Cup. The pull of our national brand is strong.

~~~~~

Manchester United plays in Manchester, England. The City of Manchester has two premier league football teams and a population of two and a half million people. You might expect United to have the support of half the City of Manchester, but rather than having 1.25 million supporters, Manchester United is said to have 659 million supporters across the World[68]. Those estimated 659 million people were from an estimated total of 1.6 billion football supporters around the World. Whilst no one can say exactly how many fans the club has in reality, it is inarguable that Manchester United has a truly global tribe. On any reckoning, that tribe is exponentially bigger than half of the population of Manchester. But why?

---

[67] From the excellent 2007 album Life With You.
[68] According to a 2012 Kantar Survey, reported on the Manchester United's website.

People like associating themselves with winners and success. It makes us feel good. Supporting a winning club links us to that success, allowing us to adopt some of it for ourselves. The highs from victories and championships can be very good for self-esteem. The more often a team wins the more ups you get and the fewer downs you have to put up with. Manchester United is England's most successful team in the last fifty years. Those trophy winning years attracted new supporters because of the strength and success of the United brand. Call it the bandwagon or domino effect, winners attract followers. And because all United's matches are shown on television in every country, they have also attracted new fans across the globe.

On current form Manchester City is now the better team in Manchester. But United is a much bigger brand. Generations of United supporters are still loyal. Maybe if City goes on to replicate United's success for itself, then in twenty to thirty years time it might be the bigger Manchester brand. Success breeds success. A long period of success will create a much larger and following. Brand followers come slowly in the beginning, but they join rapidly as the success of the brand grows. The more trophies that Manchester City wins, the bigger its brand footprint will be.

~~~~~

Consumers are capable of tremendous brand loyalty. But an organisation has to live by its brand values, or its followers will desert it in droves. Even when your brand becomes well established it has to remain consistent and authentic to keep its position. Otherwise, your brand will lose even its most loyal followers. Millennials are particularly testing, cynical and demanding. They have little intrinsic trust for business and (quite rightly) they won't buy into corporate spin without substance. Your tribe's brand has to practice what it preaches.

When a product is advertised as standing for something that turns out to be a lie, its loyal followers will question their attachment to the whole brand. Boohoo fell foul of the Advertising Standards Authority (ASA) after being caught advertising a jumper as "faux fur" when it contained real animal hair. The organisation Humane Society

International tested the jumper and reported it to the ASA as misleading. Boohoo has said that it has a strong commitment against the sale of real fur. That may be true and Boohoo itself may have been misled, or alternatively it may have been too casual and trusting. Boohoo customers will need to make their own minds up.

Brand gravity applies to commercial tribes. What goes up must come down. In our volatile, uncertain, complex and ambiguous (VUCA) World, the only question is how long you can keep your brand up. Businesses need to work tirelessly in order to delay the day when their brand loses its flavour and currency. Sometimes, despite years of authenticity and consistency, a brand can lose its reputation overnight.

*Customers will make
their own minds up*

Damaging the environment can do incredible damage to a brand. In 2000, global Oil Giant BP launched a PR campaign called Beyond Petroleum, which was designed to promote BP as a socially responsible brand. In 2009 BP's rig Deepwater Horizon drilled the deepest oil well in history at a vertical depth of 10,683 metres. Transocean the rig owner had a strong overall safety record with no major incidents for 7 years. All should have been positive for BP. But in 2010 an uncontrollable blowout caused an explosion and Deepwater Horizon sank. Tragically eleven people died. The sea was flooded with an estimated three million barrels of crude oil, causing huge damage to surrounding wildlife habitats. Reportedly, it has cost BP $30billion to try and clean the mess up.

Accidents can happen, but BP's actions were considered to have been "reckless." The co-chair of the Oil Spill Commission commented "There was not a culture of safety on that rig". BP's brand reputation was heavily tarnished as a result. As soon as an organisation is perceived to put profit before human safety it puts itself in deep water. Whether that perception is true or not almost doesn't matter. The message is clear. Being reckless with human life or the environment will cost you big time. However much brand loyalty there may be, consumers won't support a sinking brand. There are always more important considerations that making money.

~~~~~

Cheating the consumer is never likely to win followers either. Gerald Ratner's remark about his own jewellery being "total crap" was filmed and became national news. His comment instantly made all his brands' jewellery feel worthless. Deriding his own products made his customers feel cheated. Gerald Ratner's words cost him his whole business.

After a period in the commercial wilderness, Gerald has since bounced back selling jewellery online, but his personal reputation is still affected all these years later. By accepting his mistake and making humour out of it, Gerald Ratner now uses his it to his advantage. I have twice booked him as a speaker[69].

~~~~~

In 2015, the U.S. Environment Protection Agency called out Volkswagen for cheating on its diesel emissions tests. Volkswagen had seemingly installed "defeat devices" to artificially reduce emissions on nearly 600,000 vehicles sold in the United States. The devices were designed to circumvent the vehicle emissions tests. Knowledge of this practice appeared to go all the way to the top of Volkswagen. Subsequent reports seem to indicate that there were attempts to cover up the scandal before the story broke. The substantial differences in road-based emissions tests compared to official lab-based tests created a "gap" that needed to be explained. As soon as the story broke Volkswagen came under immense pressure to explain the reasons for that. Volkswagen's inability to explain the difference set consumer alarm bells ringing. No one likes being lied to.

Volkswagen sales reportedly dropped by 20% and the company sustained the worst losses in its history. The scandal has cost the

---

[69] Gerald tells an extremely entertaining version of his story.

company an estimated £22bn. No doubt it also cost some employees their jobs.

Reputational damage can cut very deep. If you can survive the immediate scandal and heavy short-term losses, you might be able to make a recovery. But to do that you need to take your medicine. Perpetuating the lie or refusing to compensate affected people can be absolutely fatal. Instead, opening yourself up to greater scrutiny and submitting to a thorough testing regime could save you. Once it was shamed, Volkswagen has worked very hard to rid its cars of the defeat devices. Car makers are now far less likely to ever try anything like that again. Volkswagen had to, to save its brand.

## *Reputational damage can cut very deep*

Perhaps as a result of making full page apologies in newspapers around the World [70] the brand's loyal customers have been more forgiving. One official comment included "We sincerely hope you see this as a first step toward restoring your invaluable trust." That's a very well structured statement. Choosing the words "you see this" indicates that Volkswagen understood its customer perception mattered most of all. The statement is a form of prayer for trust, loyalty and support. The rebuilding process worked. In 2017 Volkswagen sold a record 10.7 million cars around the World.

~~~~~

Behaving illegally doesn't help a business brand either. In 2016, Sports Direct was named and shamed by the Government for failing to pay its workers the national minimum wage. In 2017, Uber didn't have its license to operate in London renewed, after failing to treat its staff as workers. Brands do themselves harm if they are seen to be all about the money. If that comes at a human, conservation or environmental cost then self-harming can be particularly painful.

---

[70] Volkswagen took out full page advertisements in over thirty newspapers in the USA alone.

~~~~~

If an organisation can create a clear sense of tribe and harnesses that for good, it can create a combined effort of all its members and stakeholders. By pulling its stakeholders together, it can unleash an entire tribe of people to one joint purpose. To generate tribal power a tribe needs a strong brand proposition and a compelling call to action. If a tribe promotes itself as a trusted brand but has a reputation for poor customer service, its brand becomes the reality not the dream.

What does your brand say about your tribe? What does your brand stand for? Is that something worth supporting?

# 2.17 TRIBAL ROUTINES

The way things are done says a lot about a tribe. An organisation's rules, policies and procedures set out what should be happening, but what matters more is what actually happens in practice. Any behaviour that's permitted and repeated in practice becomes settled. It becomes a tribal routine.

If a company has a sign on the lawn outside its headquarters saying "Don't walk on the grass" you might expect that organisation to have a rules based culture. You would also expect people not to walk across that lawn. But if, right next to that sign, there is a well worn footpath across the grass, you'd reach the natural conclusion that people ignore the sign. That leads to a supplementary question which is: If an organisation's workers are prepared to ignore that clear and visible instruction, what else are they ignoring?

Where a company allows a great deal of flexibility with its rules and regulations one of its values becomes autonomy, but one of its weaknesses becomes too much individuality. What do your tribal routines reveal?

Researching a tribe's rules, regulations, policies and procedures allows us to understand what is supposed to happen. Comparing that to what actually happens gives an insight into the tribe's real behaviours and values. If a tribe's people regularly do something, that's what the tribe stands for.

~ ~ ~ ~ ~

In the musical School of Rock [71], Dewey Finn pretends to be a substitute teacher to pay his outstanding rent. His disinterest in anything other than creating a rock band makes him a disastrous teacher. His "stick it to the man" attitude provides a stark contrast with the austere school environment. The culture clash between Dewey Finn and Horace Green School is a major feature of the film.

We learn that the School is particularly regimented and traditional from the lyrics of several songs. Firstly in the song "Horace Green Alma Mater" the children sing "Here at Horace Green the old traditions shape who we are in word and deed." The children also "shoulder duty" and "toil and never rest."

Then in "Here at Horace Green" the Head Teacher Miss. Mullins sings of how the School is extremely strict and demanding. Sky-high expectations are a matter of "routine". Miss. Mullins expressly refers to all the pressures and demands of the parents, alumni and School Board. With the notable exception of Dewey Finn, all the staff and children are stuck on a treadmill of routines, standards and traditions.

The lyrics of "Here at Horace Green" include several other markers about how tough and uncompromising the school culture is,

---

[71] Music by Lord Andrew Lloyd Webber and lyrics by Glen Slater. The musical is based on the 2003 film School of Rock written by Mike White (who plays the real Ned Schneebly) and stars Jack Black as Dewey Finn.

including threats about non-compliance. "Greatness is routine. The Board demands it, or we will both be ripped part" as well as "While they're in our care, we tenderly prepare them to complete with the elite, till they are dispersed to Harvard or at worst Cornell." Another example is

*"Here at Horace Green we stick to custom, keep on schedule, do what must be done. Don't and it will mean I go ballistic. Right then that's all. Good luck. Have fun."*

The combination of uptight Head Teacher and highly pressurised environment is oppressive. There is no room for fun at all. The regime produces "successful" children and ever more generations of the same. That is if academic results are the only measures of "success". How can those routines really be successful when no one can be themselves and no one is happy? Having high standards does not require or justify oppression and misery.

After the impact made by Dewey Finn, the school is forever changed. Hard work should be accompanied by down time and fun. School of Rock illustrates that perfectly.

~~~~~

In business, good numbers should be viewed as the product that comes at the end of the right routines. Instead many executive reviews tend to view things from the other end of the telescope. The dangerous result is that if the statistics "look" right everything must be okay. That kind of assessment is too narrow and misses the effect that the usual ways of working are having.

Measuring employee satisfaction, customer satisfaction and supplier satisfaction produces additional numbers that are equally important to the Balance Sheet and Profit and Loss Account. Adding feedback from every significant stakeholder makes the figures increasingly robust. The combined set of statistics allows an organisation to understand the reality of its headline numbers better. With the additional information an organisation can adapt its routines to improve satisfaction levels before the headline numbers suffer. Doing it in good time might even improve those headline figures. What statistics does your organisation measure? Are those the ones that really matter?

Employees at work will routinely spend time on two things, being the things that they are responsible for and the things that they are rewarded for. Nothing else matters very much. So, quite understandably, routines build up around the things that employees believe their organisations want to see happen, not what is necessarily best. If a regular activity results in a worker getting praise and financial reward, you can expect that activity to become routine practice.

## Are your stakeholders happy with how you do things?

The public sector has been given endless new initiatives, re-structures and reforms to try and improve its performance. It has also been given endless targets and league tables to make it more accountable. With the epic scale involved and insufficient time, money, morality, emotional intelligence and strategy, the challenge seems close to impossible. But no one questions the value of having our public services. Our NHS, Education, Fire, Police and Armed services do an extraordinary job. The general public is hugely supportive of them. However despite loving their organisation's purpose, many people working in the public sector seem to be committed and frustrated in equal measure.

With so much bureaucracy to deal with and so many targets to hit, public sector management has become increasingly adept at hitting its artificial targets. That success has come at the expense of becoming more skilled and efficient at the tasks that matter most. If there is a choice between serving the public and doing administrative things that hit artificial targets, there should be no absolutely contest in what gets done. Sadly, the public's needs don't always come first.

The private sector suffers from the same problem. If a worker gets rewarded for hitting sales targets, that worker will be tempted to sell any kinds of products and services to anyone to hit the targets and earn the bonus. That will be the case even if the product or service isn't suitable, appropriate, reliable or value for money. The customer's needs don't always come first.

When hitting your targets for patient waiting times or customer sales are what count the most, the behaviours needed to achieve those targets become the organisation's routines. If on the other hand, it is public health and customer satisfaction that are judged and measured above artificial targets, the resulting behaviours would adapt and achieve more meaningful results. Which end of the telescope does your organisation look through?

~~~~~

Not all routines are positive. Some are positively harmful. Any organisation that operates on fear, manipulation or peer pressure is built like a house of cards, with no intrinsic strength. Those flawed organisations rely on routines that constantly eat away at its tribal strength.

During the time of the Roman Republic, decimation was used to punish a cohort for abandoning their arms in battle or deserting. The offending cohort was divided into small groups of ten soldiers. Each group drew lots through a process called sortition (from which we get the modern words sort and sorting) with one of the ten being randomly chosen. The selected soldier was then killed by the other nine, usually by being stoned or clubbed to death. Routinely afterwards the remaining nine soldiers were given reduced rations or forced to sleep outside the safety of the camp for a period.

Being brutal to your own people is difficult to accept, even in war. Forcing people to do anything against their will won't tap into their intrinsic motivations and inner strengths. They will give up trying as soon as they can. By dividing its own men against each other, the army of the Roman Republic cost itself a sense of togetherness and cohesion. In fact the threat of decimation encouraged early desertion when a battle wasn't going well.

Tribes should never operate based on intimidation, threats or fear. That produces the minimum energy and response in order to comply. Mere compliance with the rules is far too limiting. Fear as a motivator is self-destructive and ultimately unsustainable. Instead a tribe's core strength needs to come from a sense of shared purpose. Tribal power comes from the voluntary motivation and energy of its members.

Tribal routines that support positive and collegiate behaviour will be far more effective in building a tribe. It is absolutely no coincidence that the Romans had stopped the routine practice of decimation by the time of the Roman Empire. Rome did not reach its zenith as a tribal super-power until the abhorrent routine of decimation had ceased.

~~~~~

Certain routines and actions will contribute towards success (winning behaviours). They include repeated acts of selflessness, trust and sacrifice. Certain other routines and actions will make success far less likely (losing behaviours). They include repeated acts of high emotion, selfishness and laziness.

Values and behaviours are intertwined. Applying your values to your own behaviours will produce positive routines. But when we act, we don't always stick to our values. If our inconsistencies are the exception and not the rule, we can do more good than harm. And if over time if we develop our good behaviours, we can turn them into positive routines.

The same principle applies to any organisation. If a tribe's daily routines are based on its positive values then it will be providing continuous support for its purpose.

In Dave Ormesher's insightful book The Winning Behaviours[72] he looks at competencies. One of the core competencies for any organisation is Partnership. That is the "ability to develop and sustain

---

[72] The Winning Behaviours: Generating Performance Through Leadership

29

effective long-term coalitions and relationships" with the third parties that are "critical to achieving superior business performance."

## Develop and sustain effective long-term relationships

This routine act of 'Partnership' is a key element in building a super-tribe. It's about creating a 'coalition' of working that's broader and stronger than your tribe is on its own. Partnering involves seeking to find common ground and to build alliances. If Partnership is given genuine and consistent effort and support it will become a routine operating procedure. Partnership allows any tribe to nudge others as needed to positively influence their actions and routines with you and your organisation.

~~~~~

Meeting etiquette is can be a good indicator of tribal culture. If a meeting's agenda and papers are comprehensive and circulated well in advance, that's an indication of an open, confident and well-organised culture. However if the meeting agenda and supporting papers are late or incomplete, decision-making will be carried out in the shade, if not in total darkness. If there is no agenda and no briefing papers at all, then the meeting is merely a talking shop, or a rubber-stamping exercise that lacks any real control or influence. Any form of restriction can indicate a lack of good management, or worse a strategy of deliberate secrecy. Either way it smacks of a lack of trust from management.

## Its meeting etiquette offers great insight into a tribe's routines

A policy of secrecy can be a major barrier to employee engagement. Plants can't grow in the dark. In Marvel's The Winter Soldier [73] Captain America accuses Nick Fury of holding back crucial

---

[73] Marvel's Captain America: The Winter Soldier.

information about a mission. Fury replies "It's called compartmentalisation. Nobody spills the secrets because nobody knows them all." Harnessing tribal power is not about compartmentalisation, it is about inclusiveness and common purpose.

Are your meetings bossed by the loudest and most aggressive? Does everyone have the same level of information and understanding? Or is it the senior employees that always dominate? Is everyone's opinion heard and respected? Does each person get a turn to speak, or is it only the extroverts that get to influence your decision-making? Are the opinions of your introverts excluded by their shyness and silence? Are your meetings inclusive or exclusive?

~~~~~

At work there are many necessary routines. Unless they are structured to be engaging and enjoyable they will not be done as attentively or as enthusiastically as they could be. Work tasks can be positive, engaging and meaningful. Sadly they can also become uninspiring and dull. Worse still, where there is little or no engagement, they can become frustrating, arduous and deflating. The former aids engagement, the latter marches staff closer towards the exit door.

For example, how you advertise for new employees, supporter or members can become a good or bad routine. The choice of language can be key. Research has found that using the words like "manage" and "competitive" in job descriptions tends to attract more male candidates than using words like "support" and "develop". The word "create" has been proven to have a broader appeal than the word "build". Using lengthy bullet point lists results in more men applying, so that is to be avoided. Business is now alive to this. U.S. firm Textio provides artificial intelligence to highlight gender influencing words in job descriptions and suggest more inclusive terms in job advertisements and job descriptions.

# Are your jobs frustrating, arduous and dreary?

Initial induction, on-boarding and in-job training are also a routine part of recruitment. Done well they can really help to embed workers into an organisation, encouraging new starters to give their very best. By using follow up processes as well, new employees will be motivated to keep their good start going. When processes are applied with emotional intelligence they can be a thorough and positive experience that creates the best chance of performing well.

But when recruitment processes are done with precious little thought or enthusiasm a company's on-boarding, induction and training procedures can stifle the relationship before it's even got going.

~~~~~

A tribe's true values can be revealed by how it behaves in practice. Its routines can shed a bright light on those values. How does a tribe treat its own members and stakeholders? How does it greet strangers? How does it say goodbye to departing members? All of these tell us something about a tribe's ways of operating and its underlying values.

Do your tribe's behaviours change depending on who it is? Who does it bend the rules for? Do some members regularly get more freedom and flexibility than others? Do some members routinely get extra privileges? Does the leaver process change if a member is leaving to join a competitor[74]? How do you treat people who left and want to return? Are they welcomed back into the fold, or are they mistrusted and treated like second class citizens?

~~~~~

---

[74] Ironically, the tougher you are on leavers the less loyal the remaining members become.

Social graces like physical and verbal greetings reveal your intentions when meeting someone. Offering a firm handshake and warm words of welcome are signs of peaceful intent if you're in England. In Japan, bowing is the traditional greeting, although precise postures and degrees of bend are required depending on the formality and relative seniority of the people involved. Those different greeting routines need to be learned and put into practice.

In China bowing, shaking hands and applauding can all be appropriate. In Arab countries, male friends may embrace and kiss each other on both cheeks following a light and lingering handshake. In South Africa, handshaking, talking and backslapping all go together. Local knowledge is a huge advantage to getting on. Learning another tribe's manners and etiquette in advance shows respect. It acknowledges the diversity of life. Getting it wrong can cause great offence and break a relationship.

~~~~~

Positive ways of living a tribe's values can be repeated until they become routine. Tribes are a product of all of their signs, rituals, traditions and routines moulded together. The acid test of any tribe may be to ask the question "What has become routine for us?" Queueing is great example of a British routine, which reveals two of the mainstream British character traits of self-control and respect. What do your tribe's routine behaviours say about its values?

How well you stick to your routines matters. At the 2018 FIFA World Cup, it seemed like whenever Harry Kane was due to take a penalty he was deliberately delayed or impeded. The other team was trying to break his concentration and knock him off his routine. But each time, Harry kept himself calm, re-set himself physically and emotionally; and began his routine again. Re-establishing his well-rehearsed penalty routine gave him control of the situation. So every time he was interrupted, he re-started the process from the beginning. Every time he did, he scored.

~~~~~

Are your tribe's routines deliberate or random? Do you tribe's routines now control its actions, or are they driven by its values and purpose?

## 2.18 TRIBAL OPPOSITION

Being in a tribe means belonging to a distinct group of people. If your only tribe is everyone (the whole of humanity) then it's the most inclusive tribe possible. Any smaller tribe will naturally include some people and exclude others. In some cases the exclusion of other people is a neutral, default position (simply because they just aren't in your tribe). But in other cases some people are deliberately and pro-actively excluded because they are the opposition.

Tribes don't necessarily need an opposition, but having competitors or opponents can help to give greater focus and definition to your tribe. Finding your opposition gives you a chance to test your principles, beliefs and purpose against theirs. By studying and monitoring them, your tribe can see what it stands against. Knowing what you're not is as helpful as knowing what you are. Is your tribe the venom or the antidote?

~~~~~

Brought up on Stonegate in York, Guido (Guy) Fawkes was a staunch Roman Catholic. Faced with Protestant oppression because of his religious beliefs, Fawkes fled England. He took up arms and fought for Catholic Spain in the Eighty Years War against both France and the Protestant Dutch Republic (now Holland).

Fawkes was desperate to return England to Catholicism and save his fellow Catholics from the Protestant "heretic" King James I. So he sought Spain's support for a rebellion in England. But King Philip III of Spain was not prepared to give him the aid that he wanted.

Later, after being approached by Englishman Robert Catesby, Guy Fawkes returned home to his beloved England. Already convinced that violence was the answer, Fawkes agreed to play an active part in the Gunpowder Plot against King James I and his Parliament on the state opening of 5 November 1605. Fawkes sat under the House of Lords with thirty-six barrels of gunpowder waiting for the appointed hour. But before he could light the fuse, Fawkes was caught red-handed. He was tortured and forced to give up the names of his co-conspirators. Some were killed when they resisted arrest. The others were tried and found guilty of high treason. The punishment was a gruesome death. After being drawn, Guy Fawkes was the next to be hung. But as the moment approached he jumped into the hangman's noose breaking his own neck in the fall. After his death Fawkes' body was quartered.

## Who are you tribe's heroes?

Guy Fawkes was a staunch Roman Catholic. That was his primary tribe. Persecuted for being Catholic, Fawkes felt driven to violence against the Protestants who he felt threatened his life and religious freedom. Without a Protestant "opposition" there would have been no need for Guy Fawkes to fight anyone. That said, there were many other ways to act. Attempted murder is a crime.

On the 5th of November every year in England we have "Bonfire Night" as an act of thanksgiving for the failure of the Gunpowder Plot. A "Guy" is still being burned on the bonfire to re-establish Guy Fawkes as a traitor four hundred years after his failed plot. To Protestants, Guy Fawkes was a religious heretic and a traitor to England. To some people he was an attempted murderer and a man of violence. But to some Catholics he was a hero who died for his religious beliefs. Your view of the World depends on which tribe you're in and who your opposition is. One person's traitor is another person's hero.

Guy Fawkes was educated at St. Peter's School in York. So were his fellow-plotters Christopher Wright, John Wright and Jesuit priest

Oswald Tessimond who knew of the plot. The current school buildings are in fact built on the land that Guy Fawkes inherited from his father and sold before he went abroad. At the time of Guy Fawkes education the School's Headmaster is believed to have been a staunch Catholic and a big influence on him. Guy Fawkes' Catholic tribe may well have been adopted as a result of that influence.

As it happens, St. Peter's School is my old school too. It's a Protestant Church of England school. On Bonfire Night we were allowed to have a bonfire. But we were forbidden to burn a Guy because he'd been a pupil at the school. Guy Fawkes was part of our tribe too.

~~~~~

Businesses can motivate greater activity and urgent action by highlighting or creating an opposition. The desire to make your tribe better than the competition can drive it to greater success. Having competitors gives you a challenge to face head on. Aiming to beat your opponents gives you a reason to work even harder.

Surely the success of McDonalds drives Burger King to perform better and vice versa. The recent success of Manchester City must motivate Manchester United to re-take their Premier League mantle.

~~~~~

When you are pitching your tribe against the opposition (or competition), you need to consider how you can get ahead and stay ahead. That's done by a four step process:

(i)     Properly analysing what your own offering is (in terms of its vision purpose and values, brand, product and services specification, cost of production, distribution model and pricing strategy etc.); and

(ii)    Researching the needs and the wants of your existing and potential customers; and the future prospects of your market; and

(iii)    Evaluating your competition, especially its vision, purpose, values and competing offerings; and

(iv)    Re-positioning your own offering to make sure it meets (or preferably exceeds) your customer needs; and betters the competition in a way that's sustainable.

The four steps need to be carried out in this order. Step one is often glossed over too quickly and Step two can be missed out altogether, leaving a large degree of hope over reasoned analysis for Step four.

~~~~~

Organisations with multiple sites need a common opposition even more than single sites do. Faced with site variances, increased internal politics; and unhealthy competition for approvals and budgets; a group of individual sites can end up seeing their opposition as being the nearest 'rival' site or their own head office.

Multi-site organisations can either operate as multiple separate tribes under one ill-fitting banner, or act as one super-tribe. The former lacks collective engagement and creates unpredictable and clashing waves. The latter produces tribal waves. The trick is to learn, understand and utilise each tribe's strengths for the benefit of the overall organisation.

Creating a common external 'opponent' will help to shift each site's gaze beyond its own internal borders onto the threat outside. The greater that threat and the more common it is to every site, the easier it is for to unite against it. Promoting the same common opponents across all the organisation's sites should therefore help to foster a similar level of enmity and opposition. Being united against something means being united. The higher up the source of opposition comes the more chance a tribe can create alliances underneath that level, to form a super-tribe.

## Act together as one super-tribe

The British Army actively encourages inter-regimental rivalry. The intensity of the competition between them helps to keep each regiment fit and focused. The three Armed Services (Army, Navy and R.A.F.) pit themselves against each other too. One example is the hotly-contested Army v Navy annual rugby match. This state of constant opposition helps to maintain a state of readiness for war.

~~~~~

Who and what is your tribe's opposition? Is there a good reason for having each opponent? Can any of the opposition become an ally or partner? Would a merger be good for both tribes? Is forming a super-tribe better than taking lumps out of each other?

# 2.19 TRIBAL FRAGRANCE/FLAVOUR

Smell (olfaction) is perhaps the strongest sense of our five senses, because of its strong link with memory. Smells can be powerful enough to evoke memories of childhood events and long-forgotten times.

We detect smells by inhaling odour molecules in the air. Receptors inside our noses then relay messages to our brain to interpret. Humans are thought to be able to differentiate between one trillion different smell combinations. [75] With such a perceptive sense of smell, we use it much more than we might think. We subconsciously use our sense of smell it to help us distinguish family from stranger; and friend from foe. Although we cannot smell ourselves, we each have our own unique smell. We know this because Police sniffer dogs are used to find specific people using only their odour to go on.

---

[75] According to a survey carried out by Leslie Vosshall of Rockefeller University in New York City in about 2014.

A familiar fragrance can be easily detected. So can an unfamiliar one. Although our family members have similar smells which we could use to recognise them, it's become far more difficult to do this in recent times. That's because our natural smells are masked by all the washing powder, shower gel, anti-perspirant, aftershave and perfume we use. It is now very difficult to distinguish a person by their personal odour unless it's very strong.

Despite the limitations, different tribes and cultures can still have common aromas depending on factors like the place they live, the food they eat and the combination of fragranced products they use.

~~~~~

Smells can trigger warnings. For example the smell of gas warns us of a possible gas leak. The smell of smoke warns us of fire. Smells can alert us to food we like and need to survive. That's why restaurants pipe smells outside and why street markets seem so appetising. Fragrances can bring back memories and deeply affect us. They can also make us feel hungry. The smell of baking bread or toasted hot cross buns has an instant appeal. The smell of bacon has even been known to turn a vegetarian into a meat eater. Smells can have a huge impact on us.

By the same token, losing our sense of smell can have a profound impact on the way we experience the World around us. People who suffer from anosmia can feel isolated and 'cut-off' from the World around them. The loss can 'blunt' a person's emotions affecting their ability to form and maintain close personal relationships. Suffering from anosmia can lead to depression.

~~~~~

The World offers us a rich variety of cuisines. You don't have to visit its country of origin to taste a flavour from the other side of the World. There are hundreds of recognised dishes and thousands more variations being cooked every day.

Due to the wide range of herbs and spices available, food can taste and smell remarkably different depending on which combination of ingredients you use. If you can cook a familiar meal well people might buy it. If you have a new take on an old dish then people might buy that too. That's why Britain has so many successful Chinese and Indian takeaways. It's also why Nandos, Burger King, McDonalds and KFC occupy such prominent places on our high streets.

They have become so dominant that popular culture now reflects and enhances them. In 2003, the Fast Food Rockers had a hit with 'The Fast Food Song'. The fact that it reached number two in the UK Charts gave all the brands in its chorus enormous free advertising. The Fast Food Song no doubt strengthened those brands even further.

*"Let's eat to the beat*
*A Pizza Hut a Pizza Hut Kentucky Fried Chicken*
*and a Pizza Hut*
*A Pizza Hut a Pizza Hut Kentucky Fried Chicken*
*and a Pizza Hut*
*McDonald's McDonald's Kentucky Fried Chicken*
*and a Pizza Hut*
*McDonald's McDonald's Kentucky Fried Chicken*
*and a Pizza Hut"*

For a brand to stand out, its need great flavours and fragrances. But it also needs a great branding and leadership like every other business. Flavour and fragrance can be powerful calls to arms but they need to be part of a full tribal offering.

~~~~~

Products with a built in fragrance are made and marketed using that smell. But not every tribe uses smell to their tribe's advantage. Even basic smells can improve a working environment. Fragrances that fight and replace bad odours in your washrooms should be the absolute minimum. Displaying fresh flowers in reception, brewing fresh coffee in the visitors' waiting area; and baking fresh bread in the canteen would all lift visitors' spirits.

To stand out from the competition, you could add a fragrance to your products, envelopes or packaging. That would add an extra level of enjoyment, offering your customers the pleasure of a beautiful scent every time they receive something from you.

~~~~~

Flavour creates another potentially differentiating factor between tribes. Whilst taste will not help to describe or distinguish every tribe, the flavours of a tribe's cooking or the edible products it manufactures can set it apart from another tribe. This factor is potentially relevant to families and cultural groups that use distinctive cooking ingredients and styles.

Taste is also relevant to commercial organisations in the food and beverage sector, such as restaurant chains, supermarkets, confectioners, food and drinks manufacturers and street sellers. Flavour is the lifeblood of those businesses. Word of mouth can often spread the word about good flavours faster than any other form of advertising. Consistently good food or drink can quickly set you apart.

Several national supermarkets have offered a three tier approach to flavour and price: with lower cost own brand goods, branded goods from independent manufacturers; and high end own branded goods. Own brand goods are produced for the supermarkets and "white-labelled" to appear as their own product ranges. The high-end own brand range (such as Tesco Finest) links those flavours even more strongly with a particular supermarket, as they can't be bought elsewhere (at least as that brand).

*Word of mouth can make
or break a brand*

41

Even if your tribe doesn't produce food or drink, you could partner with an organisation that does in order to give you a new product range or a new customer gift option. Giving away a tasty free snack with your products can lift their impact. They need to relate back to the tribe's purpose. Doe sit get us closer to achieving our vision? Corporate gifts should always be complimentary and complementary. Anything that sets you apart from the competition could help you get ahead and stay there.

~~~~~

Instead of making a coffee in their kitchens and offices many people buy a coffee from chains like Costa, Starbucks, Coffee Republic and Caffè Nero. With a mug of coffee costing £2.50 or more, compared to a few pence for coffees granules, there must be compelling reasons for so many people to buy one.

The convenience from their availability on every high street is major reason. Having someone else brew it for you is another. The feeling of spoiling yourself is a third. The experience of sitting in and resting your feet is a further element on offer. The smell from a freshly brewed coffee might be a fifth reason to buy one, but where coffee's concerned taste sits above them all.

The taste of coffee depends on the choice of coffee style, the blend of coffee beans, the strength of the coffee; and whether you have milk, sugar or water with it. Coffee beans can have a smooth or a bitter taste. The choice of beans and blend makes a huge difference. A milky latte tastes quite different to a neat espresso. Both drinks will taste different depending on who sold you the coffee.

Some coffee drinkers are relaxed on flavour. To them a coffee is largely a coffee. However coffee afficionados have a clear priority order for which coffee houses to go to; and a list of ones to avoid.

Coffee chains have to find a taste that sets them apart from the competition. Then they have to provide that taste with total consistency. That way they can build up a loyal customer base. By offering a good range of products, comfortable seating arrangements; and competitive pricing they can build sales. But without flavour they have nothing.

~~~~~

Every sports club is focused on winning sports matches, but in order to generate additional revenue every club has a food and drink offering for home fans and visiting supporters. Norwich City is co-owned by renowned cook Delia Smith, who created Delia's Restaurant at the club. Having that offering takes Norwich to a level above many of its rivals and helps to improve its customer experience. Being able to eat at Delia's Restaurant must help to persuade some opposition fans to make the away trip to Carrow Road, boosting the match day coffers. The flavours on offer at Delia's must generate very welcome profits for the club.

~~~~~

Is your tribe using a fragrance or flavour to promote itself? Would either a smell or a taste add value to the tribal brand? Would members feel more unified or engaged? Would a fragrance or flavour usefully support the tribal purpose?

## 2.20 TRIBAL RECORDS

The last of the twenty factors is a tribe's records, which pull together every other factor.

The reason that we know so much about our history is that so many previous tribes have left us permanent records of their time on earth. Those records can take many forms, from annual newsletters to pottery design, books to clothing designs, architecture to weapons, board minutes to tapestries, parchments to memory sticks and photographs to cave paintings. Any details, illustrations or reports of tribal events can stand as a record of its history.

A tribe's records give us an insight into its past, exposing its purpose, values, ceremonies and routines to outsiders. The Bible is one such example for Christians. Without denigrating the Bible in its own context, having something as long as the Bible (31,102 verses) as a tribal record will be off-putting to many. There is simply too much detail to know, understand and rationalise in a record that large as an ordinary tribe member. If any organisation needs a translator to interpret its rules and values, I would argue that they aren't clear and succinct enough.

What records do you keep? Are they accurate, clear and succinct?

~~~~~

England has too many records of its history to list them in any book. Perhaps these examples stand amongst the finest.

The Anglo-Saxon Chronicle was written in the 9th century during the reign of King Alfred the Great. It is an attempt to give an annual summary (annal) of key English events from 60 B.C to the time it was written. There are believed to be nine versions produced at different times up to and including the 12th century.

The Doomsday Book is a manuscript record of the great survey of England and Wales carried out on the order of William the Conqueror in 1086. Written in Medieval Latin, the book allowed the King to reassert the rights of the crown and in particular to assess what taxes were due. It is the first national survey and gives extraordinary insight into life nearly 1,000 years ago. It was safely stored in Shepton Mallet jail in 1939 to stop it being bombed.

The Magna Carta Liberatum (the Great Charter of the Liberties) is the bill of rights and freedoms that underpins the rule of law and justice the United Kingdom. The Magna Carta was written to reflect the terms agreed between the English barons and King John in 1215. Over 800 years on there are only four surviving copies. The best preserved is in Salisbury Cathedral.

*The Magna Carta is perhaps*
*our greatest record*

The King James Bible written in 1611 is the basis for the familiar English version of the Bible we know today.

Field Marshall Montgomery (Monty) wrote a one page "Most Secret" plan in the build up to the D-Day landings on 6 June 1944. Written in pencil, the document plotted logistics involving over 160,000 men and hundreds of aircraft and other military vehicles. The key note was "SIMPLICITY".

Without these records we would have less sense of who the English (and British, and UK) people are.

~~~~~

The tragedian plays of Euripides were written almost 2,500 years ago in Ancient Greece. Euripides' three most famous plays are probably Medea, Electra and the Trojan Women, all of which are still performed today. How do we know anything about this ancient playwright or his plays?

The answer is through our written records of them. From the evidence we have, Euripides appears to have written ninety-two plays. Eighteen of them have survived pretty much intact and there are substantial fragments of the others. How is that possible over such a long period? Until the modern printing press allowed exact copies to be reproduced, the oral tradition of performers, translators, scholars and copyists kept each play alive.

Can we be sure that all ninety-two tragedies are one hundred percent the work of Euripides? The answer is no, we can't. After nearly 2,500 years, some of them will have suffered changes and adaptations (called interpolations) along the way, at least until more modern times. This tells us that the better your record keeping, the more accurate your tribal history will be.

~~~~~

Wiltshire has eight white chalk horses carved into its hillsides. The first Westbury white horse is believed to have been cut to celebrate the victory over the Danes in the Battle of Ethandium in 878AD. Local legend says that King Alfred personally commissioned the cutting of the horse, although the legend also says that he had the designer beheaded afterwards as the horse should have been riding into town, rather than riding away.

## Historian, artist or vandal?

To still have a white horse with over a thousand years of history is extraordinary. However the horse that appears today is not that original Westbury white horse. Whilst there is no record of the original horse, the story is that the earlier horse had shorter legs, a longer heavier body and a tail that pointed upwards. Why is it different now? In 1778, Lord Abingdon's steward, a Mr. George Gee took it upon himself to re-design the Westbury horse. His intervention permanently changed the appearance of the horse. Gee was labelled a barbarian and a vandal.

Since then restoration work has taken in 1873 and 1903 and in the 1950's the Blue Circle Cement Works located near by, concreted the horse to preserve it.

The re-designed Westbury White horse is itself over two hundred years old, but beneath it is a record of a thousand year old white horse. George Gee could have chosen to create a brand new horse somewhere else, leaving both horses in place for future generations to enjoy.

Maintaining your original records is vitally important for future generations of your tribe. What we destroy and replace wipes away our history. A re-boot isn't always better than the original.

~~~~

These days an organisation's external records will often be on its own website or picked up in its media and social media coverage. An organisation's internal records are different. They need to be protected and stored by the organisation itself. Those internal records could be lists of joiners and leavers, human resources files, board or executive committee minutes, stock or pricing lists, staff or product photographs, models and prototypes, supplier details, emails, letters, audio and video recordings, memos, contracts and brand designs amongst many types of other recorded information.

Tribes that have good record keeping can remind themselves and teach future generations about important tribal events. A tribe might have a long and illustrious history but without any record of it, the tribe's stories may become lost or watered down in their oral re-telling. Not everything needs to be recorded. There isn't enough time, need or inclination to record every minute detail of activity. But without maintaining the heritage and lessons of the past, there is no legacy for the future. What records do you display?

~~~~~

Employees like to be reminded of why they are working for an organisation. They want to feel proud of their organisation. Customers and suppliers like to be reminded of why they do business with a company. Manufacturers have the advantage of a product development history. Some choose to show it off. Garmin's UK Headquarters has glass cabinets filled with the generations of its satellite navigation devices, GPS watches, fitness trackers, cameras and other products. They are on view for staff and visitors alike. This display shows you how far the company has come and how many products it offers to the market. It is a reminder of why Garmin is a market leader.

Garmin isn't the only business to display its products. Britvic plc is a leading UK drinks manufacturer and distributor with brands like Robinsons squash, J2O, Fruit Shoot and R Whites (as well as exclusive agreements to make and sell Pepsico brands like Pepsi and 7UP). Britvic has a large hub area for its staff and visitors which includes multiple glass fridges full of its drink brands. This display allows staff and visitors to try every product; and acts as a reminder of how extensive Britvic's product range is.

Storck is another manufacturer with a strong UK presence that displays its products for staff and visitors to see. With well established brands like Werther's Originals, Toffifee and Bendicks of Mayfair, Storck can make a positive impact every time its staff and visitors are reminded of the organisation's brands.

~~~~~

The records of some tribes have been obliterated by their conquerors or lost to time. For new tribes, there may be no history or heritage worth recording yet. These days with so many ways to record a tribe's history, culture and heritage, there should always be written, painted, stitched, carved or other hand-tooled evidence to show you what that history is. What do your tribe's records reveal?

~~~~~

Does your tribe record its traditions, ceremonies and wider heritage? Does it record the achievements of its heroes and heroines? Does it use those records to aid its storytelling and enhance its celebrations? Do those records capture the tribe's key events for posterity? Are its records visible and accessible to every tribe member?

## 2.21 TRIBAL ACTION PLAN

The twenty signs of a tribe are wide ranging. Each combination of them makes and distinguishes each tribe from any other. As a reminder, these twenty are: purpose, heritage, structure and hierarchy, rules, nicknames, values, spiritual homeland, language, stories, art, songs, colours/uniform, ceremonies, badges/logos, symbols, brand, routines, opposition, records and fragrance/flavour.

Every tribe should regularly assess where it is with each of the twenty. Consider each one separately. Where is your tribe? The comparison should be done three ways, by asking:

i.  Where is each element now, compared to the tribe's vision? How far off its goal is it?

ii. How does each tribal element compare to the last time you reviewed it? Has progress been made?

iii. Where is each element compared to the competition/opposition?

Each tribe will have a different bias between the twenty tribal elements. Tribes don't need all twenty elements to be developed equally. The more tribal elements that your tribe develops, the more distinct it can become. If all those elements are properly aligned, then your tribe can become a super-tribe. How well do the twenty elements work together in your tribe?

The greater the alignment, the easier it will be to achieve your tribe's purpose. What needs to change? Re-work your tribal plan to include the development of the twenty elements.

For new tribes, working hard to establish a brand and develop a heritage is critically important. How much time are you spending on building these core elements? Building staff and customer loyalty through strong values and great stories will drive the brand. Supporting that with clear colours/uniform, symbols and badges/logos will help too.

For established tribes, check that your tribe's structure, hierarchy, rules and routines aren't holding it back. Have internal politics or procedures taken over? Go back to the central purpose and ask if each tribal element is advancing the cause or holding it back? Have you lost the bonds of common ceremonies, language, nicknames and stories?

Create a list of actions to develop the elements that matter most, whilst keeping all the others aligned. Then action your list.

~~~~

Taking an overview of your tribe's strengths and weaknesses is best done by asking - How well does your tribe address the six tribal concepts?

**T** **Traditions and heritage**
*(how the past affects the present)*

**R** **Rules, ceremonies and rituals**
*(how things are done)*

**I** **Illustration through stories, songs and art**
*(expressing the special and unique)*

**B** **Brand and symbols**
*(how the tribe is presented to the outside world)*

**E** **Establish a clear vision, purpose and values**
*(reason for being and direction of travel)*

**S** **Stakeholder alignment**
*(how tribal power is generated)*

Now you are familiar with the twenty elements, you can work on how they fit together to support each core concept. If all twenty tribal elements are working well, your tribe will be strong. For example, if your structure and hierarchy is unstable, you can't establish a clear vision, purpose and values. A lack of clear leadership will also threaten your rules, ceremonies and rituals too.

# 3. BUILDING YOUR TRIBE

## 3.1 TRIBES HAVE CORE INGREDIENTS

Anyone can help to generate tribal power and harness it for a wider good. No one can do it all alone. Through planning and action a tribe of yours could achieve something bigger and better than you could ever manage alone.

The planning phase of building a tribe first involves agreeing a motivational and inclusive tribal purpose. That could be obvious and widely agreed at the outset, such as a professional football team deciding to try and win the F.A. Cup. Or it may take time to debate and agree a common purpose. Either way it is essential that a tribe's purpose appeals to all of the tribe's stakeholders.

The process of agreeing that purpose has to be inclusive and involve every stakeholder. What is the single-most important thing that the tribe wants to get done? What is the higher purpose that everyone wants to see realised? A goal needs to be clear, achievable and challenging to be worthy of a tribe's purpose. A tribal purpose can be anything that ties in all the stakeholders to a wider communal benefit. Customer-centric decision-making can help build strong customer relationships, but it's not broad enough as a concept to cover the interests of all the stakeholders. That is not enough.

*Purpose has to be inclusive*
*and involve every stakeholder*

The scale of it doesn't matter, so it could be an enormous global project such as Ending World Poverty or the Campaign for Nuclear Disarmament. Or it could be starting a new business, or scaling up an existing one. Fighting to keep a local hospital or library open are other similar initiatives.

There are increasing numbers of environmental purposes, which include: The Final Straw is fighting against the damage that plastic is doing to the oceans. One of its initiatives is working to obtain a nationwide ban on plastic straws in all pubs, clubs and restaurants. On the packaging theme, in Hampshire a business called Milk & More is now reverting to glass milk bottles to save all the wasted packaging. In Yorkshire a brewer called Toast Ale uses stale bread[76] to cut down on food waste and make great beer. All their profits go to food waste charities. They have open-sourced the recipe for Toast Ale in a bid to get everyone involved in eliminating bread waste "by brewing delicious beer".

~~~~~

We are all time-thin and subjected to constant distractions. Without having a clear purpose, it is easy to wander off the path. Each tribe needs to have a single testing question to keep everyone on track. A tribe constantly needs to remind itself what it is here for. Why does your organisation exist? What is it for?

Ben Hunt-Davies was part of the British Olympic Rowing Eight that won Gold in Sydney 2000. He wrote an insider's book about his experience. The book's title is the question that the team repeatedly asked itself to keep everyone focused. The team's core purpose was winning Olympic Gold. That was easy to identify. Every stakeholder wanted the same thing. The rowers, coaches, sponsors, British Olympic Committee, National Lottery Committee and the British people all wanted it.

The question was how were they going to be in the winning lane? Every time an idea was suggested, or a change was proposed, the team asked itself a single question

*"Will it make the boat go faster?"*

---

[76] Approximately 46 million slices of bread are thrown away in Britain every day.

Absolutely everything was measured against achieving the purpose of winning Olympic Gold. If an idea helped to make the boat go faster it was actioned. If it didn't, it was binned and forgotten. That's how prominent a tribal purpose should be. If your tribe's purpose is achieving World Peace, then its repetitive question should "Will that help bring peace to the World?" If the answer is no, then why is your tribe spending any time doing it?

The tribal purpose must be something that all the tribe's stakeholders can buy into. A tribal purpose can't be so narrow that it's only the whim of its leadership. A tribal purpose must offer every stakeholder something, even if it's only the hope of a better future. It must be an all engaging crusade that reaches the extremities of the tribe. Unless every stakeholder is motivated by it, they won't lend their support.

The potential tribal power that can be generated is immediately reduced if any one of the tribe's stakeholders is not pulling in the same direction. Even worse, a stakeholder pulling in the opposite direction can divert the tribe completely off-track. Identifying and sticking to your purpose is the foundation stone for generating tribal power. As former British Prime Minister Benjamin Disraeli said "The secret of success is constancy to purpose."

~~~~~

With its tribal purpose firmly in mind, a tribe needs to agree a vision for its future. Visions require imagination, description and detail. That vision needs to offer all of its stakeholders the promise of a better future, not just a tiny few of them.

There are some simple questions to ask about a vision. If the tribal purpose is achieved, what would the future be like for the tribe? What would it look like? What would it be made of?

A tribe needs to describe its vision in words and images. The vision needs to be clear and coherent. Crucially it has to flow directly from the tribal purpose. Without a shared view of the future, each stakeholder will be heaving in its own unique direction, if it is bothering to pull at all.

A united and inclusive vision is absolutely fundamental for a tribe. Most commercial organisations fail to agree a genuinely inclusive purpose, or set a clear vision for its future. Most commercial organisations aren't reaching their potential. Facebook and its founder and CEO Mark Zuckerberg have a mixed reputation but the business is still the global leader in its field. Mark Zuckerberg is quoted as saying "The companies that work are the ones that people really care about and have a vision for the World."

## Create a shared view of the future

For example, take Portsmouth Football Club. Its vision could be layered. A short-term say five year vision could be all around achieving promotion back to the top flight of English football. A more ambitious and longer-term future would go beyond that. What would that future look like? Would Pompey be playing in a redeveloped 100,000 seater stadium at Fratton Park to full crowds? Would the next Messi, Ronaldo, Beckham and Hazard all be playing there? Would Pompey be the current holders of the Champions League, Premier League, F.A. Cup and League Cup? Would the club be the most profitable football club in the World? If they do "Play up Pompey" every game, what could that lead to?

Whatever vision the club has it needs to be easy to describe. It also needs to be agreed by all of its stakeholders including the club's owners, directors, coaches, players, commercial arm, supporters, sponsors, local council and the sport's governing bodies. That way every stakeholder can buy in and help the club to achieve its vision.

~~~~~

Once its purpose and vision are clear, a tribe needs to agree the values and the culture that it is going to live by. A tribe's values need to be suitable for the process of achieving the tribal vision. They may need to be adapted once that vision has become a reality, but ideally they will be the same. The values need to tie in the commitment of all of the tribe's stakeholders, so that everyone behaves in a similar way.

Too many commercial organisations fail this values element of tribe in several ways. Firstly, even if an organisation has some stated values, it may not have debated and agreed them with all of its stakeholders. Failing to get everyone's input and involvement will considerably limit the adoption of those values. Stakeholder involvement is especially important where there are different employee demographics within the organisation. Without generational synergy there can't be generational sustainability.

Secondly, an organisation's real values may not be sufficiently linked or tailored to achieving the organisation's vision. Living to your organisation's values should always help it to achieve its vision.

*A tribe's values should never*
*cut across its core purpose*

Thirdly, too many commercial organisations relegate their stated values to a place somewhere below making money. Positive and inclusive values produce money for everyone they don't grab and hold onto it. For example, if you claim that you put your customers first, then you genuinely need to do that. That brings a challenge. Actually putting your customers first may make you less money than if you drop them further down the priority list, at least in the short-term. But tribes ought not to be thinking selfishly about the short-term, they should be thinking more selflessly about the long-term for all their stakeholders, including their customers. Although it may sound counter-intuitive this makes more commercial sense.

Fourthly, many commercial organisations don't apply their values fairly and even-handedly. How many times has a top salesperson been allowed to behave like a dickhead and get away with it? Values should be applied fairly and equally across the tribe. No one should be above them. Having values is only part of the equation, sticking to them and enforcing them is perhaps even more important.

~~~~~

The three fundamentals of Vision, Purpose and Values (the VPV) are a tribe's essence, its DNA if you like. Without any of the three elements in place a tribe can't generate its full tribal power.

If and when a tribe has its VPV in place, it needs to formulate a strategy to allow it to achieve that vision. This is classic project management territory. There are essential elements for any project. Setting clearly defined (SMART [77]) objectives, allocating responsibilities, organising reporting lines and communication channels, providing adequate resources, setting realistic timescales and monitoring progress through key performance indicators can all help with delivery and accountability.

Project managers should constantly and consistently link the strategy back to the vision and further back to the purpose. Dealing with practical issues like the working environment, facilities and funding shouldn't be forgotten either. Before setting off after a VPV review, every organisation should carry out a sources and resources analysis (SARA) to assess and allocate delivery needs. Are there suitable and sufficient resources exactly where and when they are needed?

An agreed purpose, vision, values and strategy together create the overall Tribal Plan. So does your organisation have a common purpose, a clear well articulated vision, core values and a SMART strategy to deliver it? If so, you can turn to delivering it. But before you set off, there's one final question to ask. How committed are all the stakeholders? Unless every stakeholder is mentally prepared for a long and arduous journey you're unlikely to generate the tribal power you need.

## Why bother?

A quick explanation to everyone isn't enough. How easily do you commit to something new? Your answer might be 'pretty easily if I can see the point of it' or it might be 'not unless there's a benefit in it

---

[77] There are a few variations, but SMART objectives are Specific, Measurable, Agreed, Realistic and Time-based.

for me'. Either way, you're unlikely to set off on a journey for change unless you have bought into the point of it. Selling the tribal plan is essential to get all the stakeholders on the bus. Until we're sold on something we won't buy it.

We sell best through storytelling. So an agreed narrative is needed to explain the tribe's purpose and its vision of the future. That story arch needs to be incredibly inclusive, so that every stakeholder believes that there's a role to play for them. To support that core narrative, stories and songs are needed to illustrate and support each of the tribal values. If those values are inclusive and relevant, then sticking to them should get the tribe closer to achieving its vision. Praising members who live your values builds their conviction and helps to achieve the tribe's purpose.

~~~~~

To build a strong sense of unity and purpose, a tribe needs to offer something new and noteworthy. Unless your tribe stands for something that's different from the rest, why would anyone bother to support its purpose as opposed to anyone else's? Every tribe needs to be sufficiently compelling and identifiable, through a unique tribal offering.

Businesses need a talking point for customers to engage with. Having a unique selling point (USP) that distinguishes you from the competition could be it. Or it could be a valuable benefit that only your product or service offers. For some tribes it might be your product's user-friendliness that opens up a narrative. Other times it might be your use of technology, speed of delivery, environmental impact or price that makes you more compelling than the competition.

Finding a genuinely unique and meaningful selling point is extremely difficult in increasingly crowded, global market places. So looking to a broader difference, beyond products and services can create your story. An organisation which has a clear and agreed tribal plan (vision, purpose, values and strategy) should always be able to offer something unique. When you add a set of traditions, ceremonies and rituals to it, people will see and feel the difference. Sales people should make more of their tribe when selling. People buy people, make decisions based on emotions and crave social belonging. The chance to join your tribe may be just what a prospect is waiting for. Don't just sell the product or service, sell the whole tribe.

~~~~~

Now let's return to the six tribal concepts. How strong are your tribe's ingredients?

**(T) Traditions and heritage**
*(how the past affects the present)*

**(R) Rules, ceremonies and rituals**
*(how things are done)*

**(I) Illustration through stories, songs and art**
*(expressing the special and unique)*

**(B) Brand and symbols**
*(how the tribe is presented to the outside world)*

**(E) Establish a clear vision, purpose and values**
*(reason for being and direction of travel)*

**(S) Stakeholder alignment**
*(how tribal power is generated)*

Which of the twenty elements needs more work in order to support the six concepts? Design a programme of works that addresses the tribe's deficiencies and plays to its strengths.

~~~~~

Unless all of the tribe's stakeholders are fully committed, the tribal plan won't be achieved. Each step of the tribal plan needs to be carried out with complete conviction whilst sticking to the tribal values.

Once the tribal plan gets started, progress needs to be constantly measured. Once it's in place, the tribal plan needs to be reviewed, adapted, re-set and re-communicated throughout the process just like any other project.

Every good tribe should be doing these things. But not all tribes are good for you, or good for society. So a good tribe may form around the need to take a stand against a bad tribe's purpose.

# 3.2 GOOD, SUPER-GOOD AND BAD TRIBES

In life we have endless choices to make every day, from the seismic to the banal. Which outfit do I wear? Shall I ask her to marry me? Should I have the chicken or egg sandwich? Do I need to take the cat to the vets? Should we have another child? Is it a good time to put the house on the market? Shall we watch the original Magnificent Seven or the new one? Do I do the washing-up or hang the washing out first? Are my parents really coping on their own? Shall I apply for promotion this time? What about one more pint before we leave the pub?

The process of decision-making can be overwhelming at times but eventually we make the decisions we need to, or something happens which resolves the issue for us. Beyond all those decisions are the fundamental choices we make about which sides we're on. Our tribes reflect those higher choices. The purposes that we commit to say a great deal about us.

The winners in life may believe their own hype, but they all needed good people around them to get where they are. Footballers need ten other players to form a team. Top music artists and film stars need bands and film-makers to bring them success. The super-rich don't get rich without someone else's hard work. Even a lottery winner needs people to run the lottery and millions of others to play it. The World we live in favours the strong and the wealthy. The strong can take what they want. The rich can buy what they want. The weak and poor often have to manage with less. Making it in the World isn't easy. Making it on your own is virtually impossible. Since there is usually strength in numbers, people tend to bind together so they can have what they need and secure their own protection.

The Trades Union movement supports individual workers by creating a powerful, united voice and source of direct action. Their purpose is to protect and enhance workers' rights. Charities take causes up on behalf of the sick, disabled and disadvantaged. They use an army of volunteers to raise awareness and funds to support their chosen cause. Other groups come together to win sporting trophies, build businesses or socialise together, pulling in numbers to create the critical mass they need. Some groups put expanding their own power and wealth at the heart of their purpose. That is how some gangs, organised crime syndicates and corrupt governments operate. They use their money and influence as a sword; and the law as a shield to perpetuate their wealth.

*We all have choices to make, perhaps none bigger than which tribes are we committed to.*

Tribes can have good and bad purposes. Good purposes have benefits for the group without costing wider society in the process. Where there good purposes that also offer widespread net benefits for the many, they become super-good tribes with super-good purposes.

Bad purposes focus solely on the few and offer net losses to wider society. Tribes with bad purposes can last for a considerable period of time through intimidation and repression, through force and fear. But they will eventually fall, sooner or later. The tribes which truly generate a sustainable tribal power have a purpose and power beyond that kind of self-interest. That's because the act of chasing personal power makes a person weaker not stronger. The act of grasping selfishly for money makes a person vulnerable not rich. These may be clichés but they are also true. Greed is a weaker power than generosity. Love really is stronger and more rewarding than hate.

Where there's hope of improving things, those things can change for the better.

Choosing a communal path can bring something richer and more rewarding than power and money. With power comes responsibility and with great power comes great responsibility[78]. By making things better for society, through positive tribal movements, every community group should receive something. Super-purposes take the obvious approach of finding a win-win situation is an immensely practical one. They call for super-tribes to deliver them. The less disadvantaged that people become, the more tolerant they are of others; and the less crime, discrimination and extremism there is likely to be. Just as you sow you shall reap[79].

The more that an organisation delivers benefits for all of its stakeholders (and not just its shareholders) the more that it appeals to everyone connected with it. Then the shoulders of all of those stakeholders can be put to its wheel. Tribal power doesn't run on money, it runs on tribal purpose.

Multi-stakeholder agreements and community benefit agreements can be the paperwork which contractually ties a tribe into super-tribe arrangements that works well for every stakeholder. They are increasingly common.

~~~~~

Jim Collins' international bestselling book "Good to Great" has sold over 4 million copies. So who am I to question its central principle? The book begins with a bold statement "Good is the enemy of great" and continues "And that is one of the key reasons why we have so little that becomes great." In the sense that Jim Collins means 'good' is lower down the ladder of success than 'great'. But that's only 'good' in

---

[78] There have been different versions of this theme stretching back to the Bible, including Winston Churchill's version "Where there is great power there is great responsibility, where there is less power there is less responsibility and where there is no power there can, I think, be no responsibility" said in 1906.

[79] A line from Big Country's first single "Harvest Home" released in 1982.

the narrow sense of comparing a good performance with a great performance. In those terms 'great' is better.

However 'good' in its truest, roundest sense is where every stakeholder in an organisation is treated fairly, treated with respect and successful. Good is a shared concept. That's harder to achieve than a high share price or generating profits of the shareholders, but it's the most sustainable kind of success. Good is a tribal kind of success.

~~~~~

Star Wars is the most successful movie franchise of all time, lasting over forty years and still going strong. It pitches good against evil, democracy against dictatorship and spiritualism against selfishness, all within a multi-coloured, fictional World.

Mirroring the rise of Adolph Hitler and the Nazi party through the ascension of Chancellor Palpatine and the Empire, the films are rooted in history whilst reaching into an imaginary future.

The presence of a higher power within the universe (the Force) creates a spiritual dimension, within which the forces for good (Jedi) and evil (Sith) battle for supremacy. As well as fighting with troops, space-battleships and death-stars, each side uses either the light side of the Force (Jedi) or the dark side (Sith) to try and try and defeat the other.

## What does your tribe's dress code say about it?

Although there are many different tribes within the Star Wars universe, such as the Wookies, Gungans and Ewoks, the two tribes that matter most are the Jedi and the Sith. The Jedi dress in flowing brown robes and focus their efforts on protecting the citizens and democracy. The Sith on the other hand dress in black and their followers wear Nazi style uniforms. They seek power and control for themselves. For the dark side to gain total control, the Sith must defeat the Jedi. This selfish purpose sets the two tribes at war.

Both tribes have clear tribal signs and rituals with their distinctive colours and uniforms, values, heroes and heroines; as well as stories of past deeds. Both tribes wield huge power and influence over the present and the future. As each attempts to dominate the other, war rages between the light and dark sides of the Force.

While the Jedi quietly go about training their next generation of apprentices, known as Padawan learners, the Sith try to turn potential Jedi towards the dark side. Apologies for the spoiler, but Anakin Skywalker and Ben Solo are two central characters who fall prey to this forceful pressure from the Sith. Other Jedi like Luke Skywalker and Rey [80] manage to resist and avoid turning to the dark side. In Episode 1: The Phantom Menace, Yoda explains how the Jedi can be turned. "Fear is the path to the dark side. Fear leads to anger. Anger leads to hate. Hate leads to suffering."

## *Organisations which create a culture of fear will make their people hate them*

There is a symbiotic relationship between the Jedi and the Sith. The existence of the Sith feeds the need for the Jedi to be there, motivated to oppose and defeat them. The Sith's core purpose is to take and hold onto power. This gives the Jedi its key purpose, which is to protect the people from the Sith. Both sides openly display the signs and behaviours of contrasting tribes. One tribe is good, the other is bad. Whilst there is evil, good must face it head on and prevail.

Every worker needs to make a tribal choice about what kind of organisation to be part of. How would you make that choice? How much due diligence would you do before joining a new organisation? What questions would you ask at interview? How would you test for a tribal fit?

To attract and engage new workers, every organisation needs to be crystal clear about what it stands for and what it opposes. Make it easy

---

[80] If and when we discover Rey's parentage, we may witness another struggle of wills between light and darkness.

for like-minded job hunters to find you. At interview, employers should take the time to explain their purpose, vision and values. They should tell stories of progress towards the organisation's vision and stories of tribe members upholding the tribe's values. After an interview confirm the purpose, vision and values in writing. Don't just advertise the financial rewards of a job, always advertise the culture and values as well.

~~~~~

Each of us is responsible for our actions and omissions. We also have other responsibilities. Parents are responsible for their children. Manufactures are responsible for their products. Surgeons are responsible for their operations. Employers are responsible for their working environment. Neighbours are responsible for their community. Every one of us has responsibilities of one kind or another. We all have the choice of embracing those responsibilities or ducking them. As the supermarket giant Tesco advocates, every little bit does help. We can be a positive or a negative influence within our tribes. We can follow our tribal values or rub hard against the grain. We can treat others well or we can treat them badly. We can make bad tribes good.

Responsibility can be daunting but we shouldn't be put off by the size of our challenges. The bigger the task the more we can bring to it. Once we take on a responsibility we should do our best to discharge it positively. Our best won't be perfect because we're not perfect. The question is how hard did we try? We are hard working people living busy lives and mistakes happen. We need to aim high, but stay realistic about what's achievable. Perfection only exists in novels. If something is good enough, it's good enough. There is always stuff to fix. The question is have you fixed it up enough to win? Fixed up enough to win is all we need. Seeking perfection can be off-putting. Instead we should adopt the Japanese concept of Wabi Sabi which is about accepting that beauty is imperfect, impermanent, and incomplete.

Fearful people try to pass their responsibilities on to someone else. In the parent example, if something goes awry that might mean blaming the other parent, blaming the child's school or blaming the child. Giving a 'hospital pass' to anyone in a tribe of yours is bad for values. If everyone in society looked to themselves first, before trying to allocate blame to others, we would all learn more and develop faster. There would certainly be less conflict in the World.

## *Take responsibility rather than passing blame*

Spiritual people might pass their sense of responsibility on to a higher power. That could be faith in a God, a belief in destiny, or trusting to fate. Putting your faith, belief and trust in something inanimate delegates your freedom of choice. It gives you an excuse to avoid making decisions and taking action. If your God is all-powerful and endlessly kind then surely everyone will be saved whatever happens? And so bad logic asks why do we need to bother doing anything for other people?

By giving your freedom and responsibilities away you may feel happier. Having faith in a God, destiny or fate might bring relief and reassurance. That might come from shedding responsibility, a form of after-life, the promise of reincarnation or just from the devotion of following scripture. That trade may feel worth it. Many religious people say that you have no choice but to submit to a more powerful God in order to get to heaven. That message certainly appeals to some.

But we have a power that shouldn't be surrendered to an intangible concept of fate or divine intervention. Instead we should use our freedom of choice and decide to face our responsibilities head on. Family, work and friends need us. We can also help with a purpose that's wider than ourselves. We could give up some of our time, experience or skill for a cause that makes a positive difference for society. We could take positive action, rather than trusting in someone or something else to do it all.

Most working people are time poor. It is difficult to fit the basic jobs in, let alone something else on top. But trusting in the government, charities or the kindness of strangers to solve our problems abrogates responsibility. Within each of our tribes we have a shared responsibility as individuals to act. Businesses should think beyond their shallow interests and choose to provide a deeper and wider contribution. Asking all your staff what's important to them will create the headlines for action that you need. By listening and acting on those wider needs, you should benefit from the positive effect on engagement and performance that follows.

~~~~~

Nurses, firefighters, doctors, police officers and teachers are all good tribes whose purpose is to help the community around them. They educate, heal, protect and keep us safe. Society would be immensely poorer without any of them. They and other selfless occupations put their neighbourhoods before money; and do wonderful work. Those jobs are not for everyone but whatever job we do for living, we can help our community in a myriad of ways.

People who comply with the law and pay their taxes are solid citizens. Anyone who is in that lawful citizen tribe can settle at that level of contribution. Every net positive contribution helps. That's because there is no general legal duty to protect other people. Without a specific legal obligation such as parental responsibility or being a Police Officer we don't have to intervene. Despite that some people choose to give their time, skills and experience to help others. Volunteering to help others without payment is a selfless and generous thing to do. An estimated 14.2 million people formally volunteered at least once a month in 2015/16 in the UK[81].

## The UK's tribes of volunteers are the 'glue' that holds the country together

By contrast to lawful citizens, people who break the law are part of a different tribe. Not paying tax is unlawful, undermines government and reduces the work of local authorities and charities. We can certainly debate the fairness of taxation and how much tax people should pay, but the fact is that tax pays for essential public services

---

[81] According to the NCVO UK Civil Society Almanac 2017.

such as hospitals, roads and schools. Without any money, government cannot provide the support that society needs.

When you pay your tax you are part of the tribe that pays its way, however much income you earn. Being a net contributor puts you in the tribe which makes a financial contribution to the wider community. Being a net taker should be for those people who need society's help. Those who can afford to give should contribute at an affordable level. Those that genuinely can't shouldn't have to until they can.

Businesses have a legal and social responsibility to pay their way. That should be enough of a reason to do so. But there are commercial benefits from doing so too:

(i)     **Fines, penalties and interest add an unnecessary financial cost and can be avoided.**

(ii)    **Being on HMRC's radar could bring the distraction and cost of a full-scale audit.**

(iii)   **Paying tax indirectly helps to achieve better local services.**

(iv)    **Doing it and publicising that fact can attract the sort of workers who take pride in working for a reputable organisation.**

It's important to remember that despite the irresponsible and immoral actions of some people, big earners are not bad people by virtue of earning a lot of money. If big earners make their money fairly and lawfully without oppressing or cheating other people, pay their taxes in full; and take care of their own responsibilities they are making a positive contribution to society. We need them to carry on earning, employing others and paying their tax. Without them society suffers. We should just encourage them to give their time and support to good causes as well. That would be the icing on their contribution cake.

Busy workers who give their precious time to running marathons for charity, acting as school governors or mentoring others (amongst many different contributions) add tremendous value to society. Generally speaking (and despite the illegal and immoral actions of a few) volunteers and charity fund raisers are part of good tribes. Their efforts fill many of the gaps that government doesn't reach. Many are unsung heroes and heroines.

Anyone who earns their money through crime, oppression or cheating others is not making a positive contribution to society. Robbing from your super-tribe to benefit yourself or to benefit one of your tribes will split you as a person. Anyone who avoids paying their taxes or dodges their responsibilities isn't making a positive contribution either. They are members of bad tribes. We need to help support and persuade those people to join good tribes instead. As the Dalai Lama advocates

> *"Our prime purpose in this life is to help others.*
> *And if you can't help them, at least*
> *don't hurt them"*

An organisation that doesn't pay its workers the national minimum wage breaks the law. An organisation that doesn't pay its workers at least the national living wage takes an unfair advantage of its own people. Those owners are part of another bad tribe. There is a moral obligation to pay all workers at least a wage that covers the real cost of living. Indeed there are increasing calls for a maximum ratio between the pay of chief executives and the average pay in their organisations. Employers can create greater loyalty by paying everyone in the organisation fairly. Employers should not take the view sarcastically espoused in these Gene lyrics[82] "How you can you ask for more? If you're paid you're not poor! This is a good as it gets yeah. We've been bought, we've been sold, but at least we're not old."

As with many immoral stances, they don't make commercial sense either. How will your organisation attract and retain good people if it

---

[82] From Gene's 1999 single "As Good As It Gets".

pays below the national living wage, let alone if it is "called out" for not paying the national minimum wage undermines your brand.

A company which poisons the land or river around it takes an unfair advantage of the planet we all rely on. Similarly, a corporate organisation which screws its suppliers down to unprofitable terms takes an unfair advantage and jeopardises its own long-term future. These are further examples of bad tribes.

~~~~~

As individuals we should try to push back any undue peer pressure, selfish thinking and actively join the right tribes for us and for others. By joining good tribes, we can play to our natural instinct and work together with other people for a common good. By leaving bad tribes, we can weaken them and help to influence which tribes thrive and which don't. We should tell positive stories about good tribes to help persuade members of bad tribes to switch to them.

Good tribes have a positive focus on the many, both now and for the generations to come. Tribes which are focused on reducing energy consumption and alternative energy sources are hoping to create sustainable energy solutions. They are adding value now and into the future. Tribes which aim to minimise food waste and reduce water consumption are looking to preserve resources and provide sustainable food and clean water. Tribes which are looking to reduce consumer consumption and global pollution are looking to make our resources go further and ensure the planet remains habitable for human life. Many generations will benefit from their actions.

Tribes which keep our streets safe, promote peace, or campaign for a reduction in nuclear or chemical weapons are trying to protect the many from disease and death. Tribes which help to prevent war and terrorism are focused on the safety of the many. All of these purposes have a positive effect for the many now and in the years to come.

*Tribes of the few can protect the many*

These examples are in direct contrast with a purpose that is designed to generate the maximum short-term profit for a few, at the expense of everyone and everything else. Businesses should never be only focused on the money. Ironically that's almost guaranteed to reduce the level of profit that's actually generated.

Business should always be looking to use their resources evenly, sustainably and without waste. Take the example of tank management at petrol stations. With just under 80,000 petrol pumps nationally it's a major issue for petrol retailers. How often have you seen a pump with a "Sorry not in use" sign on it? It happens all the time. Are they always empty? No, not always. There is probably fuel still in it, but there's probably a lot more in another nearby pump. Customers prefer certain using sets of pumps to others. The set nearest the shop tends to get used first. The central pumps get more use when it's raining and cold. Also where there are multiple pumps in one set, the ones nearest to most petrol tanks up get used more heavily. People can't be bothered to stretch over to the far one. So to even-out use and stop some pumps wearing out quicker than others, the "Sorry not in use" sign goes up on the more used ones. Petrol tankers are booked to refill all the pumps equally, so petrol station managers control the levels in all their pumps by blocking the use of some pumps. By the time the petrol tanker turns up all the pumps should ideally have similar fuel levels. Petrol stations make tiny margins on selling fuel so this tank management really matters[83]. Done well it also helps with sustainability.

Organisations which are actively doing positive things for society should tell their stories. Ethical businesses have a commercial advantage over unethical ones. They attract the sort of workers who take pride in working for a reputable organisation, namely good, loyal staff who will engage and perform well. It will attract the best suppliers who know they will be paid in full and on time. It will also attract the best customers, because they will know they will buy at a fair price. Customer will also know that their legitimate complaints will be listened to and actioned for them. Being a good business is good for business.

---

[83] Petrol stations make about 3-5p a litre before tax. They can make more from selling you a coffee than from selling you a car full of fuel.

## Ethical businesses have an increasing commercial advantage over unethical ones

Even purely profit-making businesses can find a unity of purpose. That purpose might be customer satisfaction or sustainability. Concentrating the organisation's purpose on the benefits of its products or services is usually better than focusing on the money being made. That is unless a share of the profit goes direct to the staff, local community initiatives or to charity (in which case there might be a common purpose to get behind).

~~~~~

Green & Black's began manufacturing chocolate in 1991. There is no Mrs. Green or Mr. Black. The Green symbolises the company's commitment to ethically and environmentally sourced cocoa. The Black reflects the high quality of the cocoa used in their chocolate. The company was founded by Jo Fairley with support from her husband Craig Sams (who co-owns Whole Earth foods).

The company's ethical commitment was evident from the start. In 1994, Green & Blacks' Maya Gold was the first product to display the Fairtrade mark in the UK. As a result it was actively promoted by environmentalists and vicars who significantly helped to raise its profile. When your sales team is on a mission from God you've got every chance of success.

Twenty five years later the brand sells nearly £100M worth of chocolate a year. That's extremely impressive. But even more impressive is how much Green & Black's has done to support the cocoa growing population overseas. As an indirect result of the work done by Green & Black's 90% of Mayan children now go on to secondary school (from 0% when the project started). As Jo Fairley often says "Doing good is good for business."

In 2018 we booked Jo to speak at an annual event I founded and co-organise called The Solent Business Growth Summit. In the build-up I asked Jo whether she still got excited about seeing her chocolate on sale. Jo replied "I still cry when I find our chocolate in hotel mini-bars. It's like finding your child in the fridge!"

Green and Black's was bought by Cadbury's in 2005 and became part of American food giant Kraft in 2011. Now Jo actively promotes ethical behaviour within Kraft, spreading the ethical word inside a global giant. Having met Jo, I'd bet on them melting before she does.

~~~~~

The National Citizen Service for 15-17 year olds is a positive, community focused initiative. According to its website, NCS'ers come from across the country, from every background and every walk of life. They meet, they laugh, they change their communities together."

With sessions of rock climbing, canoeing, archery, public speaking, communicating and budgeting there are plenty of skills to learn. Then there are community projects to follow. One strapline alludes to the wider benefits. "Who knows, together you might even change the world a little bit while you're there?"

By building a network of like minded people NCS'ers can go on to do good beyond their 17th birthdays and into the future.

~~~~~

If your tribes are the right fit for you, then all their tribal values should make you feel good. From your smallest and most personal tribe right up to your super-tribes you should act consistently with their values. Each set of values should do mutual good, so you should never be forced to commit violence, crime or discrimination to advantage one tribe over any other. All their values should all be similar and complementary, avoiding clear and obvious conflicts.

*Are all your tribes aligned ?*
*Or are they in conflict?*

72

A study lead by Matthew Feinberg at the University of Toronto[84] has found that peaceful protests like sit-ins and marches can amplify a cause and draw in new followers for it. But where extreme or violent tactics are used, the move backfires. Those actions stop people from identifying with the cause and they put people off supporting it. Reasonable causes, supported by reasonable actions create a value worth taking up. They attract new support.

~~~~~

Hopefully the life you've chosen doesn't produce too many dilemmas and conflicts between your tribes. But that can happen as our lives are increasingly split into fractions, bringing us many different interests, responsibilities and choices. So what should we prioritise when two or more of those interests conflict? The answer comes from revisiting your personal vision, purpose and values. What do they say? Which course of action fits them best? Taking the right path should improve how you feel, by reducing the amount of cognitive dissonance you're experiencing.

Cognitive dissonance[85] is the state caused by a person having to act in a way that contradicts their personal beliefs, ideals, and values. Leon Festinger believed that every human being is looking to achieve sense of inner calm, or as he calls it an internal psychological consistency. That's because people don't want to experience an uneasy sense of conflict when they go about their lives. That should need to healthy analysis and balanced decision-making. However, instead of facing up to those differences and taking steps to address them, people tend to find ways to avoid the conflict or justify their own actions. Running away seems easier than resolving that dissonance.

## Find your internal psychological consistency

For example, if you are on a health-kick, you might find yourself at dinner with good friends who are all having a pudding. The idea of having a pudding appeals because it is sweet and delicious. It also

---

84 Reported in New Scientist No.3235
85 Leon Festinger wrote A Theory of Cognitive Dissonance in 1957.

appeals because everyone else is having one and it is the sociable thing to do. However those thoughts may conflict with your desire to avoid sugary and fatty foods. This sort of dilemma sets two opposing ideas and actions against each other, creating a cognitive dissonance. Faced with this conflict, some people will make a choice and manage the stress that it causes. That works either way, whether the decision is "Yes" (by telling themselves "I don't want to be anti-social" or "I can work it off in the gym tomorrow") or "No" (by imagining the effort required to work the fat off). Either way the short-term conflict has been resolved, even it it's a tight call.

Resolving the long-term conflict between pudding and fitness takes a deeper analysis. Which way do the person's vision, purpose and values point? Are they focused on staying healthy and independent, or on physically helping other people? If so, the conflict can be resolved with a clear "No" in order to stay fit. Where do your VPV point you to?

Other people would avoid the conflict altogether, by pretending that they need to leave before the pudding, or by pretending they can't make dinner in the first place.

The less cognitive dissonance there is between a person's beliefs and the values of the organisation that he or she works for, the easier that person's life is. The more unity there is on offer, the more engaged the worker will be in that tribe's vision, purpose and values. If you are in the right combination of tribes for you, there should be a way of achieving each tribe's purpose without great cost to your other tribes. To avoid endless cognitive dissonance and an unsettled life, you need to have core synergies between your tribes and core priorities between them. Your tribes should fit together like Russian dolls. Their purposes should be ordered and synchronised. If they can't be, one or more of those tribes is wrong for you. Good tribes complement each other.

*We need alignment in our tribes
and their values*

Taking a simplistic example, a professional Saracens Premiership rugby player tries to be the best player possible to earn a living and to avoid injury. He tries to be the best player possible to provide for his family. He also tries to be the best individual and team player he can be for the betterment of Saracens. He lives locally to Saracens and his family is provided for. Playing at club level, these purposes are all aligned.

If he does well and is selected to play for England, he also tries to be the best individual and team player he possibly can be for his country. But there is now a conflict over his availability and absence from home, but these goals are still largely aligned. His purposes, values and behaviours are all complementary. They are largely synchronised.

If instead he plays professional club rugby for Saracens and international football for Scotland then the different physical and mental demands, season dates, playing locations, travelling and training regimes involved will create far too many conflicts to be aligned.

Organisations can choose to remain neutral, blindly offering a job and pay, rather than a sense of purpose. But that isn't motivating. It doesn't fill you with pride or stir your soul to action. To attract new joiners, organisations need to take a position. They need to publicly promote their purpose and values, so that staff, customers, suppliers and other stakeholders can actively choose or reject them. The more magnetic that its moral compass is, the more attractive it can be to work with. The less cognitive dissonance that an organisation causes, the less rejection it will suffer.

The greater a tribe's social and moral impact, the greater its economic impact could be. Good tribes offer a more holistic set of rewards for all their stakeholders. But what about the tribes that cause us cognitive dissonance?

If a business sells weapons to anyone who will buy them, but it pays really well, would you work there? If the same company started giving 10% of its profits to charity, would you work there? If the proportion of its profits going to charity increased to 75% would that make a difference? If your nearest supermarket was 10% cheaper than its rivals but it had been prosecuted for polluting the local river would you shop there? Do you face your cognitive dissonances head on, or do you avoid them?

~~~~~

Geographically, the UK is part of the continent of Europe. Cut off we may be, but the UK is physically part of the European super-tribe. We cannot have our own continent.

We currently belong to the European Union, but after the Brexit vote, the UK's relationship with Europe needs to be rediscovered and realigned. The same is true of the UK's own constituent parts. Some of the UK's countries and regions voted differently to each other.

Was either side good or bad, right or wrong? Arguably not. Voting for Brexit was tribal. Everyone voted for putting their tribes' interests above anyone else's. We voted as one with the same purpose in mind. But our visions of the future and our values varied more than we realised. Our votes simply depended on which super-tribe we more closely associated ourselves with when we voted. It could have been our town, city or region pushing our vote in one direction. It could have been the needs of the organisation we work for. It could have been our country within the UK, or the UK itself. Or it might have been our European super-tribe.

## We vote along tribal lines

It seems likely that the people who voted to stay in the European Union felt just as tribal about the UK as the Brexit voters did. They just decided that being in the EU was better for the UK's wider interests. I suspect that neither side voted to put the UK second, they just didn't share the same vision about what first looks like. The tribal passion in both camps comes from the same place and that perhaps explains why the vote was so close.

Voting to leave was based an independent vision for the UK tribe. A core value was "Together we are stronger". By "we" they meant the population of the UK. To be fair to leave voters no one voting wanted to be told what to do by the EU. Remain voters just felt it was on balance better to be part of bigger club than be a separate club altogether.

Voting to stay in Europe was also tribal in the wider sense of the UK working as part of a super-tribe with all its close neighbours for their collective good. A core value was "Together we are stronger". By "we" they meant the population of the EU. To be fair to remain voters no voter wanted to be completely cut off from Europe economically or socially. Leaver voters just felt that the EU was not a good enough partner to be tied in with.

Leave and remain voters have more in common than they have differences. If we'd had time to consider the pros and cons of the different visions for its future and vote on them, we might have chosen one that the unified the country rather than dividing it.

There are many potential versions of Europe, including one where each country has its own independence, borders, language, currency and culture. There would just be a European economic community. The possible versions also include a totally integrated version where there is one shared border, one shared currency and one homogenised culture. One version of Brexit was good to someone and bad to someone else. The different versions of the European Union can all be based on similar tribal feelings. Our preferences depend largely on the scale of our point of view.

With some exceptions, neither tribe was generally more good or bad than the other. What we needed was a debate that focused around what was best for the whole of the UK. There was too much posturing, promising and prevaricating. The more information we received about the likely practical impact on our society, the wiser we would have been in voting.

# 3.3 HOW MUCH CONTROL AND HOW MUCH AUTONOMY?

No one else sees things in exactly the same way as we do. So every day brings a host of different opinions, challenging interactions and conflicting agendas. There are many pulls on our time and tugs on our heartstrings. Other people are constantly trying to grab our attention for their own purposes.

The routine requirements of work can take up most of our daily time. Urgent business needs and crisis management can drag us into unforeseen duties and delays getting home. As the majority of our day is spent at work, our organisation's rules, procedures and contractual obligations direct our actions and decisions. Work can dominate our lives. If you have no autonomy at work other people and their priorities can end up controlling your whole life. Without actively choosing what we do, we are stuck on someone else's path.

But amongst all of the pressures and responsibilities of modern life, you will have at least some time to yourself. The more autonomy you have, the more decisions you can make or influence. Having freedom of choice allows you to set at least some of your own goals for yourself. Whether those goals are for just you or others too will depend on your circumstances. If you have a management role, then you should have some autonomy. It may not be as much as you'd like, but don't write it off. You can always create a bit more space for yourself to think and act.

Being a decision-maker for other people comes with a responsibility to lead well. Good leaders love the freedom to decide what should be done and how it should be done. Great leaders are brave enough to lead the way to somewhere better for everyone, even if it is the road less travelled. Rather than being victims of circumstance, good leaders find a way to orchestrate the future.

Within the scope of your own autonomy you can decide (or at least influence) what an organisation focuses its efforts on (vision and purpose). You can also decide how that should be done (values). You can even use your autonomy to offer a path for others as well as yourself (leadership). Working your way into a position of influence will increase your autonomy.

~~~~~

The quality of leadership often affects how much autonomy a team actually gets.

Egotistical leaders tend to use control as a method of preserving their position at the top. There are many methods of control including confusion, division and destruction. Egotistical leaders don't give, they take. They create clouds and fog to disguise their duplicity and discourage others. Autonomy is threatening, control is reassuring. Egotistical leaders build the biggest mountain that they can sit on top of; and then cling on to it.

Ineffective Leaders can be better described as mere managers or even blockers. They tend not to build. Whilst they don't set out to destroy anything their lack of leadership often means that any positive momentum in the organisation fades. Autonomy and control are unused, misused or Ineffective Leaders sit on top of the mountain that they inherit, until they are replaced.

## *Leader, manager or blocker?*

Good leaders like autonomy and they understand that their team does too. Good leaders can often be described as builders, developers or multipliers. They improve and develop what they inherited. Autonomy plays an important role for Good Leaders. Good leaders build a mountain that's suitable for themselves and others.

Exceptional leaders develop others within the tribe, who then go on to develop, build and multiply. Autonomy plays a critical role. Without it leadership can't become exceptional. Exceptional leaders work with others to build the mountain that best suits the whole tribe.

~~~~~

Having sufficient autonomy is half the battle, having the courage to lead is the other half. Every tribe needs one or more people who are brave enough to articulate a vision of the future and lead the way there. Each tribe needs a leader with complete conviction in the tribal vision, purpose and values. Having an agreed vision puts a frame around a tribe's autonomy, but it also gives it greater clarity and certainty. Then its followers can decide whether they want to be part of it or not. Choosing to join is an exercise in autonomy.

A leader's conviction needs to be consistently described and consistently applied. That isn't always the case. Sir James Dyson spoke positively in favour of Brexit, saying "We will create more wealth and more jobs by being outside the EU than we will within it." He is entitled to his own views on Brexit of course. His richly deserved credibility as an inventor and business leader gave him the platform to espouse his personal views. The media listened. His views were influential on voters. Dyson had already outsourced the manufacturing of its vacuum cleaners to Singapore years before the Brexit vote. But after Since Sir James Dyson's pro-Brexit comments, Dyson has decided to manufacture its electric cars in Singapore and base its Headquarters there as well. As a result Sir. James Dyson has faced personal criticism. By giving inconsistent messages he appears to lack conviction in his own vision. He may have damaged his personal reputation and that of his company. Time will tell.

Some leaders want to have total autonomy, supreme authority and 100% control. But that approach to leadership is divine and egotistical. That exclusive kind of leadership won't bind a tribe together. A good leader is prepared to forgo total autonomy to embrace a tribal vision and use the remaining autonomy to deliver it. Leadership should mean pro-actively delivering the tribal plan and effecting change for the benefit of the whole organisation.

## Leaders have to give up some control

Leadership means giving something of yourself too. Leading puts you right out there up front. Leadership requires a leader to take assume responsibility, take calculated risks, make mistakes, learn from them and carry on with total conviction. Without a personal investment leaders can't lead. Ironically the more you give away autonomy for the common good the more credit you get.

If the tribe's vision has a collective benefit and it is being achieved, its followers will be more tolerant of mistakes along the way. A shared conviction brings a shared tolerance. Organisations need to create a clear, inclusive and motivating vision and give their staff the autonomy they need to deliver it.

~~~~~

By offering a common purpose and vision of the future, tribes can appeal to a wide range of people. A common purpose can prompt potential members to lift their core motivation past mastery, autonomy and a narrow personal purpose into a tribal purpose that can benefit the wider tribal community. Some people will forgo part of their autonomy to be part of the shared purpose.

We all have some degree of autonomy. How we use it matters a great deal. That much is in our hands. There is an exchange of words in J.R.R. Tolkien's Lord of the Rings which summarises this well.

Frodo "I wish the ring had never come to me, I wish none of this had happened."
Gandalf: "All you have to decide is what to do with the time that is given to you."

So what will you do with the time that is given to you? What springs to mind when you think abut your future? Your inner motivations could help you to define the rest of your life. If you are focused on you and just you, then perhaps change your perspective and look wider. If you are focused on you and carry on as you are, you will miss out on being part of a tribal purpose. Working alone, you have less chance of being successful, but adding your conviction to a tribe, you could make a disproportionate impact. You could be the person to light a spark under a tribal purpose and start the generation of tribal power.

~~~~~

Sustainable success is unlikely if your number one sell to your members is making them rich. For every pound or euro they accumulate, they may be sacrificing something else. That is not to say that money can't be used well. Money can be a brilliant enabler. Money can buy food, drink, accommodation and clothing to help satisfy Maslow's basic physiological needs. Money can also make life easier and free up people's time.

## Money can be a brilliant enabler

The autonomy that a job and regular income brings can be put to great use. Money buys us time to broaden our gaze and extend our vision of how things could be. But the relentless pursuit of money (especially by people who already have more than they could possibly need) misses out on something much more rewarding. If we are not careful money can become an end in itself instead of a facilitator. That's because although money is a potential source of freedom it's also a potential form of control.

~~~~~

The intensity of our conviction can make an enormous difference to whether our autonomy is used or wasted. Using a temperature scale to describe motivation, at sub-zero it might rate as an intense desire to fight against doing a thing. At tepid, motivation ranks as CBA (Can't Be Arsed) giving you insufficient motivation to either do something or to fight against it. By the time the temperature increases to warm, it starts to become a positive driving force. At scalding-hot, motivation ranks as a burning desire to get something done.

Without the autonomy to act on your motivations, you may be locked into a cycle of frustration. Without the motivation to do anything in particular, your potential autonomy is unused. We need both a driving motivation and the autonomy to take advantage of it. What is your burning desire?

~~~~~

Having autonomy gives us the freedom to really go for something. Without committing to a purpose and opting-in to a tribal vision we won't achieve everything that we can. Roger Black MBE is one of Great Britain's most successful athletes. Roger says that its' not enough to "want" to achieve something challenging. He believes that unless you "need" it you are unlikely to achieve it.

But autonomy is not a goal or an end in itself. It is a facilitator and we get to use it or lose it. The more autonomy we have, the more opportunity we have to scorch our own path. But the more autonomy we have, the fewer excuses we have for apathy and inaction. How much autonomy does your organisation give?

## *Autonomy is a great facilitator*

What positive goals do you need to achieve? Are you more motivated by mastery, autonomy or purpose? As Jessie J sang "It's not about the money, money, money." Or can't you be arsed to commit to anything?

Until you find your own mojo, you can't really know which tribes are your tribes. Considering what's on offer might lead you to adopt or reject something, which is a good start. Seeing how other people have led the way can also help to inspire us to be more influential and lead ourselves. Once we feel inspired to do something bigger, we are tapping into the feeling of tribe. Believing in yourself and in your purpose is absolutely vital to its success. In the words of Henry Ford "If you think you can or you think you can't, you're right."

~~~~~

As an individual, the more autonomy we have the more independent we feel. The idea of being in total control makes us happy. Despite knowing that we can make bad decisions for ourselves, most of us would choose complete autonomy if we could. However the reality of that doesn't match up to its apparent attraction. Total and utter freedom without any obligation or responsibility, weakens us and our sense of social belonging. Being alone is worse that giving up some of our control.

Tribes cannot operate if every member has complete autonomy without limits. We cannot be part of society without some compromise. To be part of a tribe means willingly giving up some of our autonomy for the tribe's collective good. There is a balance to be struck between having the absolute freedom but a life alone, against choosing to give up some of our autonomy and become part of a tribe.

Tribes should allow their leaders and followers sufficient autonomy to operate with agility and flexibility but they must never allow the tribe to lose focus on its overall purpose and vision. The same is true of its values.

## *Leaders should never allow the tribe to lose focus on its overall purpose and vision*

Allowing so much autonomy that the tribal core values can be ignored or discarded at will, just to get something done undermines the essence of the tribe and is ultimately counter-productive. Tribes need to have rules, traditions and rituals that everyone has to abide by. To join a tribe we have to willingly give up some of our autonomy.

~~~~~

Everything we do creates ripples. Nothing operates in a vacuum. So in truth it isn't possible to live a life of absolute autonomy even if we wanted to. What we do affects the lives of others. What other people do affects our lives, whether we want that or not.

Fighting to obtain total autonomy means fighting with everyone and everything else. That is a perpetual state of war that you cannot win. Ultimately mankind or nature will overwhelm you. The truth is that no one has complete freedom. Control is an illusion. Even Kings and Queens don't have it. Despite the flattery of his courtiers, King

Canute[86] understood that he wasn't divine and then proved it by failing to turn the Southampton waves back as they lapped over his feet. Like Canute we should also accept that we are not divine. We cannot have complete autonomy. The question we face is whether to give up some of the autonomy we do have for something better.

By the same token, tribes cannot have total control of the World around them either. The ripple effects of every other tribe's actions are constantly lapping at it borders.

~~~~~

There are plenty of examples of that ripple effect occurring in nature. For example, bees and other pollinators are vital to most of the world's food crops. Bees have been in decline in recent decades due to the destruction of their habitats, pesticides and diseases. The impact of the World around them is gradually destroying our domestic bee populations.

But that gradual destruction has gathered pace. Some bee diseases have been detected in hoverflies for the first time. Hoverflies migrate across Europe reaching thousands of miles further than domestic bees do. Scientists at the Royal Holloway University of London now think that hoverflies are spreading these diseases to reach far more bees, over a much wider area.

Without defensive cross-breeding programmes, many of our bee populations will die out.

~~~~~

Just like bees, tribes feel the ripple effect from the actions of the World around them. That's because modern tribes don't act in a vacuum. No tribe can have total freedom and autonomy from everyone and everything around it. So instead of struggling to stay one hundred percent independent, a tribe needs to take a more holistic and

---

[86] Also know as Cnut the Great lived from 995 to 1035 A.D. and was King of Denmark, England and Norway. His bones are in Winchester Cathedral.

approach and work with all of its stakeholders for their mutual benefit. That way a tribe can be inter-dependent on others, rather than outside and vulnerable.

When stakeholders give some of their autonomy to their tribe, they all receive a mutual benefit. Individuals have the choice of creating positive ripples themselves, or they can form part of a tribe and generate positive waves. It is the job of every organisation to offer collective solutions that are bigger than personal ones.

~~~~~

Tribes can't afford to be too rigid or inflexible, as they need to be able to react to changes in circumstances and take new commercial opportunities. That said, tribes need enough stability to withstand the ripple and waves of the VUCA World they occupy. Good organisations put a few sensible fundamentals in place. Good businesses endeavour to be transparent, responsible and compliant.

That means having:

- **A clear and ethical governance structure**
- **Effective audit, reporting and anti-corruption processes**
- **Well-imbedded health and safety systems**
- **Sound and dynamic risk management**
- **Legal compliance (including employment law)**
- **An ethical and transparent approach to taxation**
- **Robust waste management and energy saving schemes**
- **Deep community ties and links; and**
- **Supply chains and customer relationships built on similar principles.**

~~~~~

Giving up part of your freedom and autonomy for a greater benefit can be a very smart thing to do. If enough others do it too then a section of society can work together for their mutual benefit. Businesses that engage with their communities and other stakeholders increase their chances of prospering. If times are hard, loyalty plays a key part in where you spend your money. Mergers and acquisitions can lead to mutual strength. If everyone took a shared approach then society's ills would improve overnight.

## Giving up part of your freedom and autonomy can bring a greater benefit

Monarchies and Governments of all kinds have always relied on the goodwill of the people. In turn the people have trusted their masters to provide for them. It's only when that "trade" stops being worth it that the people vote for change or (if they can't) take up arms. Socialism and Communism have both been promoted as versions of utopia where strong, central control is good for everyone. However the practical applications of both philosophies have not (yet) proved persuasive enough for people to freely choose them long-term. The trade of giving away autonomy for a better life has to be "worth it" and produce results. Once your life becomes unbearable, or your freedom is taken without an equal benefit, the system is powered by oppression rather than choice. That is when a tribe is too controlling, has become bad and should stop.

Perhaps the longest running form of socialism was the basis for the Inca Empire. Some argue that the Inca government was more of an authoritarian monarchy. But however you label it, the Incas survived and thrived from the early 13th Century until 1572 when they were finally conquered by the Spanish. How did they dominate for so long?

The Incas were a highly administrative society, governing somewhere between 10 and 16 million people through a centralised system controlling food and commodities. In exchange for work, the people would receive food or commodities from one of the government storehouses. The khipumayuq (keepers of the khipus) carried out sophisticated store inventories and ran the state logistics and supply chains. Remarkably they did so without any written records. Inca society was not a capitalist one and didn't use money or generate profit. Despite that, the system was highly efficient and everyone received food. How did it operate without money and written records?

Historians say that the Incas used a series of knots tied in different coloured pieces of rope and string. Through the combination of knots and ropes, the khipumayuq reported on the volumes passing through all the supply chains and warehouses. Investigations are still ongoing into what all the surviving rope pieces mean. It is thought that some contain historical records and tribal stories, as well as supply chain volumes.

The Inca Empire was a tightly controlled society. The people gave their freedom to society and trusted the central authorities not to exploit their dependency on the state. It seems that 'trade' was acceptable to the Inca people for several centuries until the Spanish arrived.

## 3.4  THE BUILDING BLOCKS OF A TRIBE

The right combination of vision, purpose and values should naturally appeal to some people. If other people don't understand *what you're striving for, then* maybe your vision isn't as clear or compelling as it needs to be. If you've explained it well but there's very little support for your purpose, then maybe it isn't positive or inclusive enough to form a tribe around.

There isn't a flat-pack version of a tribe available. You can't simply buy all of the parts of a tribe that you need in a box. There certainly isn't a machine which stuffs your purpose for you to make a Build-a-Tribe. But you can plan and guide the construction of your tribe. There are conceptual building blocks to use.

The firstly stage is to plan and establish the core structural elements. A tribe needs strong foundations to be successful. The foundations of a tribe are its purpose, vision and strong and relevant values. Once they are in place you need an implementation plan. Then finally you need to adopt the signs, traditions and rituals of a tribe in order to bind it together.

The first stage is the planning phase that involves four elements. They are all critically important.

1. **Agreeing the tribal purpose.** This is the core purpose that the tribe truly and firmly believes in. It has to be genuine, authentic and inclusive. A tribal purpose should offer something meaningful to every stakeholder and it should bring hope of a better future. It is the link between the tribe and the community it serves. The tribal purpose has to inspire a motivational call to arms for the tribe's future. What wrong are you righting? What good are you doing? Are you producing an environmentally sustainable product, providing care for the elderly, or making people happy? Your tribe's vision, values, signs and rituals should all support its core purpose. What is your tribe's core purpose?

2. **Agreeing a vision of the future.** The vision needs to be inclusive and appeal to all the tribe's stakeholders. This vision should be a description of what the World looks like when your purpose has been achieved. It needs to be imaginative, detailed and compelling. It needs to cover all the facets of the tribe in question, including all of its places, resources and people. You need to be able to draw a picture or diagram of the vision and be able to describe it in words. There needs to be a quick headline description to grab attention and also in a deeper more colourful version of it to get real buy-in. You have to excite and build hope when describing the vision. What does the future of your tribe look like, feel like, sound like? Your tribe's signs, rituals and traditions should all support its vision.

3. **Agreeing the values and culture for the tribe to live by.** A tribe's values have to be clear and consistent with the tribe's purpose. They should cover all the good and bad behaviours

that members will be judged for. Making values realistic and achievable will help to get buy-in to them. There should be good consequences for living the tribe's values and bad consequences for rejecting or ignoring them. So you need to agree the rewards for following them and the penalties for failing to live by them. If you breach a core value you may have to leave the tribe. Which values are core? Your tribe's signs, rituals and traditions should all support its values.

4.  **Agreeing a strategy to get from where the tribe is currently to the agreed vision.** That strategy needs to agree which things the tribe will do and which things it will definitely not be doing. Tribes need to allocate responsibility for each element of their strategy. Set benchmarks and timelines for each stage of the strategy. As with any project, you need to provide sufficient resources to each of the actions and stages. The strategy must get you to the vision and achieve the purpose. Constantly check that is the case. Your strategy needs to actively incorporate as many of the signs and rituals of a tribe as possible. Does the strategy focus on supporting the core purpose? Will it make your boat go faster?

Your strategy also needs to include the tribe's approach to all of its partners and other stakeholders. Is the strategic approach exclusive (ignoring the power of all the available stakeholders), co-operation (working together for mutual benefit), or a form of co-opitition (turning commercial competitors into business partners)? An example of co-opitition is the tie-up between Airbnb and WeWork, who have created a partnership arrangement to serve the same customers. Airbnb provides travellers with a place to stay (accommodation). WeWork provides the same travellers with a place to work (desk space and conference facilities).

Test your purpose, vision and values by asking yourselves challenging questions. Why is that the right purpose? What will it bring if you achieve it? Who benefits? Is there enough in it for every stakeholder to get fully behind it? Is there a more inclusive purpose than this? Does everyone understand the vision? Is it clear exactly how we are going to achieve it? Does everyone understand what their role in the strategy is?

## 3.5 IMPLEMENTING THE TRIBAL PLAN

The implementation or action phase involves five elements. They are:

(i) **Messaging:** Communicating the proposed vision, purpose, strategy and values (the Tribal Plan) to all of the tribe's stakeholders (namely the owners, investors, officers, employees, workers, managers, consultants, trade unions, customers, clients, funders, neighbours, landlords, suppliers, trade associations, creditors, regulators, PR and media agency, government, local community and interested environmental groups). Present the Tribal Plan using all four VARK styles[87].

(ii) **Getting buy-in:** Seeking the agreement of all the tribe's stakeholders to help implement the proposed tribal plan. Developing an agreed narrative and repeating it regularly will help to build conviction around the strategy. Telling positive stories that appeal to all the stakeholders will support each element. Getting commitment to support it could take the plan from a dream into a reality. Moving on without this commitment will probably mean some form of failure.

(iii) **Delivering:** Progressing each phase of the strategy, staying true to the vision, purpose and values of the tribe. This strategy may have a timescale of a matter of weeks, months or even years. The longer it takes the more control and project management is needed, but the more there is that might be achieved.

(iv) **Measuring:** Progress on the tribal plan needs to be constantly measured and reviewed. Once it's in place, the tribal strategy

---

[87] See 3.13 below.

may need to be adapted, re-set and re-communicated throughout the whole process. The plan for delivery should have some built-in flexibility as long as it stays true to the tribe's VPV.

(v) **Recruiting:** By recruiting tribal members for their attitude (commitment to the purpose and values) you can often get the best long-term candidates. The maxim "Recruit for attitude, train for aptitude" requires a commitment in time and effort, but the mutual rewards should be far greater. Short-term, stop-gap thinking can produce longer-term problems. Hiring and promoting people with similar values gives you a solid base. Sustainable growth is powered by people with positive values. A tribe's direction should be set by a clear and inclusive purpose and vision, but the tribe won't go anywhere unless its culture attracts and retains good people. A job candidate's character and values should always come before any other attributes. Good values create happy employees, which creates good finances. Recruitment should never be rushed or done in a hurry.

The recruitment process should be **CALM**:

**C - Character.** Only recruit good people who are good team-players. Strong individuals who are not good team players might produce a pocket of excellence, but all around them will be distrust and dissatisfaction. Competency is really important but it can often be taught and trained. Without character led recruitment the organisation will under-perform compared to its potential.

**A - Ambition.** Target the very best people you can. Always offer to pay them fairly, but don't recruit based on money. Sell the tribal plan. Not everyone wants to be a business owner, director or partner. Many want a balanced lifestyle. So you can persuade people to join you by explaining your organisation's vision, purpose and values. To the right person, your opportunity will prove very attractive. By explaining and illustrating your organisation's Match M) good candidates will be able to see what the future could look like. If they like it and share the same ambitions they will help to align their personal EFGH to the organisation's own EFGH. If they don't share the same expectations, fears, hopes and goals they won't join (which can save considerable pain later).

**L - Leadership potential.** Recruit for today and for tomorrow. Everyone joining the tribe should be good enough to train and manage others one day. The characteristics that make a good leader also make a good team member.

**M - There needs to be a Match of personal and organisational purpose, vision and values.** Make sure there is a fit between what the candidate wants out of life and what and the organisation is aiming for. In addition, there needs to be a match of EFGH (expectations, fears, goals and hopes). Those expectations will include realistic targets, manageable responsibilities and achievable outcomes. That can be done by highlighting up front the organisation's vision purpose and values, job role and description, responsibilities, targets and budgets; and then testing for a suitable match.

If your recruitment is CALM, your organisation should thrive. Interviews should not be a one-way process. "Interview" is not an inclusive term. Calling those meetings something else like "Getting to know each other chats" can remove one of the barriers to achieving the alignment that's needed.

~ ~ ~ ~ ~

With regard to recruitment it is worth remembering that there is rarely a 'perfect' candidate. Gaps in experience are opportunities to gain it; and gaps in skills can be development opportunities rather than weaknesses.

Keeping a Talent Pool Database can help to fill vacancies with suitable candidates. A Talent Pool Database could include (i) current employees, (ii) external candidates (who've let you keep their details); and (iii) alumni who have left but might return.

## 3.6 EVERY TRIBE NEEDS A GENUINE PURPOSE AND CONVICTION

Apathy, enmity and distraction are the enemies of getting things done. The ideal tribe member feels a natural conviction, compulsion and commitment to the cause. If multiple people feel the same impulse there are the seeds of a tribe. Establishing and communicating the tribe's vision, purpose and values to potential tribal members are critically important to building conviction and commitment. Selling the dream will help to enthuse, inspire and generate membership growth.

The feeling of achievement is only a temporary effect. The sense of accomplishment from making a big sale, or giving a winning performance fades with time. Without an underlying purpose to keep us going, our happiness and motivation fades. Without having like-minded people to work with, we end up struggling on alone. We are looking for people with the same shared purpose. We are waiting or leadership that takes the lead on our own agendas. But that leadership has to be genuine and heart-felt.

To attract potential new members, the conviction of the tribe's leadership has to be total and authentic. Without genuine commitment from the chief storytellers a tribe won't properly form and won't last. Leaders have to be able to offer a certainty about the future that they are proposing. Their belief in the cause has to be heart-felt and honest. It cannot be switched on and off, or faked for commercial purposes. We are cynical enough to challenge what we are being sold. Even the billions of pounds spent on branding and advertising can't pull the wool over our eyes. We can see through purely commercial pitches and spot inconsistencies in a brand.

### *Total and authentic leadership*

Millennials in particular can easily spot a liar. They have a healthy cynicism and sense of fairness which allows them to ignore the person completely (if they can't be bothered), or call them out online and watch the resulting feeding frenzy (if they are feeling contentious), or fearlessly tackle them head-on (if they are fired-up). Whichever way millennials deal with fake news and fake news-feeders it is not going to be supportive. By using progressive and passionate messages that advocate positive change you can pull millennials into your tribe.

We are all pretty good at spotting a dodgy salesperson who is peddling a broken brand. The absence of authenticity and conviction is telling. Our antennae can see through politicians, advertising executives and company representatives who are selling something they don't believe in. Discovering when someone is downright lying to you about their purpose is even more important; and there are telling signs.

Our body gives away our lies, even when our words don't. We need to pay close attention to other people when they sell a vision to us. Liars often lick their lips, swallow nervously, clear their throat and breathe more unevenly. They cross their arms and legs, or point their feet towards the exit (in the act of trying to get out of the situation). There are other signs too. A liar's posture will be unnaturally stiff and controlled, to try and hide the lie. He or she may literally give you the cold shoulder and partially turn away from you. Avoiding eye contact is another sign of discomfort and a possible lie. When people lie they reduce the number of gestures they are using. Instead they tend to touch their face more often, obscuring the mouth that's telling the lies or rubbing their nose. The more often it happens, the more likely that the speaker is lying.

As well as the physical contortions, a person's speech can be affected when they lack conviction in what they are saying. A voice can seem flatter and more monotonous. Mistakes can creep in to what's being said too. An accomplished liar will try and control their body before it gives the lie away, so speakers might put their hands deep inside their pockets or even sit on them.

Liars like Iago[88] can become powerful influencers, but they cannot lead a tribe on a quest towards a better future for everyone. That's

---

[88] Iago is the leading antagonist in Shakespeare's Othello, believed to be written between 1601 and 1604.

because their self-interest and dishonesty will reveal themselves. We won't give our trust to people who lie to us. As Homer wrote in the Iliad "Hateful to me as the gates of Hades is that man who hides one thing in his heart and speaks another."

If a leader doesn't have the belief and passion in the messages being given, the tribe will feel that and know it lacks sincerity. Belief runs downhill. If a leader doesn't believe in the cause, no one else will. Although you can fool some of the people some of the time, you can't fool all the people all of the time. If a leader is discovered faking it or lying, the tribe will lose its belief. A loss of faith is always a risk, because followers study the words and actions of their leader very intently.

In contrast, genuine speakers are naturally calm and at ease in their posture. When their passion comes out the movements are expressive, open and fluent. Their voices are animated and clear. Rater than ducking awkward questions, they are happy to answer them directly, eye to eye.

Unless a leader is committed there won't be any followers. If you aren't fully commitment you may be in the wrong tribe.

~~~~~

Forest gorillas typically live in harems, Group numbers tend to be between four and ten gorillas, although numbers can be larger and sixty-five gorillas were counted together in Rwanda. The leader is always a male silverback[89] and the rest of the harem is made up of several adult females and their offspring. The silverback is much bigger and more powerful than the female gorillas and his chief role is to protect the group. However it is the female gorillas, by forming the tribe around him, that have ultimate control.

A silverback leader has to be the best gorilla in the forest to hold his harem together. He can never show any self-doubt or lack of

---

[89] Literally because of the colouring across his back.

confidence. He cannot back down from a confrontation or he might lose his whole group.

## Leadership brings pressure

With many more females in groups than males, there are plenty of lone male gorillas who wander the forest looking drive a silverback off and take over another gorilla's harem. So a game of cat and mouse ensues as the silverback leader tries to keep his group moving away from trouble. Big harems can become separated when they move quickly and ultimately the silverback cannot keep running away.

As the leader he is under immense pressure. If challenged, a silverback has to stand his ground by warning off his rivals by chest-beating or emitting a hooting or grunting sound. If that fails, he will have to fight any lone silverback that tries to overthrow him. The silverback leader cannot back-down. If any female gorilla loses faith his ability to protect her, she will leave him. If he isn't strong and brave enough as a leader, he will have no harem to lead.

Without having real conviction, a leader won't inspire faith in their leadership. Without clear leadership a tribe will struggle. If a common conviction in the purpose is lost, there probably won't be a tribe at all.

## 3.7 REWARD THE MANY

Organisations can focus their rewards too narrowly on the few and not on the many. The modern tribes that function well get that balance right. They don't let some members starve while others live like Kings and Queens at their expense. That's not acceptable or sustainable. It's also a self-defeating logic, as it has the ironic impact of limiting the rewards for everyone.

Under-paid people feel under-valued and demotivated. When our intrinsic motivation is missing, we naturally produce less effective and energetic performances. Quality, output and profits become suppressed. Opportunities are missed or dealt with half-heartedly. An organisation can't maximise its potential output if it doesn't have a fully engaged workforce.

## *Maximum output comes from maximum engagement*

Owners and shareholders are best to focus on staff rewards, not their own earnings. If you build it properly the rewards will come. Many senior people in businesses do care and would happily share profits wider that they do, especially if they also did better as a result. But the arbitrary self-imposed pressure of achieving profit this year brings a singular reference point. Businesses develop tunnel vision, losing their peripheral perception and focusing far too much on increasing short-term shareholder profit.

~~~~~

Setting business targets based on incomplete figures or an artificial "need" for growth will make them unrealistic. Monitoring performance data is important, but so is understanding what the business can actually achieve. The latter understanding requires honest, two-way communication with the 'shop-floor'. Trying to force a level of performance that's beyond the reasonable and realistic won't inspire or build engagement. It will have a positively demotivating effect. This is especially true where those performance expectations are linked to pay rises.

It is vital to have a sense of both operational and market reality when target setting. The split second between one financial year ending and the next one beginning is not the time to start planning for the new financial year. In practice, business plans need to be in place much earlier than that, but the earlier that happens the more unrealistic they'll be. So business plans and targets should be set early, but be contingent on how the year is actually going. The Q2 targets should therefore be at least partly contingent on what happens in Q1. Working to an unachievable target all year is hugely demotivating.

This is especially true where those targets are directly linked to staff bonuses or commission.

~~~~~

The John Lewis Partnership has recently rebranded John Lewis as John Lewis and Partners; and Waitrose as Waitrose and Partners. The brand change was to emphasise the contributions of all the people who make the brand as strong as it is.

With over 80,000 partners (staff) there is a big pressure to maintain jobs, wage growth and profits in tough economic times. But the Group is not immune to wider market conditions. Over the twelve months to June 2018, the group made over 1,800 people redundant whilst at the same time creating 700 new jobs. Managing Director Paula Nickolds commented "We are determined to play the long game and our ownership model means we can. While others are investing in drones, we are investing in people. Where others are cutting back, we are investing in the very thing that is our point of difference." The John Lewis Partnership has set high standards in employee value, involvement and reward. Steering the ship on the same course, through big economic waves, is some challenge. If Paula Nickolds can achieve this, the business will continue to thrive.

~~~~~

Businesses also tend to limit what they reward too narrowly. These days data tends to drive decision-making and rewards. Some assume that if it can't be measured financially it's not worthy of reward. That is of course wrong. Transparency and objectivity are vital, but every contribution can and should be 'scored' and included in a data lead approach.

Firstly and more importantly, the reward structure must directly link to the vision, purpose and values of the organisation. A contribution which helps the organisation achieve its vision is worthy of reward. A contribution which takes the organisation further away from achieving its vision, or undermines its purpose, or which breaches the organisation's core values is not.

# With responsibility must come reward

Any scheme must be fair, objective and transparent. The rules must be clear and agreed in advance, not left deliberately woolly or brought in part way through a financial year. Any scheme must be so easy to follow that everyone in it can work out how it's calculated. The rewards and rules of any scheme need to mutually benefit the organisation's owners, customers and operations teams. If in theory everyone wins, in practice everyone will probably win. Reward schemes can drive an organisation towards its vision and provide fair rewards for that. Consulting on them first will increase the chances of that.

Once the reward scheme's fundamentals are established as the starting point, a fair bonus scheme or profit allocation system should have both credits and debits. The level of reward should be linked to the balance between the credits and debits. Without debits, no one checks and controls their behaviours. Together they should combine to produce a net reward figure.

Credits should be given for certain financial aspects of performance such as:

1. the amount of profit generated by the person, team or organisation[90];

2. the amount of profitable new business generated;

3. the growth in profit (taking into account any investments made, what happened in previous years, comparables in the same sector and the state of the economy);

4. the growth in profitability (through operational efficiencies and organisational improvements);

---

[90] Depending on who the scheme benefits.

5. but growing turnover without adding to profit (Fool's Gold) arguably shouldn't be rewarded.

Good people management should be given credit too, especially for managers, for measurable success like:

1. how many staff are under a person's management;

2. how quickly new staff (are helped to) get up to a satisfactory performance level and hit their minimum targets;

3. retention of key staff;

4. low staff turnover generally (especially in high turnover sectors);

5. good staff survey feedback;

6. good external stakeholder relations; and

7. living and displaying the organisation's values.

Operational efficiencies and improvements that should be credited too:

1. reduced time from order to delivery;

2. reduced costs of development, production and delivery; and

3. increased sustainability.

Where a person actively ignores the organisation's values and displays the opposite values, each instance should be penalised with a debit. This will help to reduce the bad behaviours that help some people and teams artificially profitable. So debits should come from elements like:

1.  the number and seriousness of customer complaints (together with the value of any payouts);

2.  the effect of insurance claims on the organisation's claims record and premiums;

3.  upheld staff grievances (together with the value of any payouts);

4.  upheld employment tribunal claims brought against the organisation (together with the value of any payouts);

5.  upheld complaints to any regulator or other authority such as the Information Commissioner (together with the value of any payouts); and

6.  upheld complaints from creditors or suppliers (together with the value of any payouts).

Staff benefit schemes should always provide a mutual benefit for the person and the organisation.


# 3.8 INVOLVE YOUR ELDERS

Having thought about your own heroes and heroines, who do you inspire? For many humble people the answer will be "No one." But I bet you have offered inspiration to other people from time to time. Inspiration doesn't have to come from a tub-thumping speech. It can be a few quiet words, an example of resilience and stoicism, a moment of guidance or simply leading by example. Great leaders inspire others to follow and some to lead. More people will be inspired by you than you think. People often have more to offer than they realise.

In a VUCA World, we can all be blown off course by events outside our control. To counter that, we should aim to both find inspiration for our own lives and also to be inspirational to others. We should do more to connect the energy and wisdom of the generations by blending the best of their attributes. The raw naivety and exuberance of youth offers bravery, determination and high energy. The calm experience of age offers guidance, support and wisdom. As Winston Churchill famously said "When youth departs may wisdom prove enough." The combined strengths of youth and experience are much better than either of them individually. The collaboration brings energy and wisdom and provides the engine room to generate tribal power.

## Do more to connect the energy and wisdom of the generations

The Native American Indians understood the enormous value they could gain from regular conversations with the elders in their village or tribe. The elders passed on their guidance and life experience to the next generation. That way their wisdom was transferred on and wasn't lost. Does your tribe tap into that kind of experience? Your story can inspire someone else. The telling of someone else's story can have the same effect too. Stories can provide knowledge, insight and reassurance.

~~~~~

Traditional mentoring of others helps you to learn more and pass on what you know. Some employers offer an internal mentoring scheme, with allocated training and mentoring time for anyone who volunteers to be a mentor or who volunteers to be mentored. Sometimes that's Induction Mentoring to get the new employee off to a good start. Other times its Development Mentoring with a longer term set of aims. Mentoring can offer mutual insight, encouragement and rewards, but it doesn't always work. So rather than forcing a mentorship that isn't bonding, changing partners should be encouraged.

Peer to peer mentoring can allow a mutual respect to become a mutual benefit. Top down mentoring (from a more experienced/more senior person to a less experienced/less senior person can provide great assistance downwards but it's perhaps less beneficial for the mentor.

Reverse mentoring is becoming increasingly popular, with the less experienced person giving a different insight and approach up to the current leadership. That can provide leaders with a new form of inspiration and focus to carry on their good work. Whichever kind of mentoring it is, it should offer a win: win solution to the mentor and mentee.

By choosing to take part in mentoring, you have to take on a responsibility and give a slice of your autonomy to the process. But you will hopefully be doing so for a larger slice of mutual gain. Mentoring is a growing trend. All leaders should have a mentor and all leaders should be a mentor for someone else. Learn, pass on what you learn and keep learning. Many great business people had a mentor.

## *Mentoring brings a mutual benefit*

Mark Zuckerberg has openly credited the late Steve Jobs with mentoring him in the early days of Facebook. "I went and I met with Steve Jobs, and he said that to reconnect with what I believed was the mission of the company, I should go visit this temple in India that he had gone to early in the evolution of Apple, when he was thinking about what he wanted his vision of the future to be." Mark Zuckerberg took the advice and returned with a new found confidence, purpose and sense of direction.

According to an article published in Forbes magazine, Sir Richard Branson credits the late Sir Freddie Laker with being his mentor saying "We wouldn't have gotten anywhere in the airline industry without Freddie's down-to-earth wisdom. He helped shape our vision for high quality service at competitive prices, and was the first to bring my attention to how fiercely we would have to battle with other airlines to make a success of our airline."

In sport, mentors are very common, which should tell business the value of them. Sir Bobby Robson mentored Jose Mourinho, Glenn Hoddle and Andre Villas Boas amongst many others. Arsene Wenger has mentored Patrick Vieira and Thierry Henry amongst others. Sir Alex Ferguson has mentored too many players and coaches to mention including the likes of Cristiano Ronaldo, Ryan Giggs, Bryan Robson and Steve Bruce. Great leaders can leave a legacy and create great leaders of the future through mentoring.

~~~~~

What I call MRC mentoring can be very effective. MRC stands for Mentoring Reinforcement Circles. It also represents Mickey, Rocky and Creed. In the Rocky franchise Mickey Goldmill mentors Rocky Balboa to win the World Heavyweight Boxing Championship. Mickey explains his mentoring approach to Rocky "...I'm gonna stay alive and watch you make good. And I'll never leave you until that happens. 'Cause when I leave you, you'll not only know how to fight, you'll be able to take care of yourself outside the ring too."

Through Mickey's wisdom and guidance, Rocky is set up for life inside and outside the boxing ring. Six films into the franchise, Rocky goes on to mentor Adonis "Donnie" Creed. Rocky calls on his experience of Mickey's mentoring to help him do so, adding his own experience into the mix.

## Circular mentoring can enhance the learning process

Donnie Creed gets his mentoring from Rocky, but also indirectly from Mickey. He therefore learns from both of them. But even better what if Creed had been able to mentor Mickey, to complete the circle and reinforce all the good learning? Creed could have imparted all his experiences back up to Mickey. That would have helped Mickey improve the way he mentored Rocky. And in turn, Rocky would have learned more from Mickey and mentored Creed better. MRC mentoring can create a virtuous three-part circle.

Mentoring doesn't have to be generational (but it is often beneficial where it's from an experienced person to less experienced person). Mentoring just needs to pass useful guidance, training and support to someone else inside the organisation. The three-person MRC mentoring could offer all three people the chance to give and receive mentoring. That should improve the way they each do their jobs and the way that they mentor.

~~~~~

Any tribe can benefit from listening to the feedback of all of its stakeholders, which may be made up of its owners, investors, officers, workers, managers, trade unions, customers, clients, funders, neighbours, landlords, suppliers, trade associations, creditors, regulators, PR and media agency, government, local community and interested environmental groups. Together they provide a collective sounding board.

~~~~~

Leaders should hold regular sessions to get feedback from each of the tribe's stakeholders. These meetings will all transfer available experience to the organisation's leadership. They will bring a wide range of benefits to play.

Business leaders shouldn't let years of experience leave their organisation without tapping into it first. Succession planning and formal handovers are necessary to protect a tribe's future. One idea is to ask each leaver to write down what they've learned and can pass on. Some leavers will completely ignore the request or write something facetious, but others will see it as an opportunity to leave their own legacy for other employees to benefit from. Another alternative is to ask your organisation's leavers to give (or record) a leaver's presentation, talking through the key things they've learned. Both options are a good opportunity to pass on their knowledge and experience to those who follow them. It's certainly not too late to gather experience from an exit interview.

## Leave a legacy, pass your knowledge on

Good leavers will welcome the opportunity with open arms. That means they will always leave a part of their spirit within the organisation. They will leave proud and happy, wishing the organisation well. Then they will actively recommend people to go and work there. If a worker's contribution is respected on retirement, he or she will remember work fondly and would probably come back and help the organisation in a crisis. Employers need to do more to ensure that their leavers leave well. They need them to leave so well that they doubt their decision, tell everyone how good their time was, sell the brand, make recommendations to others and then become a 'boomerang' returner.

Creating alumni associations can retain links between the tribe and its former tribe members for many years to come. They tend to operate in larger businesses, but there's no reason why every organisation can't have one. Maintaining those tribal bonds after leaving has mutual benefits. Alumni news, updates and events are popular because they maintain friendships and offer networking opportunities. It's worth it for employers too as they get a free team of advocates.

## 3.9 TEACHING OTHERS HELPS WITH LEARNING

There is surprising value in sharing what you know with other people. I remember reading Paul Arden's thought-provoking book "It's not how good you are, it's how good you want to be". One idea in it immediately jumped out to me "Give away everything you know and more will come back to you". It made me think, how does that work?

Ever since then I have used an adapted version of that maxim myself, namely "Teach everything you know, so that you'll have to learn something else." Since reading Paul Arden's book I never hold back any advice, pearls of wisdom or secret tips in the hope that I will stay ahead of the pack. Instead I regularly give away all my best thoughts and share all of my best and worst experiences. That has achieved exactly what I hoped. It has forced me to do more, listen harder and read endlessly in order to learn more.

My knowledge has undoubtedly increased because of this philosophy. I have forced myself to improve. The cycle of learning, passing on and learning more, provides a similar virtuous circle to MRC mentoring which is good for the teacher and the student.

Now I definitely know more than I would have done if I'd held back my knowledge. This book is another attempt to give away everything I know. Now I will be forced to learn lots of new things.

# 3.10 HOW WILL YOU MEASURE SUCCESS?

Bhutan is a neighbour of Tibet and Nepal. It isn't a major capitalist power. So you wouldn't expect Bhutan to be leading the way in how to measure success for states and companies alike. However it very well might be.

Bhutan has been following a development policy based on Gross National Happiness (GNH) for several decades. Gross National Happiness is not just a gimmick. It is measurable and looks long-term. According to the Economist, some companies are emulating Bhutan and adopting a Gross Organisational Happiness philosophy, using the same 9 key areas of data measurement that Bhutan uses.

The 9 metrics for Gross Organisational Happiness are unsurprisingly much wider than profit. The data comes from two sources. Data for (i) psychological well-being, (ii) health, (iii) time use and (iv) education is gathered from the organisation's workers.

## *Gross Organisational Happiness*

The data for (v) community vitality, (vi) cultural diversity, (vii) good governance, (viii) ecological diversity and (xi) living standards is typically gathered from the organisation itself. Each metric is measured, converted to numbers and benchmarked. Steps are taken to keep all 9 in balance. With a focus on the future, long-term planning is seen as the right approach and investment doesn't have to have an instant profit and loss account benefit.

Your tribe is free to measure its own success, however it wants it. I have personally used what I call the Magnificent 7 Measures. They are benchmarks for People, Culture, Products/Services, Brand, Customers, Systems and Finances. But whether you use the Magnificent7, the 9 Gross Organisational Happiness metrics, or an individual formula of your own, you need to define what success looks like and what you are measuring. Measuring profit alone is far, far too narrow. What data will you use to make measure success?

~~~~~

Spartan soldiers fought together in a phalanx. Each soldier held his bronze shield (Hoplon) in front of the Spartan to his left. The whole phalanx moved as one, carrying out well-coordinated manoeuvres in unison[91]. A Spartan shield was therefore a symbol of teamwork and collective strength. Losing your shield risked the life of a fellow soldier and was a mark of great shame. When a Spartan man left for war, his wife (or another significant woman) presented him with his shield. She handed it to him ceremonially with the words "With this or upon it." Success for a Spartan soldier was extremely simple. Either return triumphant with your shield, or die in battle.

## 3.11 TELL THEM A STORY

Providing raw data can inform but it doesn't illustrate a point or elevate it into a guiding theme. I have tried to use analogies, references and stories to illustrate points in this book. Stories can make data memorable.

---

[91] Spartans The True and Brutal Story of How the Spartans become the strongest warriors in history, by Patrick Auerbach.

James Kerr, the public-speaker and author of the inspirational book Legacy[92] told me that telling great stories can be the secret to success. James is a fantastic storyteller and he seems to have an almost endless series of stories to tell. Told well, good stories can be very powerful.

The stories that work best are genuine, natural and speak the truth. They offer authenticity. The kind of stories can vary tremendously. Some are of achievements against the odds. Those stories can fire us up and help us to face our own challenges head on. Other stories can bring us back down to earth and restore our humility. Using stories requires the same focus as every other aspect of building a tribe. You should only tell stories that fit your vision, your purpose and your values.

## Stories have power

There is a common saying "Fake it until you make it" which encourages people to sell themselves as successful, in order to become successful. Faking anything is generally not a good idea. It is true that by acting as if you can do something, you take sometimes manage to get things done. But faking or lying isn't authentic and any positive effect is limited. Tribes won't have the glue of unity if its members are faking their commitment.

Being yourself is much better than being a pretender. Many people have personal stories to tell which can help others. If you feel you haven't achieved much yet, then tell stories about the successes of others which echo your philosophy and approach. Give those other people credit. Some of their positivity and success will rub off on you. As you gain more experience yourself, you can mix in some stories about your own successes as well.

~ ~ ~ ~ ~

Having a good storybook will definitely help to persuade other people to choose your tribe. When your organisation is interviewing for job

---

[92] The full title is Legacy: What the All Blacks Can Teach Us About the Business of Life.

vacancies, make sure tell stories that make it seem attractive. Give examples of when you've helped workers who were struggling (it's comforting), how you reward staff fairly (it's reassuring) and how you've achieved things together as a team (which pulls on social belonging).

~ ~ ~ ~ ~

In the 1960 film the Magnificent Seven, a group of seven gunfighters defends a small Mexican village from marauding bandits [93]. The villagers are poor farmers and cannot fight. Chris Adams (Yul Brynner) is given a handful of coins and valuables by two villagers with the words "This is everything we have". Moved by what they are offering him, he responds. "I have been offered a lot for my work, but never everything."

One by one Chris uses the villagers' story to persuade five other gunfighters to join him in defending the village. With only a tiny amount of money available to pay the gunfighters, the telling of the villagers' story and the credibility of the story-teller are crucial in pulling a team together. Because of their own needs and motivations, each gunfighter hears the words of the story slightly differently.

Vin Tanner (Steve McQueen) has lost his money gambling. He is working in the local Store and desperate to get out of his dead end job. When asked later why he took the job, Vin tells his own story about a man falling from a building with the punchline "It seemed to be a good idea at the time." The villagers' story appeals to him because it offers him a change of scene and potentially a change of luck. It was also appealed because it was Chris Adams who told the story to him.

*Everyone has different motivations. Tap into them*

Chris's friend Harry Luck (Brad Dexter) is motivated by money. When Chris tells Harry the villagers' story, he doesn't have any sympathy for their plight. But Harry is a cynic and doesn't believe that so little money could have persuaded Chris to help. So Harry ignores what he's

---

[93] The 2016 film with the same name has a different premise.

being told and comes to the conclusion that it's not the real story. He makes up his own version for himself. Wrongly assuming that there is a secret hoard of gold, silver or diamonds, Harry joins the gunfighters with his own agenda. Later when Harry dies, Chris doesn't have the heart to tell him that the story he told him was true. So Chris tells Harry what he wants to hear, so Harry can die happy. Thinking that he could have become rich is enough for Harry to accept death.

Britt (James Coburn) is a gunfighter and a knife thrower who likes testing himself against the best. As we meet him he is trying to avoid killing a man who's challenged him to a knife against gun duel. Pushed and goaded into fighting the man, Britt kills him with his knife. When Chris tells Britt the villagers' story, he is up for the challenge precisely because the odds are against them. Britt has immense pride and confidence in his own ability. Britt certainly isn't scared and won't back down. Later when the gunfighters are taken by surprise and forced to leave the village, Britt wants to return saying "Nobody throws me my own guns and says run. Nobody."

An Irish-Mexican called Bernardo O'Reilly (Charles Bronson) has fallen on hard times. He is chopping wood for money when Chris and Vin find him. For him any pay is better than nothing. Defending the village is initially just a job, but he warms to the villagers' plight and begins to care. His true character comes out when a village boy calls his father and the other villagers "cowards" for not wanting to fight. Bernardo scolds the boy with a speech that includes the words "You think I am brave because I carry a gun? Well your fathers are much braver because they carry responsibility. They do it because they love you and because they want to. I have never had this kind of courage."

Lee (Robert Vaughan) has lost his confidence and is trying to escape from his many enemies. Hiding in drink, he is wracked with fear. When Chris tells him the story he hears it as an opportunity to go South into Mexico and hide. It is a good opportunity to run again. Lee desperately wants to regain his nerve, but he is full of self-doubt. Eventually faced with having to fight, Lee says out loud to himself "The final supreme idiocy. Coming here to hide. The deserter hiding out in the middle of a battlefield."

As the gunfighters head towards the village they are followed by a seventh man called Chico (Horst Buchholz). Earlier Chico failed the reactions test when interviewed for the job by Chris. He is embarrassed but still follows the group as it travels towards Mexico. Impressed by his persistence, Chris eventually invites Chico to join the group. Chico is in awe of Chris and the others and wants to be part of what they are doing. Utterly convinced by the group's purpose, Chico helps to rouse the villagers from their fears, in order to help themselves. He finds love and stays in the village after the battle.

Each one of the Magnificent Seven has a different motivation. Pulling them together into a tribe wasn't easy. The purpose is dangerous and the money on offer wasn't persuasive on its own. The story-telling and conviction of their leader is what brings the Magnificent Seven together and binds them as a group. Without the power of the story and the storyteller, the Mexican villagers would not have had the Magnificent Seven to defend them.


# 3.12 FIND PEOPLE WITH A SIMILAR VISION

Until you know what you want the future to look like you can't be sure which tribes are your tribes. Formulating your own ideas is really important.

What does your ideal vision of the future look like? Is it just about you, or is there a wider concern for others? Are you sitting in a luxury mansion, surrounded by beautiful people who adore you, counting your shares and gold reserves? Are you working in your current job concentrating on your family? Are you helping others in the evenings and weekends? Are you working in a not just for profit (NJFP) organisation, doing great work and surrounded by people you have helped to achieve equal success? Are you not working at all? Or are you living in a ramshackle hut, helping in a poverty stricken area in Africa?

You need a personal vision to have something to aim for, something to compare your progress to. Without a vision any success will be accidental or random. For an increasing number of people, their wider sense of purpose is about creating something which has a social, environmental and financial benefit for more than just themselves. But some people aren't driven by any of that, their vision is about their own career, status and earnings. Other people have a fairly neutral approach, which is not to harm other people, but not to particularly help them either.

## Whose kind of future do you like the sound of?

If you have a wider point of view, then the phrase People, Profit and Planet might apply to you. That summarises a holistic approach. The people element involves everyone that you want to help and provide for; as well as everyone who could help to make things better. The profit element is about making something economically sustainable, so that it lasts and provides the means to help other people year after year. The planet element is the need for environmental sustainability, so that future generations can live at least as good life as we do and preferably better.

To help to fulfil your own ideals, you need to search out people with a similar vision to you. In a phrase, you need to find your tribe. By choosing a vision that has a wider benefit at its heart, you should be able to find other people who will help you build it. Ask other people what their hopes for the future are. Do you share your vision with any of them?

## 3.12 FIND PEOPLE WITH SIMILAR VALUES

In 'Legacy', James Kerr describes the motivations and values of the New Zealand All Blacks and where their source comes from. As the World's most successful international rugby union team, the All Blacks offer us a great example of a winning culture. Rather than being a team based on personal strength and ego, their core characteristic is humility (mana).

The team's present performance is powered by its respect for the past and its responsibility to the teams of the future (Whakapapa). The All Blacks also use the phrase "A better person makes a better All Black" putting a person's character before their ability. This is the smart thing for any organisation to do. In recruiting other lawyers I have always used the mantra "Good person, Good lawyer in that order". Both are important, but good character is vital. In other contexts you could talk about it being "Good person, Good skills" in that order.

### *Character first, skills second*

When recruiting I always try and wait for the right character, or I'd even change the job specification to fit the right character. In a group environment an exceptional CV full of personal achievements is not enough. Does the person tell stories that illustrate their role in team-working? Or are they all "me" based?

Employers should actively test for a team-working attitude and skills during the recruitment process. That doesn't happen often enough. One way of doing this is the obvious but rarely taken option. By asking candidates to perform a series of tasks with the team they might join, you can observe how they interact with that team before you offer them a job.

~~~~~

Character matters enormously. A person's character influences their interactions with everyone else. If you recruit a bad worker you need to act. You should give everyone a fair chance to reach the required standards, but you'll need to act if they can't. No employer can afford to ignore bad character.

If a good worker becomes selfish and disengaged after joining your organisation, you need to address that. There could be many different reasons for a change in attitude and performance. So every tribe should try and offer support first before judging (as well as complying with employment law). Many decisions are tough, but the workers you help through crises of health and personal circumstances can go on to become some of your highest performers. Don't tolerate poor character and behaviour. Operate a "No dickheads" rule. Overall your recruitment rejections, performance turnarounds; and tough goodbyes can be some of your best decisions.

Egos and mercenaries have no place in a tribe. There's a saying that you get what you pay for. In the case of buying favour, paying someone to secure their "loyalty" costs a heavy price and still leaves you vulnerable, because it creates no intrinsic loyalty. If someone else offers a mercenary even more money, there's nothing to hold them to you. Instead of paying ever more money, leaders have to create a purpose, vision and set of values to include and excite their team members. Fair pay is essential, but excessive pay is not the answer.

*Ask this question.*
*Why do you want to be here?*

Imposters have no place in a tribe either. You can't rely on anyone who's faking the right thing. You are either in a tribe or you are out. Employers need to set out their vision, purpose and values and then test every candidate for fit and suitability. Never make a job offer based on an unchecked C.V. or application form. A bare question and answer session doesn't constitute a proper process. If you're planning to ask someone to join your tribe for years to come, shouldn't you spend more time getting to know them properly first.

Work out what character you need and find out what character is on offer. Recruit for the growth stage that someone's reached and not for the bullshit that they've preached.

~~~~~

Similar values can be narrowly focused and local, or they can be much broader than that. As Legacy also flags, the South African cricket team adopted the African concept of Ubuntu, the inter-connectedness we all have with the World around us. The Proteas didn't just play for themselves, or each other. They played for their whole nation past, present and future. That inclusiveness was truly inspiring.

That was recognised as being powerful motivation by their opponents. Richie McCaw on the All Black de-brief after the 2009 year. "It soon became apparent to us that the South Africans were playing for transformation, they were playing to advance the cause of the Rainbow Nation, they were playing for something bigger than themselves.[94]" That's an admission that the opposition had

## Play for something bigger

No wonder they became the first international cricket team to be number one in all three formats of World cricket. To play for yourself may make you good. To play for your team mates or the ones you love, may make you better. But to play for your whole nation, all your ancestors and all the future generations to come, must surely make you the very best you can be.

~~~~~

The Finnish have a national characteristic known as sisu which combines resilience, determination and bravery in a single concept. Anyone who has sisu has indomitable courage against the odds. The harsh Finnish Winters may be partly responsible for this defiant outlook. But however this characteristic developed, it has made the

---

[94] "The Real McCaw: Richie McCaw: The Autobiography" by Richie McCaw.

Finns a hardy people with great inner strength, perseverance and sustained courage.

~~~~~

Your values matter to your colleagues; and theirs matter to you. For me kindness is King not cash. Show me someone genuinely kind and you're likely to have a thoughtful, selfless team player. Genuine humility is very valuable too. No one likes to work with someone who is arrogant. Mental strength is often more critical than physical strength, so loyalty and reliability are valuable characteristics. You also need emotional resilience and a determination to get the job finished. Together these go a long way to describing someone you should recruit, someone who is tribal. Focus your search on people with good values and characteristics to help you build your tribe.

Sir. Steve Redgrave is quoted as saying "It's the iron in the mind, not the supplements, that wins medals." Recruiting for character rather than for reputation will set any organisation up for success.

People can have different and competing opinions on many issues. There is an expression "Money talks." It does, because it speaks of character. How people react to money can reveal their inner values. In business, decisions with regard to investment and tax planning can be very divisive. A longer-term approach to investment is consistent with tribal values. At the other end of the investment spectrum is a short-term view that puts maximising this year's profit for the owners before sustaining the whole tribe's future.

## Mental strength is often more critical than physical strength

With regard to tax, most people have no choice but to pay their tax in full. Some people happily insist on paying their tax for legal and moral reasons. Other taxpayers will use all lawful means to reduce their tax bill, stopping short of anything illegal. Finally some people will use any tax avoidance schemes possible, whether or not those schemes are lawful. Every year people are caught evading tax. A common justification is to claim ignorance and blame the financial advisers who set up the scheme. But every taxpayer should agree with their advisers the principles they want to be applied and check that is happening.

Choosing your advisers, fellow business partners, shareholders and colleagues wisely is vitally important. Money can break relationships. A number of business people, celebrities, sports stars and others have had to work very hard to unravel their tax avoidance schemes, in order to stop their reputations from unravelling.

~~~~~

Where selfishness and narrow-mindedness are prevalent, the offer of a better way of doing things will appeal to people with similar values. Where the current direction of travel doesn't help the many, offering to do things differently may bring new hope to the whole tribe.

One person can effect a dramatic change in a tribe's sense of purpose and widen the impact of its success.

## 3.13 EVERYONE IS A POTENTIAL TRIBAL MEMBER

Although we have our own individual aspirations, inspirations, vision and values, we don't want to be alone. We don't want to be the only one who thinks like we do. So we want to find and associate with other people like us. Unsurprisingly, the reason is one of self-interest. There is more chance of being fed, watered and clothed if we are part of a tribe. Tribes also offer us social belonging and protection. Being part of a tribe is good for us and everyone else in the tribe.

Whether it's loving our own family, supporting our favourite sports team, or promoting the company we work for, we tend to operate in a tribal manner. There are always exceptions, but most people gravitate towards other people. The tribes we are allocated by our birth are often deeply ingrained in us by the time we reach adolescence. After that, we tend to choose our tribes for ourselves. Well, at least we think we do.

## *Which tribes are for you?*

We are free to make our own choices, but in making decisions we are subject to a large number of internal biases and external influences. Many of those influences are known to us and we can consciously assess their impact. But other influences affect us subconsciously. Every bias you give in to limits your opportunities.

~~~~~

For decades, psychologists have tried to understand why some people commit crime and some people don't. Even where teenagers come from a neighbourhood that's dense with crime, only some of them will go on to commit crime themselves.

The root causes of crime vary from person to person. They can include: poverty, a lack of hope, boredom, self-protection, a bad experience with authority, standing up for your friends or local area, seeking notoriety, peer pressure and gang initiations. But why doesn't every teenager come from a crime-ridden neighbourhood go on to commit crime? There is a credible theory that some teenagers are insulated against the criminal influences, when other unlucky teenagers are not. That protection appears to come from one of three roots.

1.    A personal guiding purpose which the person perceives to be worth more than the upside of crime and not worth the risk of getting caught. That personal guiding purpose could be: aiming to go to university, aspiring to have a specific career, wanting to play sport at a high level or a strong personal desire to avoid prison or death. For hip-hop star Loyle Carner it was a love of cooking that kept him out of trouble.

2.      A collective guiding purpose which the person perceives to be worth more than the upside of crime and not worth the risk of getting caught. That collective guiding purpose could be finding an escape route out of the neighbourhood for your whole family. The fear of having your parents or siblings family at risk daily risk of harm could drive anyone to change their family's destiny. Another collective guiding purpose could be helping your sports team to have success and not wanting to let your team mates down.

3.      The constant positive nudging of a relative, a good friendship group or the encouragement of a teacher. Those nudges could be enough to keep someone on track and out of serious trouble.

Whichever it is, there's a tribal influence involved. Whether we are giving or receiving help, we all need positive tribal influences to keep us on the straight and narrow.

At home, school and work, positive influences, interventions and offers of help can make a telling difference to our lives. The World is full of negative influences, but there is often a way out of the present and there is almost always the hope of a better future. We can be wooed and persuaded to follow our dreams if someone is offering us the prospect of positive change. We can be led away from trouble by a kind and helpful influence; and we can be that influence for other people too. Finding another person who sees the future in the way you do, can bring you both the hope of something better. It can be the start of a tribe.

A tribe that has a clear VPV and appeals to logic, hope, aspiration, support and belief could secure widespread support. If a tribe can appeal on all those levels it should grow quickly.

~~~~~

How a purpose is sold matters a great deal. We absorb information in one of four main ways: Visual (show me), Auditory (tell me), Reading/writing (let me read it) and Kinesthetic (let me find out for myself). We tend to prefer one style of learning most. One or more of these VARK learning methods will appeal to most people.

If a pitch is made to us in our preferred learning style, we are much more likely to receive it well. To attract as many people as possible, any appeal for support should be pitched using all four methods.

## Pitch to everyone

Use pictures, graphs, charts and other images to appeal to visual learners. Use seminars, presentations, audio books and question and answer sessions to appeal to auditory people. Use books, notes and online guides for people who prefer reading/writing. Use hands-on activities, physical challenges and memory tests for kinesthetic learners.

Make sure any appeal for new tribal members is VARK friendly. If someone is pitching to us and the delivery method strikes a chord, we are going to hear those messages much more clearly. So make sure that all tribal updates are given in a VARK friendly way.

~ ~ ~ ~ ~

Life dishes out inequalities at birth. It also dishes out even more through life experiences. The presence of inequality creates a sense of fairness and justice; and the need for some to support others. When people are suffering from inequality they may be more open to joining a tribe that offers help and hope of change. There are far too many inequalities in life to list, but they include physical disability, illiteracy, low income, learning disabilities, unemployment, culture and language barriers and mental health problems. Other examples of personal characteristics and situations that make us vulnerable include being the victim of a serious accident or crime, being agoraphobic, divorcing, the frailty of old age, being threatened with deportation; and living or working remotely away from your family. A genuine offer to help people in need may have wide appeal. An offer which really just amounts to helping yourself will not.

There are lots of people hoping for change. There are also lots of people capable of providing that change. Bringing them together can be the start of a new tribe. The have-more could be extremely useful stakeholders in improving the lives of the have-less. Getting their time is the biggest challenge. But once it's being given it can be invaluable.

# 3.14  USE CALLS TO ACTION

In the corporate world, securing new business is a primary focus. Every method of increasing sales needs to be utilised. Every potential customer has an invisible target centred right on them and every sales tactic needs to be employed to reel them in. For tribes and their followers the position is essentially the same. Every opportunity to deepen the relationship with an existing follower, or attract a new one, should be taken and not be ignored. Winning people to a cause takes a great sales pitch.

Calls to action can be used to persuade people to buy something or buy into something. Many successful brands have a strap-line which is as well known as the brand itself. These are often referred to as tag-lines and sit next to the brand's logo. Three good examples are Nike's "Just do it," McDonald's "I'm lovin' it" and Kit-Kat's "Have a break, have a Kit-Kat."

Due to the strong emotional connections we make with brands, just re-reading one these familiar strap-lines can increase the chances of you buying a product from that brand. They are a call to action, whether that call to action is "Buy me" from retailers, "Use this" from service providers, or "Join us" in the case of a tribe.

~~~~~

In the charity sector, a strap-line can help to pull-in new donations or attract more volunteer time. Stonewall's strap-line "Acceptance without exception" makes the organisation's purpose clear and at the same time calls out for your support. A good strap-line like that silently whispers to our inner motivations.

## *Are you with us?*

The Fawcett Society achieves a similar effect, with "Equality. It's about time." The charity calls out to people that their purpose resonates with. This is another call to arms, a higher level of strap-line. They can have a tribal effect by pulling people in to support the cause. The Suffragettes used "Deeds not words" as their call to action.

~ ~ ~ ~ ~ ~

Calls to action can be focused on a few targeted people or to the general population. The Labour Party's strap-line addresses that distinction head-on, with its tag-line "For the many not the few." Depending on whether you classify yourself as being one of the "many" or one of the "few" the strap-line either calls directly to you. For some the point will be lost and it won't call at all.

Ironically, the MPs who defected in 2019 seemed to consider that the Labour Party was no longer speaking for quite so many of the "many".

~ ~ ~ ~ ~

Using words that invoke a sharp, emotional response can generate a powerful and compelling argument to get involved. Everyone has different intrinsic motivations and so each call to arms will only speak to some people. So the call to arms has to be quick and attention grabbing. The more succinct and punchy the words are, the more powerful the calls to arms can be. The more that a tag-line offers hope, the more of a reason there is to respond. A great example of a call to arms backed by an appeal to hope is "Extinction is forever. Endangered means we still have time."

In the banking world, Lloyds Bank and Mental Health UK produced a joint television advertisement in 2018 with the hashtag #GetTheInsideOut. It aimed to raise the profile of mental health issues amongst the bank's staff, customers and the wider general public. If the bank genuinely followed through and used education, training, flexible terms, individual rewards and tailored environments for its staff and customers, it will have been a good initiative.

## *Appeal to hope of a better future*

You could theoretically reach everyone with a call to arms. But in reality many people won't even notice it. Of those that do hear it, not everyone will feel its importance or care about its outcome. Of the people that it does resonate with, only some will be prepared to offer their time, money or expertise. Despite those limitations, there are always people out there who will step up for a good cause. There are lots of money rich, but time poor people with a head for business and a heart for their community. Causes should tap into our intrinsic human needs, to help persuade us to contribute and to give something back.

Reaching out to potential followers requires a good strap-line. In 2012, the London Olympic Committee used the call to arms "Inspire a generation" and they did. What is your tribe's call to arms?

# 3.15 TRIBAL ACTION PLAN

Tribes flounder without a clear and agreed purpose, vision and set of tribal values. Is your tribe's purpose clear? Is it still relevant? Are all the stakeholders supportive of it? Does the tribe still believe it is achievable?

If the tribe's leadership needs reassurance that's there's still support for the tribe's VPV, it should call a meeting for all its stakeholders. If you need to, get your directors and shareholders on the same page first and then bring everyone else in. Imposing unchecked authority from the top has very limited value. Being inclusive is being tribal.

1.  Test the stakeholder needs that underpin the tribal purpose. Do all those needs still exist? Are they aligned or in conflict? Does the purpose need to be adapted? Will that tighten or splinter the tribe? Is the purpose inclusive enough? Does it need to be broadened?

2.  Test that every stakeholder is still invested in the vision. Does the vision need to be re-imagined or better explained? Is it appealing enough to all stakeholders? Does the vision need to be re-established? Does it need to be modernised or updated? Can that be done whilst still sticking to the tribal purpose?

3.  Test that everyone is adhering to the tribal values. Is anyone behaving as if they are above the rules? What needs to be done about that?

Once the VPV has been re-tested and re-worked, use strong calls to action to get the tribe formed back into line. Everyone needs to re-commit to the tribe's purpose. How do you gain that commitment?

Publicise the vision and try to bring in new tribe members. What are your calls to arms? Why should anyone join your tribe?

# 4. GENERATING TRIBAL POWER

## 4.1 GETTING A CONNECTION STARTED

Every adult over eighteen has the vote in a general election or referendum. Voting is one of the greatest rights and responsibilities we have. The voting process is individual and secret. We have the freedom of choice. However, in the same way that we have our own views and opinions, so does everyone else around us. We are subject to those views on a regular basis.

During the build up to an election we are all put under pressure to vote in a particular way by: party political broadcasts, political leaflets, door to door visits from local party members and the views of family and friends. Still, despite those pressures, we get to choose how we vote. That decision ultimately comes down to us. We get to decide who governs us and the outcome of a general election or referendum can dramatically change the course that the UK is heading on.

Voting is an individual responsibility but it is a tribal process. The collective will is what wins the day. It is a tribal act to choose a side. It is a tribal act to vote with your values. That's why we should always make a choice, even if it is for the lesser of the evils on offer. It is precisely because we have both a mind capable of choice and the freedom to choose that we should always register our opinion.

*Make your choice*

If there is nothing on offer for you, then spoil your ballot paper. Voting for none of the options is still far better than not voting at all. Registering our objection to what is on offer is essential and absolutely justified. Expressing what we oppose is as important as what we support. If enough people vote for none of the available options it will help to create change.

Amongst all the political noise and pandering to us, we get to decide what to support and what to oppose. Other than through general elections and the occasional referendum we don't get to make the really big decisions. Our politicians do that for us.

But we are free. In between elections, we can campaign for change and try to influence government policy. We can build a consensus around social improvements and find individual causes to support and believe in. We can join with others who feel the same.

~~~~~

As human beings, we are able to think for ourselves, which creates our own unique view of the World. We have the freedom of choice. With the exception of people suffering from a restricting mental illness, disability, oppression, poverty or imprisonment, most people get to choose what to stand for, what to believe in and what to offer support to. We cannot go through life without having views and opinions about the World around us. It's what we do with those opinions that count.

One individual can't be a tribe, but a single person can lay the foundations for one. By setting out a clear vision and purpose, together with clear supporting values, anybody can stick a flag in the ground and let it fly. A single person can be the cell nucleus for a tribe (the control centre that establishes the cell's DNA).

## Be the flag bearer

One person can also take an existing tribe and lead it onwards to its existing vision. Or one person can take an existing tribe and help to re-position or re-invent it.

Whichever scenario it is, every tribe needs two things. The first is a powerful and inclusive VPV and the second a leader with the skills required to deliver it. In short, someone needs to propose the way forward and raise a call to arms for help.

~~~~~

Once we find things we feel passionately about, what do we do about it? Something? Nothing?

Some people spend time thinking about a cause but haven't got the time, energy or inclination to get involved. Other people will share their views in person and online and then stop. Some will act on their views by trying to change things for the better. Others will look beyond themselves and sell the cause and garner support for it. The more passionate that someone is about a purpose, the more likely that another person listening will recognise their own passion for it.

Until we are shaken and stirred we are probably content, happy enough to carry on as we are. Many people settle for only a fraction of what this wonderful World has to offer. Events around us may need to change before we feel compelled to react. Our leaders may need to fail before we make a stand. Our tribes may need to flounder and run aground before we are driven to change.

## Don't wait too long

An awakening can happen at any time. There is a cause for everyone. That could be running an ethic and moral business, starting up a not just for profit business, helping with disaster relief, promoting peace, defending human rights, conserving wildlife, protecting animal welfare, supporting causes for children, saving the environment, assisting with medical research, providing education or advancing the arts. For some people, the cause could stem from a pride and commitment to how things are and their opposition to any change. It's out of shared views, opinions and votes that people come together.

~~~~~

Tribes are formed when people find a cause and find each other. Together they can combine their energies and resources to generate a tribal power. When people with a shared purpose seek each other out, they are already starting to bind themselves to a common purpose and pool their resources. When a tribe's purpose, vision and values are well articulated, people will understand what the tribe stands for and what it stands against. Explaining the tribe's VPV can be empowering to the story-teller and to the listener. Using clarity and passion to articulate the need for the tribe to exist will help to persuade people to choose to join it. When a cause starts to generate a wider profile and interest, others will join it.

When enough people join a tribe, they can collectively align their thinking (through debating and agreeing their tribal plan), resources (through a form of stock-take) and actions (through implementing the tribal plan). That process of combining the group's collective thinking, resources and actions provides the base from which tribal power can grow.

## *Pool resources and spirits*

Once people start coming together around a tribal plan, then a tribe can begin to develop its own hierarchy and structure, heritage, language, rules, nicknames, spiritual homeland, stories, art, songs, colours/uniform, ceremonies, badges/logos, symbols, brand, routines, opposition, records and fragrance/flavour. The more its members feel part of a tribe, the more they will generate tribal power.

## 4.2 TAP INTO A SHARED MOTIVATION

As individuals, we can be quickly stirred to anger, revenge and fear, but the effect of these emotional states can quickly fade. A tribe cannot rely on simultaneous anger and fury to power itself. A group on the rampage trying to force change is merely a mob. Undermined by its temporary state and lawlessness, a mob rarely achieves sustainable change for everyone's benefit. Achieving a tribal vision usually needs a coordinated approach and consistent effort over the medium to long term. Where a vision is hard to achieve, followers need a deep, long-lasting motivation to keep going. External pressures to act are often less durable than internal ones. We need to want it for ourselves.

The more of ourselves we bring to everything we do, the more our intrinsic motivations can power us on. The more of ourselves we leave at home, the less we give at work.

Tribes must therefore tap into their members' intrinsic motivations, the ones which help those people to last the distance. Corporate tribes should have a purpose that motivates and inspires all of their stakeholders to put their collective shoulders behind the wheel. Tribes fire-up more easily when their members bring their full selves to the party and not just a watered-down "work" version. Businesses therefore need to tap into the intrinsic motivations of their employees, or they will have a workforce of corporate shadows dressed in suits or company uniforms.

## *Don't be just a shadow*

Tribal leaders can question their employees to discover their intrinsic motivations. This can be done during appraisals, performance reviews and more general conversations. Good managers will show a genuine interest in their team members, finding out what Culture, Opportunities, Rewards and Environment each of their employees needs to operate at their best. Really good managers will use this information to examine themes of satisfaction and dissatisfaction amongst their teams. By understanding what rewards their team is expecting, managers can work out what staff think is motivating enough to get traction.

Even if managers can fire-up their teams, unless the tribe's goals are inclusive and beneficial the interest that's been sparked will be fleeting or aimless. There are enough potential followers out there that any tribe could possibly need, but too many tribes are strong on purpose and weak on vision. Moaning about the way things are is just whinging in the wind. Action is needed for something better to grow and take hold. Find a vision, purpose and set of values that will spark you into action. Finding like minded people to take action with can be the spark of tribal power.

~~~~~

If someone isn't sufficiently motivated to do the job in hand, he or she will procrastinate before starting and then become easily distracted. Finding shared motivations empowers tribe members to help each other stay on track. Knowing exactly why they are there together helps each tribe member to focus and re-focus. Connecting what each person does care about to the purpose is crucial if it is ever going to be achieved.

The biggest reason for lacking motivation is that the purpose and vision is not worth the effort to make it happen. To be worth sacrificing time and effort for, a purpose has to be something you deeply care about. How much effort is required is directly proportionate to how much you need to care about achieving that goal.

Making tasks fun, challenging and core to the purpose will make them feel worthwhile. Making goals realistic and achievable will give tribe members the confidence to take them on. Giving adequate guidance, time and resources will help to keep task performers calm and composed. Providing monitoring and review processes will offer help anyone who is struggling, before they give up.


# 4.3 BUILD A SHARED CONVICTION

Without the central threads of vision, purpose and values to pull everything tightly together, there is just an idea, a loose alliance or even less. Unless everyone yearns to achieve the same things together, the effort being made won't be sufficiently coordinated or aligned to generate tribal power.

In order to reach agreement over a tribal plan, there should be a constructive and healthy debate. There are two compelling reasons to let dissenting opinions have their voice. Firstly, we can get greater clarity in our thinking by forcing ourselves to hear and process what we don't necessarily agree with. In this regard, the tribal elders can often provide a useful sounding-board or challenge, as well as hearing feedback from people with staunchly opposing views.

## *Properly test your plan*

The second reason for asking for both positive and negative feedback is that a tribe has to respect the views of all of its stakeholders in order to harness tribal power. We are all people, not sheep. We are human beings, not automatons. You cannot expect a person to give everything to the cause, without allowing them to express their views and have a say. People don't like being subjected to enforced rules and policies. We like to choose what we support. Tribes only stick when there is a shared conviction.

All tribal members need to regularly ask themselves whether they have a genuine and natural commitment to their tribe's purpose, vision, strategy and values. If not, why are they still in that tribe? Trying to stick to a steep, winding path when the wind is blowing and you don't care about reaching the destination seems pretty pointless. In reality, if you aren't driven to reach the summit you're highly likely to give up somewhere along the way.

Where you have a natural deep-seated conviction in a purpose there is no sense of sacrifice. That's because people with a heartfelt conviction in something don't feel like they are giving anything up by working towards it. They feel the opposite. Someone with conviction doesn't just stop their journey because it gets difficult. That merely drives them on.

Winning over someone's belief in a tribal plan can create a new follower for the tribe. Turning that belief into a strong conviction can produce a follower who lasts the course. It could even produce another leader for the tribe.

*If you don't have a genuine conviction
in your tribe, then you either need to change
your tribe or change your tribe*

Throughout history there are innumerable examples of extraordinary human endeavour. In virtually no cases was that achievement completely accidental. That isn't possible without personal conviction. There are too many examples to refer to, but one example of how conviction defied conventional thinking took place in 218 BC.

Hannibal the Carthaginian is said to have taken nearly 40,000 infantry, 9,000 Numidian cavalry and 37 elephants from North Africa to Italy through the Alps mountain range. Recent evidence has now emerged that the journey through that perilous mountain range took the hardest possible route over Col de la Traversette[95]. At the time the journey would have been deemed physically impossible, but Hannibal was convinced that it could be done. He also knew that if they achieved it, the Carthaginians would have the element of surprise, as the Romans would never expect such a treacherous crossing. Despite the cost in horses, elephants and men, the Carthaginians completed the journey and took the Romans completely by surprise. The Carthaginians had total conviction in their leader Hannibal. Filled with belief they won several great victories and occupied part of Italy for fifteen years. Hannibal is revered as a great military strategist, but his conviction in an Alps crossing is perhaps even more impressive.

## 4.4 LEADERS NEED OTHER LEADERS

However good a leader is, he or she inevitably needs help to achieve the tribal purpose. Leadership support is crucial. There are always a range of skills hidden inside any organisation and ideally those

---

[95] The evidence emerged from a scientific expedition filmed for Channel 4's documentary Hannibal's Elephant Army: The New Evidence.

leadership skills will come from existing tribe members. But if you have to get external assistance then you should always get that person's buy in to the tribal plan first. No one in a leadership or influencing position should be allowed to stand independently or maintain competing allegiances.

Unless the tribe is very small (2-6 people) or everyone works communally (e.g. in a small factory) then having more than 12 people to lead is hard. Creating an organisational structure and leadership for it is important for clarity, communication and delivery. Using a very basic example, where an organisation comprises a headquarters and three operational locations, a genuinely empowered sub-leader will be needed in each of those three operational locations.

~~~~~

When a business or sports club performs well we like to attribute that success to the individual powers of the organisation's chief executive, managing director, sporting manager or head coach. We laud them as a 'great' individual. In doing so we transform the organisation's combined strength into a personal one.

Even where it's acknowledged that there's a special leadership group within an organisation, the chief executive or manager still tends to be given a disproportionate amount of credit for any success. Often that's unfair and the other group members should have more individual credit. But that said we need to give due credit to the visionaries and catalysts who can assemble a group of people and mould them into a tribe.

## *Credit doesn't come from titles, it comes from action*

Success only comes when the right skills, experience and attitude are present throughout the whole organisation. Not even Eddie Hall could carry an entire organisation. No single person can win a football, rugby or cricket match. In sport, unless the coach or manager is also a player, he or she can't even play in the matches.

We need to stop looking for a single individual to credit with everything. That is the hallmark of ego, imbalance and dysfunction.

9

Success usually comes where there are two, three or even more leaders working together. Often it is many more people working in harmony. When every tribe member is given responsibility, support and reward you have the hallmark of a tribe.

For strong-minded people to work well together there needs to be a mutual respect and trust between them. In sport, those relationships can come between owners, coaches and players. Choosing the right people can create a powerful spine of leadership and character through out any organisation. Sometimes there is a symbiotic link with each leader interdependent on the other.

~~~~~

Sir. Steve Redgrave won five Olympic Gold Medals rowing for Great Britain. Each one was won in consecutive Olympic Games, stretching from 1984 to 2000. He is the only person to have ever won five Gold Medals at consecutive Olympic Games in an endurance event. He is literally in a league of his own. Sir. Steve Redgrave is British hero. His is probably the most extraordinary sporting achievement.

Sir. Steve was born with an extraordinary physique. That was personal to him. He also has an extraordinary grit, resilience and determination. That is his character, no one else's. Sir. Steve put in extraordinary levels of mental dedication and physical practice on and off the Thames. No one else did that for him. Sir. Steve Redgrave won his Gold Medals. No one else rowed for him.

## Greatness isn't a solo achievement

But where would Sir. Steve Redgrave have been without Lady Redgrave, Jürgen Grobler, Andy Holmes, Patrick Sweeney, Matthew Pinsent, James Cracknell, Tim Foster, Ed Coode and many others? Every day he had his family's support. Every one of his boats had a coach. Every boat he won Olympic Gold in had at least one more rower in it. Even Sir. Steve couldn't have beaten two men in an Olympic Final (although I would have loved to see how close he took them).

Every sporting great is great because of their own physicality, skills, resilience and dedication; and also because of the people around them. Sir. Steve would be the first to credit everyone around him. Which only confirms the extraordinary person he is.

~~~~~

Sometimes great partnerships are given public credit like Sir. Brian Clough and Peter Taylor. As a pair they had tremendous success at Derby County and Nottingham Forest during the 1960's, 70's and 80's.

Working together for the first time, they managed Hartlepools United (now called Hartlepool United) from 1965, where a young 16 old John McGovern was on the books. But it was when they took over a Derby County team facing possible relegation from the Second Division that they really started to build some traction. They won the old Second Division title in 1968–69, the First Division (the former Premier League) title in 1971–72, and got to the semi-finals of the European Cup in 1973.

After falling out with the Derby owners, both Clough and Taylor left to go to Brighton. But then the partnership split up. Sir. Brian Clough famously went to Leeds United in 1974 (to replace Don Revie who'd left for England). Peter Taylor chose to stay behind and take over as the Manager at Brighton.

Without Peter Taylor to help him, Sir. Brian misfired from the off. Speaking about the Leeds players in a television interview before he'd even arrived at the ground, Clough accused his new players of winning through dirty play and cheating. His words echoed his earlier criticism of the Leeds players and alienated them in an instant. His approach backfired spectacularly. Results quickly went against him and Sir. Brian Clough lasted only 44 days at Leeds United before he was sacked.

## A tribe of two is still stronger than one

Clough headed off for Nottingham Forest and in 1976 Taylor joined him there. Re-united the old chemistry returned. The two of them repeated their achievement at Derby by winning promotion into the old League One in 1976/77 and then winning the League title in 1977/78. They also won the European Cup in 1979 and 1980. Forest also lifted the Anglo-Scottish Cup, the F.A Charity Shield, the European Super-Cup, and the League Cup twice in 1978 and 1979.

Peter Taylor retired in 1982 leaving Sir. Brian alone. Without his partner the trophies didn't come as readily, although Sir. Brian eventually won the League Cup twice more in 1989 and 1990.

Peter and Sir. Brian had a symbiotic strength when they worked together. Neither was able to draw enough power to operate successfully alone. Giving due credit to Peter Taylor is a great step forward from giving all the credit to Sir Brian. But is that giving enough credit elsewhere? Were those championships and cups won by them alone? What about John McGovern? He played for 'Cloughie' at Hartlepools United, Derby County, Leeds United and Nottingham Forest. Would Clough and Taylor have won two League titles and two European Cups in 1979 and 1980 without their captain and talisman?

Neither Sir. Brian or Peter played in their Derby or Forest teams. Their coaching, guidance and tactics undoubtedly helped to create many wins, but they didn't kick a ball between them. You need leaders on the pitch as well as off it. You need leaders within every team, location and level of your tribe.

~~~~~

Leadership shouldn't be limited to one person. Ben Ryan successfully coached the Fiji's Rugby Union Sevens team to two Rugby Sevens World Series' wins and an Olympic Gold in Rio in 2016. Ben has a very clear view about needing more than one single leader. "The greatest teams have both a great coach and a great captain."

There are many successful managers, coaches and business leaders. But none of them did it all themselves. Sir. Alf Ramsey coached England to win the 1966 Football World Cup. But how far would England have got without iconic captain Sir. Bobby Moore? Sir. Alex Ferguson is the most successful manager in British football. Where would he have been without Roy Keane and Steve Bruce? The same is true of Arsene Wenger and Patrick Vieira. After Vieira left for Juventus in Italy, Arsene Wenger and Arsenal lost their power.

In rugby league the same is true of Brian McDermott and Kevin Sinfield at Leeds Rhinos. Brian McDermott was able to get the best of a team where egos could have been a big issue. On the pitch "Sir Kev" was probably the most influential British rugby league player of all time and therefore perhaps the greatest. Together they were a powerful combination.

## *The greatest teams have both a great coach and a great captain*

In rugby union think Graham Henry and Richie McCaw of New Zealand. It's not always a coach and captain. In Motor Racing, it was the partnership of Technical Director Ross Brawn and driver Michael Schumacher which won five World titles at Ferrari[96]. In Boxing think Muhammed Ali and his trainer Angelo Dundee. Each relationship was a close and powerful alliance. Each person drove the other. Each of these leadership pairs also needed help from many others too. That shouldn't be forgotten.

There are also plenty of successful groups combining great on and off the field leadership. They can be all shapes and sizes. In rugby union there was Sir Clive Woodward, with massive on-field leadership form Martin Johnson and Jonny Wilkinson. At Chelsea it wasn't just about Jose Mourinho because he had John Terry, Frank Lampard and Didier Drogba as his on-field leadership team.

There are many other examples of joint leadership in sport, with even more examples in business. The truth is that no single leader can take 100% of the credit for any team's success.

Which other leaders haven't been fairly credited in your tribes? Which combinations will bring the most success?

---

[96] Michael Schumacher also won two World Titles at Benetton.

## 4.5 APPEAL TO LOGIC, EMOTION AND INTRINSIC MOTIVATIONS

With a growing number of media channels and increasing volumes of content, there is more information available to us than ever before. There is already far too much data to contend with. It is impossible for us to process it all. New information is fired at us all day, every single day. We are drowning in a flood of supposed facts. Sleep is our only release.

Stitched into each fact comes the influence and thinking of others. Sometimes that additional layer of opinion is immediate and obvious. Sometimes it is more clandestine and controlling, masquerading as fact. That's because the information we're given passes through the prism of values, beliefs and experiences of all its messengers as it travels towards us. Those influences are only rarely explained to us. So as the receiver of the news we can be unwittingly subjected to social or political bias, sales techniques and peer pressure. The truth can get lost in all the spin. This phenomenon is well recognised. When mere opinions are presented as facts, it is now nicknamed 'Fake News'.

With so many external factors pulling and pushing us at every point, we are close to losing our freedom to think for ourselves. Resistance to fake news and undue influence is absolutely vital, as tribal power can't be generated without a clarity of vision, purpose and values. If we allow our freedom of choice to be hijacked and over-ridden by the opinions of others, we will become sheeple. We need to challenge and test what we are told, to find the truth. We have to use our minds and freedoms to think for ourselves and to choose what is right.

*We need to choose our tribes for our own reasons,
rather than other people's*

The good news is that as human beings we have a brain, a heart and a soul. If we can find a tribal purpose which appeals to our logic (brain), emotion (heart) and soul (which produce our intrinsic motivations) we will find it hard to resist. Tribes have to appeal to all three.

Even though we inherently understand and feel what matters to us, we can lose our grip on our own motivations because of all the external pressures bearing down on us. That can happen despite knowing that we are permanently under the influence of advertising, political manipulation and emotional blackmail. To try and combat this external challenge to our intrinsic motivations, we have developed a defensive cynicism which critically examines anything that doesn't seem genuine or real. That cynicism actively tests any information that challenges our views and beliefs. Testing the logic of what we're told can help us make true sense of it.

We have a fundamental and daily challenge to protect the essence that makes us who we are. To be our happiest and most productive we must stay true to ourselves.

Alcuin was a teacher and philosopher born in York born in 735 A.D. He wrote "Quadpropter potius animam curare memento, quam carnem, quoniam haec manet, illa perit." which means remember to care for the soul more than the body, since the former remains, the latter perishes.

~~~~~

Tribes need to find and develop common views, to develop common action. Logic can be very powerful, but tapping into a person's emotions and intrinsic motivations is stronger than an appeal based on pure logic alone. Although people are open to new ideas, they are not easily persuaded by anything which contradicts their existing beliefs. Trying to win over people with diametrically opposing views is extremely difficult, as most people don't switch their values and motivations very easily. Persuading cold hearts and closed minds is time consuming, with no guarantee of success.

All this means that it is difficult to get messages and appeals through today's mass of information and existing biases. Even if you can pitch them well, those messages have to pierce the minds of people who don't like change. So when you're building a tribe, finding people who already have similar beliefs and sympathies is a good place to start. With global social media, finding and contacting other people has never been easier. But convincing someone that you have a tribe worth joining has never been more difficult. Persuading people to exercise their freedom of choice in favour of your cause can require a long-term view and hard work. You have to influence people on two levels, by stirring the passions inside their fiery red emotional hearts; and explaining the benefits of the change to their cool blue logical minds.

## Use logic powered by emotion

The energy needed to effect change comes from the combined power of a shared purpose and a passionate call to arms. A tribe should set out the bare facts, offer its vision for the future and allow for a healthy discussion. Within that debate a tribe has to be able to quickly and clearly explain its 'truth' or it will get lost in all the cacophony. The richer the debate around its purpose, the more likely that common thinking can crystalise. Re-proving and re-establishing the basis for the tribe's purpose and vision can be a very constructive process. It can help a tribe to tell its story and re-build conviction amongst its members.

Any tribal sales pitch should be made using logic, emotion and an appeal to a person's intrinsic motivations. The combination can help to pull potential tribe members into the fold.

# 4.6 REACHING OUT

We all want to live free from imprisonment and oppression. We all want to be financially independent. We don't want to rely on anyone else for our basic physiological needs. We all want to choose which tribes we belong to and which we don't.

Where we have achieved economic, legal and social independence we don't want to lose it. We cling to it and resist any change that might jeopardise it. If someone tries to take away your freedom or independence you would strongly defend your own position. You would fight to defend yourself. But who else would you fight to defend? Your family? Your friends? Beyond them, would you work with others to defend everyone's interests?

~~~~~

In 1762 Jean-Jacques Rousseau wrote The Social Contract. In it Rousseau describes how people have gone from being free and happy to suffering from the "modern condition" of inequality, dependency, violence and unhappiness. The Social Contract includes the famous line "Man is born free and everywhere he is in chains." Faced with an alienated society of individuals, Rousseau's solution was for everyone to give themselves to the "general will" and regain their freedom through being part of a collective social contract. Rousseau felt that society could solve its own ills and social alienation by acting as one and focusing on the general interests of all.

There are people who would immediately benefit from a more selfless, collective effort. The people who are in most need would probably be the fastest to rally to a cause offering hope of change. People whose physiological needs are not being met will be desperate for aid. So anyone that is struggling without food, water or housing will instantly rally to the promise of it. The same is true of anyone who is being forced to live without rights and freedoms. They will quickly support someone who is offering equal treatment, the right to vote, or job opportunities. Using Rousseau's logic, those with less could rally to the idea of a collective social contract.

# Focus on the interests of
## every stakeholder

In a hypothetical society where it's every man, woman and child for itself, the twin threats of theft and violence would be ever present. Some people would use force to take more than their equal share. Without the protection of the Police and the law, other people would be forced to go without enough to meet their basic physiological needs. In that primal environment, there would be inherent instability and innumerable conflicts of interests. Faced with daily fear and uncertainty many people would be hoping and waiting for a tribe to come along and offer hope for the dispossessed.

The same principles apply with regard to our health, safety and security. Paying tax to fund the Police, National Health Service, the Armed Forces, the Fire Service, Government, and Local Government is part of an existing collective social contract.

~~~~~

Similarly, the staff of a modern business which operates with Victorian working practices will impose a sense of fear and oppression on its workers. Those who can leave will leave. Those who can't leave will give the minimum amount of effort they can get away with. Customers and suppliers will question whether they want to deal with that sort of employer. In that unstable environment, another rival tribe could come along and offer hope to the disillusioned.

Happy people stay, work hard and add value. Unhappy people either leave or offer reduced value. Businesses that are fair, open and inclusive will reap the rewards as their competitors fail to see the holes springing up in the bottom of their boat. On a modern working level, if you offer the prospect of more openness, more shared rewards, a better working environment or more opportunities for advancement you will appeal to anyone who is striving for those things and hasn't achieved them yet.

There will always be people who are in need of assistance and other people who are willing to provide it. Good causes produce both the aided and the aiders. Connecting them up is a constant challenge. Finding sufficient time and the inclination to help can be a problem. We can't help but witness the issues of the day playing out around us. But all too often the idea of doing something to help fades away to nothing. Expressing our feelings out loud to family and friends, shouting at the television news or ranting online can get the frustrations out of your system. However unless we do something to make a difference, our views and principles will remain stuck in limbo. Until you are part of a tribe, with a clear vision, purpose and values you will just be stirring up ideas, causing waves or feeding hope to an online crowd. That won't help you to deliver on your ideals.

## Do something to make a difference

The worse that someone's personal situation is the more they will be looking for a reason to believe in something better. People will put their hope and faith in a tribe that's authentic, passionate and realistic. Desperate people are prepared take help from anyone. That's why extreme political views always attract more support during economic and social crises.

Ideals are a much higher level of need than our base needs for food, water, housing and the paid work that keeps us out of poverty. So our physiological needs will always come first. But once we have provided for them, we can refocus our minds back to our ideals.

But a belief in something needs a movement to make it become a reality. Whoever is offering help has to deliver it. Broken promises and false hope will eventually crush support for anything. People are cynical through experience, because too many politicians have made offers and promises of a better life without delivering fundamental improvements. Hope is in short supply.

When it comes to political or business change, there has to be a fully costed and resourced plan for delivering on the ideas and embedding them afterwards. When it comes to social change, it's easier. People power can drive change and embed it within almost every organisation.

~~~~~

Theraputic Communities is a group-based approach to dealing with deep-seated social problems like mental illness, alcoholism and drug addiction. At its height, patients and therapists lived together in residential units 24/7. With some success in rehabilitation and patient satisfaction, these groups provided the safety of living in a supportive community. There was no need to reach out for help, it was there on hand.

Government budget cuts have resulted in residential therapeutic communities being replaced with cheaper day units. The benefits of therapeutic communities have (at least temporarily) been lost. Now patients and providers have to reach out to connect with each other. Communication has been become much more important. The further away from the organisation's epicentre a tribal member is, the harder he or she needs to work to make their relationships work.

~~~~~

Human beings like to be liked. We like to like people who like us. We don't normally care about anyone else unless and until we know that they care about us first. So if you are trying to appeal to potential tribal members, you need do something to show that you come in peace. You need to prove that your purpose is inclusive and genuine.

Doing something kind and unexpected normally earns a warm and generous response. If you make an offer of help with commitment, passion and determination it helps to build trust and faith in you. That faith and trust will grow if your efforts are sustained and persistent. Then the people you are helping will believe in your ability to deliver and they will follow your lead. But any faith and trust will soon dissipate if your ideas have no substance and no delivery. To create a sustainable tribe, you have to sell your image of the future, prove your credentials, stick to your purpose and use your stakeholder group to make your vision become a reality.

# 4.7 NOT EVERYONE WILL JOIN YOU

Just remember that not everyone will support the vision that your tribe's proposing. There will always be some opposition.

If your tribe is advocating change you will face determined resistance from the people who have a vested interest in retaining the status quo. Some people who are already independent and self-sustaining won't want to lose out if things are shared more widely. The have-mores won't ignore your tribe's call to arms, they will rise to oppose it.

If you have a commercial tribe then there will always be commercial opposition. If you are trying to start a new business or increase your market share, then the existing providers will compete to see you off. They won't just let you muscle in and take business away from them. Those competitors will use a combination of lowering prices, improving quality, adding features, increasing advertising, offering customers more deals; and paying their staff more to force you out of the market. The more unscrupulous competitors will misrepresent or denigrate your quality and service levels. Don't expect the commercial competition to join you, or do you any favours.

~~~~~

In simple terms, your vision is where you're going to; and your strategy is how you're going to deliver that vision.

Your tribe's vision needs to be quick and easy to describe. Every member of the tribe needs to know what the 'promised land' looks like, so they can aim for it and spread the word to other people. Producing a written manifesto is one way of explaining what you intend to do, but to bring it to life your description of the future requires a physical telling. Any vision needs to be explained, illustrated and sold.

A personal appeal is far more powerful than a lengthy email or a series of Powerpoint slides. You need to capture your listener's' imagination and give them an insight into what the new world would look and feel like. Your purpose and vision must reach the intrinsic motivations of your tribe to gain its support. The substance and content of a vision is obviously key, but the storytelling process is absolutely vital too. A passionate, determined and authentic pitch is needed to fire each person's emotional red heart. A fair, realistic and measured pitch will appeal to each person's logical blue mind. Storytelling is a vital skill to plan, practice and improve.

Each person listening to your pitch needs to know the answers to the following ten questions:

1.   **What is the purpose behind what we'll be doing?**

2.   **What does the future look like if we manage to do it?**

3.   **What are the benefits of that alternate future?**

4.   **How will those benefits be shared?**

5.   **How hard will it be to make the world like that?**

6.   **Is that new future likely to happen?**

7.   **When is it likely to be achieved?**

8.   **Who has already agreed to help?**

9.   **Why should I bother getting involved?**

10.  **How could I help?**

The clearer and fuller the vision is, the easier it is to produce the strategy that's needed to support it. The strategy should include what needs to be done, by when, in what order, by whom, with what resources and to what standard. It should plan for delays and set-backs. It should also set out exactly what each stakeholder is going to contribute. The more complete the strategy is, the more likely it is to happen. If a group of people sets off on a journey to an agreed place, using an agreed route, at an agreed pace, there is a good chance everyone will arrive in the same place at the same time. If instead the group has no idea of its destination, has no agreed route and everyone is allowed to travel at their own speed, what is the chance of any of the group arriving in the same place at the same time? A clear vision and strategy are absolutely essential. Clear and regular communication of the tribal plan is vital to maintain both the tribe's understanding of it and its conviction in it.

If a group of fellow travellers agrees how to behave with each other and anyone they come across on the way, their journey will be more harmonious and enjoyable. With a set of agreed values there's more chance that a group will stay together and fulfil their vision. When journeys are arduous and challenging, people will only stick at them if they intrinsically want to. People tend to carry on with a difficult project when finishing it really matters to them; and when they are travelling with people that they care about. A person's voluntary consent is only given when it is worth giving it. Some people will buy-in fairly quickly after a strong pitch. Other people will need to be heavily persuaded. Not everyone will think it's worth it.

## *Finish things that really matter*

We like spending time with other people who care about the same things, value the same behaviours and work in a similar way. The opposite is also true. Having to work with difficult, selfish people, who care about very different things can make people change their path or stop travelling altogether. Tribes should avoid trying to bring along people with opposing values. Formulating the tribe's positive values up front will give clarity, which will encourage people with similar values to join in. Having a set of agreed values will also discourage people with opposing values from joining. Why set off with an opponent in your midst? Clear, agreed values can pull a workable team together. Clear, agreed values can also be policed by the rest of the tribe.

There is an expression 'You can't push string.' The implication being that people won't do something unless they are persuaded to. Leaders need to offer positive reasons for calling someone to action (to 'pull' them) rather than just telling them to do it (to 'push' them). Offering an inclusive set of values is appealing. Knowing everyone else will behave in the same way as you is a definite pull factor.

~~~~~

As a matter of respect and inclusiveness all senior Japanese business people expect to be briefed before significant change takes place. If there isn't a proper briefing, those senior business people will take it as a slight and won't back a project even if they support it on its merits.

This stage in Japanese decision-making involves speaking to each of the key leaders and uses their feedback to test and shape the proposals that are going to be made. This process of taking soundings and laying the groundwork is called nemawashi. It helps to make stakeholders feel part of the change process.

In the UK most business decisions are taken by a few owners or senior leaders without enough stakeholder involvement and feedback. Is it any wonder why tribes can be so underpowered?

## 4.8  TWO EXAMPLE VPVS

There is a need to reduce the presence of artificial additives, including salt and sugar, in manufactured food products. With statistics showing every greater medical problems and rising healthcare costs, that would suit the people and governments. At the extreme end, humanity will poison itself to death unless change occurs. The issue is therefore real and urgent, which is why support for it is gathering.

So if we take an example food manufacturer, what is that tribe's purpose? To produce healthy and natural food, so that our customers live long, healthy lives (and therefore buy more of our products).

So what is that tribe's vision? A planet, where food is grown or bred locally and eaten naturally and fresh; and where our products lead the way in healthy eating.

So what are the tribe's values?  They could be:

1.  We will respect our customers (by only feeding them healthy, natural food without additives).
2.  We will protect our sources of food (to ensure we have healthy, natural ingredients).
3.  We will advocate healthy living (as we want our products to form part of a healthy lifestyle).
4.  We will promote natural farming methods (so our ingredients can be produced naturally).
5.  We will help our customers to live long, healthy lives (by only offering products we would fee our own children every day).
6.  We will produce manageable product sizes (so we don't waste food).

The business structure is formal and subject to exacting quality standards. Its tribal colours are natural food colours. Its spiritual homelands would be anywhere and everywhere that natural ingredients are produced and sold. Its routines and ceremonies include promoting natural food production and consumption.

Its branding strap-lines could be:

1.  Evolutionary version "Live a long life. Only eat food that's healthy and tasty."
2.  Revolutionary version "Bad parents poison their children. Check your food's ingredients."
3.  Thought provoking version "Cars don't run on sugar and salt. Nor do people."
4.  Directional version "Always insist on natural, healthy food."

This is just one simplified example of the VPV of a business tribe. Every tribe needs to develop its own VPV.

~~~~~

Outside of business (and as an increasing part of business) there is a fast-growing movement to reduce our global consumption [97] of plastic. High profile television programmes and other media coverage are helping to highlight the issue. What is the issue? Plastic is suffocating our planet and causing a major health risk to all our planet's inhabitants. Our oceans are becoming a plastic soup. We are breathing, drinking and eating plastic particles every day. In 2019 a dead whale was found to have 40kg of plastic inside it. Choking from the inside the whale starved and died. Every other sea creature is being similarly affected. When we eat those creatures we ingest our waste plastic too. The Earth cannot cope with all the human-made waste we're producing. Humanity will choke itself to death unless change occurs. The issue is therefore real and urgent, which is why support for it is gathering.

So this kind of tribe would have a different purpose to the manufacturing business. What would that be? To heavily reduce (if not eliminate) the plastic being manufactured, used and consumed.

So what's the tribe's vision? Its vision is of a plastic free planet, with clear blue oceans and healthy people, animals, birds and fish.

So what are the tribe's values? Its values include:

1. **We will respect our planet (as it is our home).**

2. **We will respect and protect our sources of food (as they are our food).**

3. **We will advocate healthy living (as we want to live long, healthy lives).**

4. **We will conserve nature (as we want to live in a healthy world).**

---

[97] Consumption in terms of manufacturing, use and ingestion.

5. **We will protect our planet's wildlife (as we don't want to adversely affect our own eco-system).**

6. **To all these ends we will aim to eliminate man made waste.**

The movement's structure is informal and fluid. Its tribal colours are nature's greens and the oceans' blues. Its spiritual homelands would be anywhere and everywhere that's threatened by the effects of plastic. Its routines and ceremonies include collecting plastic waste; and reusing or recycling it.

Its branding strap-lines could be:

1. **Evolutionary version "Protect the planet, reduce plastic."**

2. **Revolutionary version "Save yourself. Boycott plastic before it kills us all."**

3. **Thought provoking version "Convenience now is very inconvenient later."**

4. **Directional version "Always insist on plastic free packaging."**

This is just one simplified example of the VPV of a tribe. Each tribe needs to develop its own VPV.

# 4.9 DEVELOP A FLOW

Tribes are complex, living things. They don't ebb and flow like inanimate fluids, they have a complicated and turbulent flow to them. The combined human energy within them directs the tribe's speed and direction of travel, which is in a constant state of tension. Sometimes that energy is relatively steady, creating a manageable swell; and other times it can be flowing in raging torrents. A tribe's momentum can change dramatically and unexpectedly depending on the balance of its circumstances.

As a result, a tribe is capable of being influenced and lead. A person or people can help to ease that turbulence by creating an outlet and funneling the tension away in the chosen direction. However, without clear leadership and direction, tribes are capable of splintering or going to war with themselves. One single determined person, who offers genuine hope and a tribal plan, can hugely influence a whole tribe's flow. That person can win the tribe's hearts and minds through coordinating a common purpose, providing authentic leadership and creating a clear and agreed tribal plan (purpose, vision, strategy and values).

## 4.10  A TRIBAL PURPOSE UNDERPINS TRIBAL POWER

Profit creates real money that can be re-invested or distributed. It is a vital component of business. However, making profit shouldn't be an organisation's core purpose, or there will be less profit. Profit should be one of the positive results of a bigger, more rounded purpose.

To have sustainable success (and greater profit) an organisation needs to have a purpose which appeals to all of its stakeholders. The power generated from a whole group of interested parties pulling everyone together as a tribe is far beyond what any individual or small group of owners can achieve by concentrating all their efforts on making money. By identifying all of an organisation's stakeholders, listening to them and giving them a part to play, an organisation can find a collective purpose for everyone to get behind.

In a business sense, a tribe's stakeholders are always a much wider group than the organisation's owners and executives. Stakeholders aren't just the shareholders. Stakeholders include owners, investors, officers, employees, workers, managers, consultants, trade unions, customers, clients, funders, neighbours, landlords, suppliers, trade associations, creditors, regulators, PR and media agency, government, local community and interested environmental groups. Depending on the nature of the tribe, there may be other stakeholders to add to that list.

A tribal purpose is the mutual purpose of a tribe's members and stakeholders. So creating a unity of purpose that involves all of an organisation's stakeholders is the beginning of tribal power. It is the virtual thread that pulls everything together. Once its purpose is clear, a tribe can create a vision for its future and the tribal values it will operate by. That trio creates clarity and certainty. It is important to note that making money for the business owners will almost never be broad or inclusive enough to be a tribal purpose.

Organisations that continually provide positive answers to the four engagement questions create worker loyalty.

*"Where is my organisation headed?"*

*"What is my role in the future development of my organisation?"*

*"Does my organisation reward me fairly for what I do?"*

*"Are my values and my organisation's values similar enough?"*

That's because feeling you're like an integral part of your organisation is empowering. Being valued by your organisation offers social belonging and provides a form of "glue" that binds a worker to the organisation. A worker's engagement is not automatically given. It is a voluntary gift from workers to their organisations.

A fully engaged worker is thought to offer something in the region of 15%-20% additional, discretionary effort compared to an average employer. A disengaged employee with offer less still. The more organisations build employee engagement the more discretionary effort they'll get in return. Businesses can therefore invest more in worker benefits and rewards and still increase their profitability.

As a worker's engagement has to be earned, employers should plan for delivering practical answers to these four key questions. If they don't, they risk a high turnover of staff. It is insufficient to have one quick chat once a year that's labelled an appraisal. That's because working with uncertainty about your role or your purpose is highly unsettling. Lone-working is lonely. Co-working is tribal. Organisations with poor planning, poor communication or poor rewards fail to involve and integrate their workforce. They cannot generate tribal power.

# TRIBAL ACTION PLAN

The foundation stone for generating tribal power is a shared conviction in the tribal purpose. Does every stakeholder share that same level of conviction?

How do test for conviction? What level of graft and financial investment is required? Is that enough to secure someone's buy-in?

If someone doesn't share that conviction how do address that? Do you take them through the tribal plan and re-sell the purpose?

# 5.  SUPER-TRIBES

## 5.1  MAKE LINKS AND PARTNERSHIPS

Joint-working with other stakeholders can create an enhanced performance and a mutual benefit. Whenever your tribe needs skills, experience or resources that it doesn't possess, it can look outside itself to trade for them or gather them in. Collaborating to achieve a collective goal or project can build relationships beyond tribal boundaries. A tribe can therefore borrow and adapt ideas from outside. Plenty of bright ideas have been borrowed and adapted from other places. Owen Maclaren, a retired aeronautical engineer and test pilot borrowed the concept of an aircraft's retractable landing and created a lightweight retractable baby buggy.

Plenty of real partnerships have produced great results, such as the collaborative working on Live Aid. In fictional terms, the Mexican farmers in The Magnificent Seven hired professional gunfighters to help them defend their village. They knew a great deal about farming their land, but they did not know anything about gun-fighting.

In business, commercial competition is faced with legal and ethical boundaries. In order to combat unscrupulous employers paying fashion workers less than the national minimum wage, a super-tribe of interested parties is openly working in support of each other. Those parties include leading high street retailers such as John Lewis and M&S, the UK Government (through an All Party Working Group), the UKFT (United Kingdom Fashion and Textile Association), Homeworkers Worldwide and the Ethical Trade Initiative. With the same shared purpose, their efforts are providing open debate and positive action.

~~~~~

On 14 April 1912, the Titanic set off on her maiden voyage from Southampton to New York. Just before midnight she hit an iceberg in the North Atlantic Ocean and sank. There were approximately 2,200 passengers and staff on board. Over 1,500 of them died. The sinking shocked the World.

In the aftermath, questions began about how so many people could have died. There was outrage about the lack of lifeboats and lifejackets, as well as the favouritism showed towards the highest passenger class during the evacuation.

*Every passenger deserves the same chance of safety*

In 1914, representatives from thirteen countries met in London at an International Convention for the Safety of Lives at Sea (known as SOLAS). The Convention agreed a new code of safety standards for merchant ships, including a major increase in the number of lifejackets to be carried. By agreeing minimum safety standards for all sea travel, it became instantly safer to board a ship.

Moving straight to an international code allowed everyone to share the same benefits, learnings and developments. A modern updated SOLAS code is still in operation today.

~~~~~

Tribes can often benefit from developing strong links and partnerships with other tribes and individuals. But these potential links and partnerships must always help your tribe to work towards its vision, purpose and values. Your allies and partners should always help you to achieve your vision. Otherwise they could be undermining your purpose and knocking you off track.

Unless your vision, purpose and values are shared by all your stakeholders (namely the owners, investors, officers, employees, workers, managers, consultants, trade unions, customers, clients, funders, neighbours, landlords, suppliers, trade associations, creditors, regulators, PR and media agency, government, local community and interested environmental groups) they could be the anchor slowing down your progress and working against you.

*Every tribe needs to decide who its supporters are and who the opposition is.*

If a potential partner stands for opposing ideals and inconsistent values, then why would you build any links with it? Surely you shouldn't. Analysing all of your existing relationships and only building on the positive and complementary ones is crucially important to your tribe's success. Every tribe needs to decide who its supporters are and who the opposition is. If your tribe stands for something, then it must stand against something. It is as important to know what a tribe opposes, as well as what it supports.

Properly assessing partnership opportunities before you commit is very important. External link-ups need to add missing skills, determination and impetus to the cause. Does a particular partnership make your 'boat' go faster? Having links to groups that divide public opinion, could divide opinions about your tribe too. Guilt by association may be unfair, but it is the risk any tribe runs by linking-up with anyone else. Why would you risk it if they don't share the same ideals?

~~~~~

With the growing urbanisation of the World, there will be increasing opportunities to work together. In 2000, approximately 2.9 billion of the World's population lived in urban areas. It's predicted that will have become 4.3 billion by 2020. That trend is due to continue and by 2045 it's predicted that 6.3 billion of the World's population will live in urban areas. With social media in overdrive too, access to other people is becoming easier and easier. More tribes can their pool resources and partner together to become super-tribes. That trend will only increase.

~~~~~

In 2019 the UK Government committed the UK to a range of international partnerships to meet shared challenges and drive growth. Its key purpose is to ensure that the UK "remains global leader in science." Rather than going it alone, the UK has chosen to develop and implement an industrial strategy called The International Research and Innovation Strategy. This is because the UK's best interests are served by global partnering.

In practice this super-tribe strategy means active involvement in a host of collaborative activities and taking a leading role in coordinating them. The UK has made a number of specific commitments including: hosting a Global Innovation Summit in Manchester, Chairing the EUREKA programme [98] for 2018/19; and setting up innovation hubs across the UK for global innovators, entrepreneurs and investors.

There are multi-million pound investment funds earmarked for projects like an Artificial Intelligence collaboration with Japan's 'Global Brain', a robotics collaboration with a Chinese company to run an assembly and testing facility in Birmingham; and investment in Technology Accelerators in partnership with Africa.

The UK has also committed to "build and invest in collaborative partnerships to tackle the greatest global challenges" such as climate change, energy security and environmental sustainability (including moving to sustainable development goals ('SDG's)). This strategy will help the UK to fulfil its vision of remaining a global leader in science.

Science is a leading proponent of super-tribe working. One obvious example is the World Health Organisation pulling research and researchers from all over the World to decide which four strains of flu should to be included in the Worldwide flu vaccine each year. Every tribe can learn from this kind of working. It's the level of connection between a tribe's stakeholders that matters. Where there is a high level of common purpose there is likely to be greater unity and a higher level of performance. The opposite is also true. The greater the self-interest and disconnection between stakeholders, the weaker the joint-working will be.

---

[98] A European inter-governmental initiative to create innovation across European borders and other key partners.

Understanding its vision, purpose and values allows a tribe to centre itself and find its place in the World. An agreed vision gives a motivational Finish Line to aim for. Analysing where the tribe is now gives it a Start Line to head off from. Both the place of departure and the destination are needed to create a tribal plan. That process of centering before the off will give any tribe a strong sense of meaning and direction. An agreed plan helps a tribe stay on course and not head not 'off-road'. Staying focused on that Finish Line takes a collective effort of all the tribe's stakeholders.

Gathering up those stakeholders for the off will create the tribal power needed to see its vision become reality. There should be plenty of stops to pick up other passengers along the way, to add more stakeholders. The more difficult the vision is to achieve, the more that human effort and collaborative working are required.

## *A vision provides the motivational Finish Line*

Having a shared vision, purpose and shared values with someone else creates a potential joint-working opportunity. Once the core elements match, clear communication is absolutely vital in operating that partnership relationship. Ensuring that you both speak the same language and use the same terminology is therefore critically important. But despite the need for growing strength, not everyone is a suitable partner for your tribe. If another person or organisation has an opposing vision, purpose or values, they will not be a good fit. Numbers matter, but alignment matters more.

~~~~~

If another tribe stands against you, they will have to be defeated or become part of the managed opposition. In peacetime there is tolerance and acceptance of opposition. In peacetime your opponents don't have to be destroyed, they just have to be kept under control. Governments, for example, have to accept that there are held to account by opposition parties. Businesses have to accept that they have competitors trying to win the same customers. Sports teams have many rivals to beat in order to win trophies. The process of learning how to beat your opposition helps your party, business or team become competitive and maintain its competitiveness. Success comes from using and developing your tribe's strengths to overcome its competition.

## 5.2 TEMPORARY BONDS CAN BE TIED AND UNTIED AS NEEDED

Permanent partnerships can be very valuable, but they are not the only kind. Temporary bonds can add expertise, experience and skill when it's needed. Those bonds can be tied and untied as needed. If temporary ties work well for the parties, then why not work together on one-off or occasional projects.

There is an increasing trend for bespoke teams to be pulled together for each project, depending on fit, expertise, availability and price. Project management still requires a tribe approach. Temporary tribes don't have a collective group heritage or set of traditions to fall back on. Temporary tribes need to be formed quickly, so their structure, rules and values are particularly important.

~~~~~

International rugby union teams train together all year round, season in season out. They practice as a unit and work out their best combinations over time. Taking their players from club rugby, each international team has to blend the best of its country's players. Each club has a different playing strength and culture. Each club side has a proud heritage and set of rituals. Each club is a different tribe. To blend the best team from all the club players, each international side has dedicated coaching and backroom teams who know the players' personalities, playing statistics and their injury history. International rugby teams have one advantage over club sides, which is an intrinsic national passion. Playing for your country is the greatest personal honour there is in sport. International teams are examples of partnership working. They are the best of the best, they are super-tribes.

The British and Irish Lions began their first tour in 1888. Captained by Robert Seddon, a party of English, Scottish, Welsh and Irish rugby union players took part in 35 matches in Australia and New Zealand, winning an impressive 27 of them. Now every four years, a touring party of British and Irish players visits Australia, New Zealand or South Africa in rotation.

## The best of the best of the best

By contrast to international teams, the British and Irish Lions are made up of players, coaches and backroom staff from the four Lions nations, who have been adversaries for most of the previous four years. Giving everything physically and mentally to beat each other in the Six Nations Championship, the touring squad has to re-focus on a higher level. Made up of staunch opponents, the squad only has a few weeks to gel as a group.

Despite the unique challenges, the British Lions have had some famous victories over the years. When managed and coached well the quickly selected combinations click and the best of the four "home" nations come together as a collective force. When that happens the British Lions are the best (of the Lions' squad) of the best (of the four international teams) of the best (club teams). They are a super-tribe, one tier above international and two tiers above a club team. The British Lions produce a rugby form of tribal power.

# 5.3 TOO MANY GROUPS AND NO SENSE OF TRIBE (SUPER-TRIBES)

Within every community there are groups of all interests, backgrounds and denominations working to different purposes. Some of those groups are working directly against each other, often without realising it. When there are tribal waves crashing against each other a community can't act as one combined force for good. Despite the very best of intentions too many disparate groups can create an awful lot of light and noise without producing much motion. We need to foster a sense of super-tribe to pull different communities together.

Necessity is a powerful binding force. In the animal kingdom, a wolf is a fantastic hunter, but wolves have learned that they eat more and stay safer if they live and hunt in a pack. The collaborative working is far more powerful than each wolf working alone. In 2011, when the temperature got so low it had killed all their usual prey, more than four hundred Siberian wolves came together to create a super pack. By hunting together en mass their prey had no chance.

Joining forces with people who have a similar vision, purpose and values can grow your tribe in a quick and sustainable way. And it's often only when lots of people with the same purpose converge and join forces that big change happens. Far more tribal power can be generated from tribes forming a super-tribe, rather than going it alone.

*Collaborate, combine, join forces*
*and build a super-tribe*

Inside organisations, teams, departments and cliques can be the enemy of their organisation if they allow silo thinking to dominate. Corporates that are split into separate divisions can suffer from fierce internal politics and competition which hold them back. Egos, selfishness and personal fiefdoms can undermine any organisation's collective goals. By clinging tightly to the vision, purpose and values of their own divisional tribe, divisions and teams can damage their wider organisation. Team and divisional leaders need to buy-into whole organisation thinking at the highest level. That way they can by part of a super-tribe. I describe this mindset as CAST thinking. CAST being a structure that's been designed, moulded and then solidified; and which is also the acronym for Creating A Super Tribe. Committing to the highest level of tribe usually harnesses the most power.

~~~~~

On Sunday 25 June 1876 in modern day Montana, the Sioux, Cheyenne and Arapaho nations were in camp together by the Little Bighorn River. They had come together as neighbours to discuss how to protect their people, food and sacred Black Hills from their common enemy, the white man. Without that common opposition this gathering may never have happened. It certainly would not have happened on the same scale. The shared sense of fear and loathing resulted in what was probably the biggest ever Indian encampment, of between 6,000 and 7,000 Native Americans. Of them, about 2,000-2,500 were men and boys of fighting age. All the main Lakota Sioux tribes were present, including the Hunkpapa, Oglala, Minniconjou, Blackfoot and Crow. Tatanka Yotanka (Sitting Bull) was the Chief of the Hunkpapa.

The U.S. Army had been gradually driving the Native Americans further and further West, making false treaties, breaking them and killing Native Americans as it went. The Fort Laramie Treaty of 1868 established the Great Sioux Reservation which included the sacred Black Hills. Under the treaty, white settlement was forbidden on the reservation. But greedy businessmen spread rumours of gold in the Black Hills, which sent white settlers heading onto Sioux land in breach of the treaty. The U.S. Army didn't discourage those settlers and some say that they even encouraged it. The result was inevitable. Eventually some settlers were killed by Native Americans and the U.S. Army immediately sent in soldiers to protect the settlers. The Fort Laramie Treaty became yet another worthless piece of paper.

One of the most famous Sioux tribal stories is about Sitting Bull's vision of white soldiers falling from the sky. This was interpreted as meaning there would be a great Sioux victory over the white soldiers. Inspired by his vision, the Sioux, Cheyenne and Arapaho nations bound themselves around a single purpose. It was simple and fundamental, it was their very survival. By coming together to protect their sacred people and their homeland, they had combined their strengths. Despite all their differences, past squabbles and rivalries, they knew that had a more dangerous enemy than each other.

## *The shared threat, gave them*
## *a shared purpose*

Whilst the Sioux, Cheyenne and Arapaho were peacefully in camp, U.S. Army soldiers rode out towards them, sent with their own single purpose. That was to fatally defeat the Sioux Nation. Seen as a threat to white settlers, the decision had been taken to kill their fellow Americans. Those U.S. Army soldiers included General George Armstrong Custer and his 7th cavalry. General Custer was desperate for battle and personal glory.

Wrongly believing that the Native Americans knew he was coming and were leaving camp, Custer's singular focus and closed mindset made him rush his 7th Cavalry into battle before reinforcements arrived. Without properly scouting ahead, Custer hugely underestimated the Native American numbers. When their lodges were suddenly attacked, the combined force of 2,000-2,500 Sioux, Cheyenne and Arapaho warriors came out to fight. They fought together, side by side and won their most famous victory. Custer's Last Stand was told as the story of a hero who fought bravely against the odds. The bigger truth is that it was also the last great stand of the plains tribes and the Native Americans. Each tribe fought valiantly against the white man's "progress" but separated from each other, each tribe lost its fight.

If more Native American nations had come together many years earlier, then maybe the white settlers would not have been able to take hold of North America. But they did not see or understand the threat until it was too late. Had they united when the first ships arrived, they could have easily defeated their white enemy in battle. Instead, picked off one by one, each nation was defeated and restricted to small, imposed reservations. The power and strength of hundreds of Native American nations such as the Algonquin, Apache, Arapaho, Cherokee, Cheyenne, Comanche, Mohican, Navaho, Nez Perce, Pawnee and Sioux, was divided and conquered.

Eventually, nearly 30 million buffalo were slaughtered to starve the Native American tribes into reservations. Their modern day descendants are trying to grow their numbers once again. They look forward to the time "When things are set right again."

~~~~~

In the Monty Python film, the Life of Brian, we get a sense of how different tribes behave. The comedic reference to the splintering of the opposition to the Romans is amusing, making reference to a Judean People's Front, Judean Popular People's Front and a People's Front of Judea. But it highlights the disadvantages of going it alone. Faced with oppression, the opposition parties should have got together to become one Judean super-tribe. Even then it may not have been strong enough to battle the Roman Empire and hold onto its own lands. Only Scotland held out against the might of Rome. But a united Judea could have achieved more than its individual splinter groups did.

~~~~~

In 2010, Nick Clegg was the leader of the UK's Liberal Democrat Party. After a closely fought general election the UK had a hung parliament. No party had the majority needed to form a government. The Liberal Democrats were traditionally the third party in terms of MPs, infrastructure and influence, but after a very a positive election campaign they had amassed 56 seats.

Nick Clegg and the other senior members of his leadership team faced a major dilemma. They were being asked to form a coalition government with David Cameron's Conservative Party. The

Conservatives had won the most seats but needed Liberal support to govern effectively. The debate was around which option to take. Was it best to accept the Conservative offer, or to try and force through a Government with the Labour Party instead, or just stay in opposition? For the first time since the party's inception in 1987[99] the Liberal Democrats found themselves in a pivotal position. They could not become King[100], but they could become Kingmaker.

The UK was in the throes of the worst global financial crisis since the 1930's and national stability was absolutely vital. Although there hadn't been a coalition government since Churchill's Second World War ministry, a coalition government with the Conservatives offered the greatest chance of national stability. That option could provide a more constructive approach than the usual antagonism of three-way party politics. The Liberal Democrats knew they were in a relatively strong bargaining position. With some power and influence, the Liberal Democrats could at last have a direct bearing on UK politics. Being on the inside of government gave the party much greater ability to curb the elements of Conservative policy that it didn't approve of. On the face of it the decision was easy. Opportunity pointed straight towards David Cameron's offer.

## *Mutual compromise can hurt less than no compromise*

But it was not such an easy decision. There were large differences of political philosophy between the Liberal Democrats and the Conservatives. Being the minority partner[101] any deal on policy would be difficult to enforce. In addition, the election had been very hard fought and there was a lack of understanding and trust between the two parties' leaders. What was best for the UK (a super-tribe approach) might not be best for the Liberal Democrats.

---

[99] The party was formed when the Liberal Party merged with the Social Democratic Party.

[100] Or Queen.

[101] The Conservatives had 16 Cabinet members to five Liberal Democrats. Nick Clegg was Deputy Prime Minister.

Undeniably torn, Nick Clegg and his team decided that the needs of the UK had to come first. So, they agreed to form a coalition government. That decision created the stability that the nation needed. The Conservative manifesto was watered down, but the Liberal Democrats also made sacrifices which lost the party credibility and voters in equal measure. The big moment came when the Liberal Democrats voted for an increase in university tuition fees. That was part of the wider coalition deal, but it directly contradicted a Liberal Democrat election pledge. That was a compromise too far for many voters and caused huge consternation in young party voters in particular.

As time went on, there was increasing frustration from being the minority partner. Cracks started to appear in the coalition, but the Liberal Democrats somehow held it together for the country until the next General Election in 2015. When that election came along, the Conservative vote went up. But Liberal Democrats lost 48 of their 56 seats. The voters had spoken. Now they were no longer needed by the Conservatives. They came out of government and returned onto the backbenches with only 8 MPs. Nick Clegg was forced to resign as party leader. The Liberal Democrats remained in the doldrums for four years afterwards until local elections in 2019, when the two main parties both lost some of the middle ground to them.

Political reporting at the time was hard on Nick Clegg and the Liberal Democrats. History is likely to be kinder to Nick Clegg and his party. They offered their commitment to a super-tribe and made a brave an impressive self-sacrifice for the benefit of the UK.

~~~~~

Bonding together with similar tribes where there is a united purpose and vision, can get bigger things done. At the Olympic Games and World Championships the English, Scottish and Wales compete together as Great Britain and 'Team GB'. The combined capability of these nations has produced sensational performances at the London 2012 and Rio 2016 Olympic Games amongst others. Together these three proud nations are part of a sporting super-tribe.

The name Great Britain isn't as inclusive as it could be. It does not expressly include every part of Team GB. The full name would in fact be Team Great Britain, Northern Ireland, Isle of Man, Channel Islands and UK Overseas Territories (including the Falkland Islands and Gibraltar). That name is a mouthful, but it would be more accurate than Team GB. Also, somewhat confusingly, competitors from Northern Ireland can choose whether to represent Ireland or Great Britain. As the team is named Great Britain and not the United Kingdom, most Northern Irish competitors tend to represent Ireland. Despite these issues, Team GB inspires magnificent performances from all its competitors. Great Britain is a great Olympic power.

At the Commonwealth Games, all of the nations within Great Britain compete against each other. The experience of a Games environment, the pressure of competition, the pride in representing your country and the opportunity to win medals are all on offer. All of these collective experiences then benefit the super-tribe of Great Britain at subsequent Olympic Games and World Championships.

# 5.4 BRITAIN AND THE UK

Millions of people are both English[102] and British. Many are proud to be both, but the distinction doesn't affect their daily lives in practice. You can be both English and British without much conflict. When it comes to sport, most of these people support England and Great Britain.

Many of the same people are also proud to be from the UK too. Some are proud to be from the EU as well. They may be staunch supporters of their town and county too. Often their interests are aligned. Can you feel equally strongly about all of these tribes? Do you ever have to choose between them?

England is made up of multiple regions, with multiple accents, dialects and histories. People from Cornwall, Yorkshire, Merseyside

---

[102] Substitute Scottish, Welsh or Northern Irish if you wish.

and many other English places have immense pride in their county or regional roots. Even now in the global village we live in, where we are from matters. In modern England all of these regions work together for their mutual betterment. England is a super-tribe. Those same people may be proud to be from say Cornwall, from England and from the same unified Kingdom simultaneously. That doesn't seem to produce an obvious conflict or opposition. Historically it would have done. Until King Alfred united England Cornwall, Yorkshire and Merseyside were all separate Kingdoms.

## Look to how your different tribes' interests can align

The United Kingdom is made up of England, Northern Ireland, Scotland, and Wales. The UK is another super-tribe. All four countries have different values and traditions, but they are working together for their mutual betterment.

So long as our tribal interests overlap and offer us consistency without conflict, we can be proudly belong to more than one. We can be part of several tribes and super-tribes as long as their and our interests align. Taking the same hypothetical Cornish person, that list of tribes might be Truro, Cornwall, England, Great Britain, the United Kingdom and Europe. All of them, with the possible exception of Truro, are super-tribes, tribes which are made up of smaller tribes. Each layer of super-tribe adds potential inconsistency of vision, purpose and values but if they can be aligned it adds greater tribal power.

~~~~~

The English in particular like to beat France and Germany at sport. We see the differences of our territory, languages, histories and traditions as keeping us apart. But we are close in the way that matters most, family.

The peoples of the United Kingdom have DNA that stretches back thousands of years to the same original source as every other people across the globe. The history of the Y chromosome is indisputable 103. We are related to everyone else on Earth. More specifically, Europeans are all believed to descend from one or other of seven 104 clan women, who each head a different DNA haplogroup. The seven are collectively known as the daughters of the Eve. No actual names are known of course, but Eve is the name given their mother and the original source of all European mitochondrial DNA. With such close biological connections between us, the European super-tribe seems entirely natural.

## *We are all related to each other*

Great Britain may be an island now, but it was physically joined to mainland Europe, through an area called Doggerland, until the Mesolithic period about 8,000 years ago. Hunters moved freely across the whole continent until the Storegga landslides (in what is now Norway) created a tsunami that permanently flooded Doggerland. At that point our land connection to Europe was removed and Britain became the disconnected island that forged our Britishness. That separation reduced dramatically with the advent of passenger ships, commercial air travel; and the opening of the Channel Tunnel on 6 May 1994. We are geographically connected too.

Even after the United Kingdom physically separated from mainland Europe, we have continued to share our DNA with other Europeans through invasion and travel. We are part Celt, Roman (Italian), Viking (Swedish, Danish and Norwegian), Angle (German), Saxon (German) and Norman (French). That's just the European mix. Every other country in the World has added to the British gene pool to a greater of lesser extent.

Being English is not an exact or finite state of being. Our family tree and DNA arguably matter less than ever. Everyone born in England

---

[103] Thank you to the late Dr. Mark Goodwin, Associate Professor in the Department of Genetics and Genome Biology at Leicester University for his explanation.
[104] The precise number has come under question ever since The Seven Daughters of Eve was published in 2001. Some alternative thinking means that there may have been nine daughters.

can be English and yet everyone has a different string of DNA. We are not tested and judged on that. That level of detail doesn't matter.

If we are all inter-related why do borders, flags and nationalities matter so much? That's because we are inherently tribal. Our direct family and spiritual homeland must be protected. Our basic tribal units come first. They are our priority tribes. But if we widened our 'border' beyond the UK we are part of the European super-tribe. That's so long as our tribes don't conflict. Either way we are a polymorphous people. Complete independence from our European or World neighbours isn't geographically or biologically possible. We are European too; and as long as those interests don't conflict with our other tribes, we can happily be European too.

The UK's Brexit vote showed there are clear differences of opinion on whether the level of conflict between the UK and Europe too big for UK people to feel part of both super-tribes. Some feel it is. Some feel it isn't. Either way they are both tribal views.

~~~~~

Arguably the most difficult tribe to describe is the British. Much has been written about what it is to be British. But the characteristics of the British tribe have changed as society has evolved. What it meant to be British in 1918 is utterly different to what it meant in 1968 and what it means today. The biggest contributor to the changing nature of Britishness has come from the effects of globalisation. Ironically Britain has itself played a critical part in that.

There has been a dramatic growth in both population and the number of different nationalities inhabiting Great Britain. The first national population census was taken in 1801 when there were 10.5 million people living in Great Britain. That figure has risen sharply to about 67 million people today.

In 2016 the Office of National Statistics reported that around 1 in 7 of the usually resident population in the UK was born abroad, and 1 in 11 had non-British nationality. By country of birth, there are more than half a million people originally from each of Poland, India and Pakistan. In 2011, the Evening Standard reported that London included people with over 270 nationalities and over 300 languages were being spoken in the capital city.

## *Globalisation brings us together like never before*

British culture has traditionally been very welcoming of foreign visitors and immigrants. Since the Brexit vote on 23 June 2016, the traditional warmth of the British people has felt a bit more like a cold chill. Maybe that played a part, maybe the vote was more about jobs and economics. Either way, hopefully it won't be a permanent freeze.

Like many old tribes, the traits of being British are heavily influenced by history and tradition. Those characteristics are a mixture of positive and positively unattractive. Being British is a broad church. There is a down to earth humility in some, an arrogance born of empire in others. Over recent years a suspicious, fearfulness seems to have shown its head. There is peaceful tolerance in many; but there is a vitriolic and bitter intolerance in others. We have much in common, but also a whole spectrum of difference to manage.

Amongst the British, a sizeable minority of the English in particular seem to revel in a feeling of superiority over other nations. Fired by historic power and influence, the English can have an inflated sense of our standing and importance in the World. Mocking the Germans, French and Australians is a form of national pastime. In pure sporting terms that is understandable (within limits). At those times we are opponents. But the arguments of genetic superiority are deeply flawed. I once overheard someone arguing that the English were better than the Germans because we (the English) come from "good Anglo-Saxon stock". I would have laughed if it hadn't been so laughable. The Angles and the Saxons were invaders into Britain. Most came from where modern Germany is now. To be Anglo-Saxon is to be partly German. British people mocking Germany and the Germans are partly mocking themselves. British people are descended mainly from the ethnic groups that settled in Great Britain before the 11th Century. They included the Celts, Romans, Angles, Saxons, Jutes, Vikings and Normans. The British are what might be termed a mongrel nation in genetic terms. Whilst that might upset some people, it is the truth. We are still a very distinct people in many other ways like so many others and we are all the better for that.

Our language gives our genetics away. The earliest form of the English language is called Old English or Anglo-Saxon. Old English developed from a set of North Sea Germanic dialects originally spoken along the coasts of Frisia, Lower Saxony, Jutland and Southern Sweden by Germanic tribes such as the Angles, Saxons and Jutes. The Saxons gave us common words we use everyday like 'what, where, when, why and who'. After them the Normans' arrival in 1066 added a French influence. Words like 'chef, omelette, fiancé, restaurant, chic, coup and silhouette' are now part of our vocabulary. Interspersed are words influenced by Roman, Greek and many other languages.

## We share the same genes

We can enjoy the banter that celebrates our differences of modern nationality, but our genes and history are shared. We only have a Prime Minister because King George I was German and didn't speak very good English. As a result, George I needed to rely on his ministers in Parliament much more than previous monarchs. So, he needed someone to represent him in Parliament. Sir Robert Walpole became our first Prime Minister from 1721 to 1742 and we have had one ever since.

Britishness is a blend of history, tradition and modern multi-cultural life. Pining down the exact values of the British tribe is hard. Being British is being part of a larger and more inclusive tribe than being Cornish or English. It is a broad and colourful banner to unify under. We can be local (e.g. Glaswegian), national (e.g. Scottish) and international (British). Unless there is a conflict between their vision, purpose and values we don't have to choose one or the other. We can belong to tribes and super-tribes.

After all we are a race made up of the finest blend of roots and genes. We are product of the toughest conquering people. Invaders brought strong gene pools to our shores and left them with us. They have made the British tolerant, fierce, fair, proud and compassionate.

By comparison to the elusive description of what 'British' means, the English tribe is more easily recognised. Englishness has the distinctive elements that a tribe really needs. They include:

**Colours:** *Red and white.*

**Symbols:** *St. George's Cross, red rose, V sign (both ways round), black cabs, Stonehenge.*

**Logos and badges:** *Three lions, the red cross on a white background.*

**Stories:** *Robin Hood, King Arthur, 1966 World Cup.*

**Brands:** *Aston Martin, Burberry, Barbour, Rolls Royce, Jaguar Land Rover.*

**Uniforms:** *Coldstream Guards, Morris Dancers, white cricket kits and white Wimbledon tennis gear.*

**Spiritual homelands:** *Wembley, Wimbledon, Glastonbury, Yorkshire Dales, White Cliffs of Dover.*

**Songs:** *Jerusalem, Three Lions on a Shirt, anything by the Beatles.*

**Nicknames:** *Tommy, Pommy and Sassenach.*

The Scots, Welsh have their own unique version of all these elements too. Each nation within Britain is its own strong and proud tribe. Each one of those three nations is made up of many smaller tribes with common land and common goals. These tribes can be independent (as England, Scotland and Wales) and collaborative (as Great Britain) at the same time. Adding Northern Ireland into the mix produces the same result with each individual nation and the UK (as the super-tribe).

Hearing the anthem 'Land of My Fathers' sung at the Millennium Stadium is a wonderful thing. The English translation reveals the passionately tribal lyric "Land! Land! I am true to my land!" This is the Welsh national anthem, not the anthem of everyone in Britain. It is also wonderful to hear Flower of Scotland sung at Murrayfield and its tribal call to arms "But we can still rise now and be the nation again." That is not the anthem of everyone in Britain either, only the Scottish. Despite both songs being inherently anti-English, I can appreciate and celebrate the passion and difference they bring. They are a powerful reminder of the pride burning strong within both of those tribes. Together the three nation tribes are one super-tribe. When we all come together as the British, we are immeasurably stronger precisely because of those differences, traditions and passions. No one wants to be partnered with a weak nation that lacks self-belief.

A Britain based on the strengths of all of its nations, regions, cities and tribes has enormous strength, shared tradition and shared potential. Britain's collective sense of tribal passion and determination is what gives Great Britain its tribal power. That strength from its differences is superbly demonstrated during the Six Nations. That said, the divisions between the individual nations and regions of the UK currently feel too wide. There are some good reasons for frustration and dissatisfaction. Government has to address those so that we do not lose the combined strength of a genuinely united Britain. That would be immensely powerful and would undoubtedly thrive whatever Brexit brings.

~~~~~

The Home Office has published a Guide for New Residents to the UK, called Life in the United Kingdom [105]. It is the only official guide to help new migrants pass the Life in the UK test.

The opening pages include a list of the fundamental principles of the UK. They are the UK's values in all but name. These principles are said to be: democracy, the rule of law, individual liberty, tolerance of those with different faiths and beliefs; and participation in community life. The book then goes on to list the expectations of a permanent resident or citizen of the UK. They include respecting the rights of others and looking after the area in which you live and the environment.

---

[105] The Third Edition was published in 2017.

In summary, the Home Office appears to be saying UK residents need to be tolerant of each other and participate in helping their community and the wider UK. The Home Office seems to be promoting positive values and a vision for the UK that could accord with the values of many tribes. The Home Office is reflecting a UK super-tribe.

*"Democracy, the rule of law, individual liberty, tolerance of those with different faiths and beliefs; and participation in community life"*

In order to pass the Life in the UK test, a person needs to speak good enough English and needs to answer questions about UK history, society and government. Many existing UK residents would pass without much revision. But there are facts inside this guide that people who've lived their whole life in the UK may not know. Examples include What is the Council of Europe? [106] How many member states are in the Commonwealth? [107] What is Northern Ireland's flower? [108] Who was John Petts? [109]

Being able to correctly answer those questions might win you the prize of citizenship, but how much does it contribute towards you being a good citizen? Does not knowing the answers make anyone a bad person? Frankly no. Learning a set of facts won't make someone a good citizen, but a test which makes applicants familiar with what life is like in the UK is a good start.

~~~~~

We take pride in buying British. But too much of Britain's industrial heritage has been sold to international investors. Some of those overseas investments have created thousands of direct jobs and tens of thousands more indirect jobs. Some overseas investments may

---

[106] The Council of Europe sits outside the EU and is responsible for the protection and promotion of human rights in the 47 member countries.
[107] There are 52 member states in the Commonwealth.
[108] Northern Ireland's flower is the Shamrock.
[109] John Petts was a Welsh artist best know from his paintings and stained glass.

have taken major Government concessions and hand-outs, but some have been net positive for UK plc. On the face of it, car maker Nissan's Sunderland plant which employs approximately 4.500 people is a positive example. Whilst Honda's decision to close its Swindon plant which employs 3,500 people may not be.

The merger between British heavyweight confectioner Cadbury's and U.S. giant Kraft took place in 2010. It was highly controversial because there was not a real merger. It was a takeover. Promises about chocolate production were made by Kraft to take away the deal's sour taste. But according to a 2016 Dispatches television programme and other reports, key promises not to close UK plants and not to transfer production outside the UK have been broken. Despite its wonderful British history, Cadbury's place in the British hearts and psyche is weaker for compromising on its promises and values since the takeover. If Kraft interferes too much with its products, then it will slip further out of our hearts.

Buying British still has a cache around the World. We sell our industrial and economic strength at our peril, because we lose more than ownership.

~~~~~

What then is British? Is it just a simple blend of the individual nationalities, with everything that is English, Scottish and Welsh being added together to become British too? Similarly, what is being from the UK? Is it just everything that is English, Scottish, Welsh, Northern Irish, Manx etc. all rolled in? Or is the uniqueness of each blend that creates the British or UK super-tribes? Is it even possible to describe Britishness or UKness?

## What do you feel?

This seems to be a question without a determinative answer. Passing a factual test isn't it. Simply living in the UK isn't it either. Ultimately it comes down to a sense of belonging that people either feel, or they don't. Being British or from the UK is about feeling a personal commitment rather than meeting a fixed set of criteria. The core test of any tribe is whether you feel you're a member of it or not. Do you feel British? Do you feel part of the UK?

~~~~~

Is UK society too splintered to stay bound together as one super-tribe? It feels like we have moved closer to that in recent times. Modern life itself is more splintered than ever. Our ties are perhaps more fluid than ever before. How many families all live in the same town or city? It used to be vast majority, now it's the minority. Our national borders have always created an arbitrary form of disunion. There's the geographical divide between territories and parliaments. But it's not just the borders and geography between the four countries that cause segregation. Differences in language, accent, dialect, history and tradition act as further impediments. There is also economic separation, caused by regional wealth differentials.

To some these are all reasons for the UK to 'divorce'. But to others, the strength of our diversity and the underlying alignment of our core interests are precisely the reasons to stay 'married'.

## United we stand

There has been talk of moving the UK's parliament somewhere more central to the UK's geography. With London being the capital and economic epicenter of UK, Parliament's current home is logical, but it feels remote for most of the UK. Locating it more centrally in a city like Leeds would make Government seem more relevant accountable. That might help to hold the Union together. But it would mean politicians voting to head north, miles away from the spiritual home of Westminster.

~~~~~

Most people have a core humanity. Most people agree that everyone should have food, water, clothing and shelter. Most people agree that peace and harmony is better than hatred and war; democracy is better than servitude; and mutual respect is better than committing crimes against each other. Our common ground could provide a powerful consensus about how society should operate. And yet there are people living on our streets, people who are hungry every day and people suffering from the effects of crime. A super-tribe could be formed which transcends politics, religion and every other form of difference between us all. Society could peacefully demand what society actually wants. Pluralism has greater strength than factions and division.

Putting humanity into practice is where things tend to go awry. Even if the majority could be harnessed behind these core fundamentals, there are endless different versions of how this should work in practice. So, despite all the common thinking, cracks can start to appear when it comes to implementing those principles. This is especially true when we don't understand what options are really on offer and what the future holds.

*A super-tribe could be formed which transcends politics, religion and every other form of difference between us all*

Some political parties may claim to share those values and have humanity as its core purpose. However, none of them can (or dare) describe their vision for the UK. What would it be like to live in the UK if we had ten years of your Government? That can't be hard to describe if a party has a coherent plan. If a political party is not making its vision, purpose and values clear then either confusion or subterfuge reigns.

Without a clear vision to vote for or against, people will vote for what's best for their personal tribes and not what's best for the UK's super-tribe. Will it be a traditional or a new party that takes the middle ground and offers us a clear tribal plan?

~~~~~

The UK Labour Party under Jeremy Corbin feels there is too great an imbalance between the owning and working classes. As a result, it is proposing to engineer fundamental social change through enforced economic change. As I write, a current proposal seeks to introduce a 10% shareholding on businesses with over 250 employees. This form of representation and taxation would seemingly be shared between the employees (who would get more say in business decisions and up to £500 each) and the Government (which would receive the rest of the money). If would effectively make Government a 10% owner in every business with 250 or more employees.

Hard-wiring the economy is a draconian measure. Time will tell if it becomes law. Business owners who have worked hard to create an employing company and who pay substantial taxes already will understandably complain about the infringement of their rights. Some will invest less and employ fewer people if this becomes law. Many, many employers are decent people who run good tribes. But some owners don't pay their workers fairly for what they do. If that latter group shared the fruits of their workers' labours more evenly with them then this proposal might not have been suggested.

The increasing gap between the highest and lowest paid earners is evidence of the disparity that Labour wishes to address. Gender Pay Reporting has shone a torchlight on pay from an equally compelling perspective. On top of that, the employers who have tried to avoid paying even the national minimum wage have poured fuel on the fire. They have fed the distorted image of employers being unfeeling, Victorian factory owners.

## Inclusion brings greater partnership working

It is of course true that some employers operate illegally. There is an undeniable case for Government and the law to intervene where that happens. Some employers operate immorally. There is a case to be made for Government and the law to intervene here as well. However, to repeat, many employers are fair and decent. A one-size fits all approach is too simplistic, in the same way that the Victorian factory owner image doesn't fit every employer. Legislating for every business just to tackle the bad apples means both wins and losses for everyone. Some illegal and immoral organisations will be forcibly re-balanced for the better, whilst other good but low profit employers may be forced under.

Where there is less company profit to be made and higher personal taxes to be paid, less risk will be taken and less investment will be made in UK business. That is obvious. Shackling UK business is not the right way to help it to grow. The national minimum wage needs to be increased over time and set at the right level. Holding unlawful employers to account for not paying it is fair and vital too. However, care is needed to get the right balance. A form of reward communism will diminish effort and risk, two key elements in wealth creation. Two little reward for investors will ultimately lead to fewer meaningful jobs and slower pay rises. Reduced profits will push some business owners out of their employing organisations, switching their investment into property. That will ironically drive house prices up for the workers that need them.

If, instead of just being a tax collector, Governments used their enormous tax receipts to generate income and create more job opportunities, they could create more wealth for the UK, rather than just re-distributing it. When insufficient tax exists to pay the UK's bills then Governments could work to create more income, rather than taxing their people more.

## 5.5 HERD IMMUNITY

Measles is a contagious disease that spreads quickly between people. Before the measles vaccine was first introduced in 1963 everyone who caught the disease typically infected another ten to twenty people. Since then fewer people catch measles and therefore fewer people pass it on.

Where there is a vaccine against a contagious disease, the number of people being immunised has a direct affect on the spread of the disease. The more people that are immunised the slower and narrower the spread of the disease. If the vast majority of the population has the vaccine, then the spread of the disease can reduce. The percentage needed to halt the progress of a disease altogether depends on how contagious that disease is. Every additional percentage point of vaccination constrains the disease even further.

## The many can save the rest too

Measles is very contagious. As a result, at least 95% of the population would need to be vaccinated before measles stopped spreading. Polio is less contagious and perhaps only 85% of the population would need to be vaccinated for the disease to be stopped in its tracks.

The benefit of mass vaccination is that eventually even the people who haven't been vaccinated stop getting the disease as well. By a widespread programme of immunisation a community can protect everyone in it. By getting 90% of society immunised against Polio, the other 10% probably won't catch it either. This phenomenon is called herd immunity. By getting sufficient numbers of people to adopt a course of action, there can be wider benefits for everyone. Once an immunisation tipping point has been reached there could be safety for everyone.

~~~~~

It's rare for everyone inside any organisation to fully buy into its vision, purpose and values. For some people work is just a way of paying the bills. For others it's a stepping stone on to something else, something 'better'. Some people are happy to work hard without caring a jot about the bigger picture. The truth is that not everyone is bothered enough to keep the organisation's vision and purpose in mind.

Even so don't give up on anyone. A disengaged employee just needs to start believing. A new employee just needs to understand why to care. Every additional person who catches the 'tribal bug' gets you closer to the tipping point for success. Tribalism is contagious. Building tribes gets easier with every new convert. One can inspire a few. The few can create the many. The many can do it for the whole community.

The good news is that not everyone needs to be constantly referencing the purpose for an organisation to have some success. That's because the tipping point of forward momentum comes before you hit one hundred percent buy-in. So organisations can run at far less than 100% and still make some progress. However, tribal power is only unleashed when the vast majority of employees actively engage with the purpose.

# 5.6 ONE TRIBE

Some people see tribes as aggressive and divisive. They argue that tribes perpetuate and encourage differences. Shouldn't we all try to be the same, to become one homogenous tribe?

If everyone in society agreed the same core values and had the same vision of the future then the highest possible super-tribe could follow. A global super-tribe is certainly possible around global warning. That threat creates a single unifying threat and purpose. One tribe could step out of the pack and pull us all together.

Generally it is difficult to find a universal consensus on anything. Maybe if one national political party adopted a set of complementary, common sense, common purpose policies we could all get behind them. If it then actually delivered on those policies, that party could act as a social magnet pulling us all together as one tribe.

*Common purpose,*
*common sense, come on*

How can everyone agree the same vision and values when we all see the World through our own unique prism? The reality is that we won't all agree on everything. But we don't have to. We just need enough buy-in to reach the tipping point. Most people can accept a form of compromise where it is in the common good. Unfortunately, a version of that common good hasn't been sold in realistic and compelling terms yet.

To bind everyone together, there would need to be something on offer for every social group. If any tribes that feel disproportionally disadvantaged or ostracised wouldn't lend their support to a super-tribe. We need more focus on the highest prizes. In the meantime, we can celebrate the positive contributions that other tribes can bring. We can appreciate difference as long as it doesn't threaten our tribes and their visions. Where there is similar thinking and a common purpose, we can form super-tribes out of a collection of smaller tribes. In a corporate context, that means mergers and acquisitions where two organisations' tribal plans can be aligned.

A single tribe that offers a community-focused vision, purpose and set of values would perhaps be the ideal, as long as its tribal plan was genuinely inclusive and good. But a World without tribes and just one global super-tribe would be compromise to the point of extreme. All we'd have left is a bland, vanilla coloured World. The beauty of our diversity would be lost.

~ ~ ~ ~ ~

By committing to its own tribal plan, each tribe implicitly excludes every other combination of vision, purpose and values. So, when another tribe comes along with a different mix, that tribe will be a form of opposition. That creates competition and a risk of conflict. As the other tribe's purpose is different, can it be rejected as wrong? Right? The answer is not necessarily.

Despite the obvious differences between tribes, they are rarely diametrically opposed. Sometimes there is more in common than not. So instead of looking to defeat other tribes, trying to find common ground with them may bring opportunities for both tribes, creating a super-tribe effect. When two tribes go to war both may end up weaker as a result. When two tribes create an alliance, both may end up stronger as a result. If a combination of tribes can be aligned and form one tribe focusing on common purposes, that super-tribe will bring positive and lasting benefits for them all.

If, however the other tribe wants to beat you or take your customers, you need to defend yourselves. That's when your VPV will be tested. If there's nothing at your organisation's core, no reason to stay, no intrinsic motivation to belong, then you will lose. How loyal is your tribe? How well can you gain new ones? Keeping followers is essential. If you can retain your own people and building followers faster than anyone else, you will over-power the opposition.

~~~~~

One tribe means everyone being in it together. To be one tribe everyone needs to benefit from organisational improvements and changes. The reward gap between owners and workers can't continually grow without challenging the tribal fabric of the organisation.

Sharing the rewards, as well as the hard work, keeps everyone moving committed. Unfair distribution threatens the bonds of work. With little to lose and everything gain, disenfranchised workers will react to ever growing separation. Some will suffer presenteeism, some will work 'to rule', others will go on strike; and many will leave their jobs. Some of those leavers will become your competitors.

~~~~~

In the inspirational 'Legacy', James Kerr investigates the strength of the New Zealand rugby union team, the All-Blacks. James spent five weeks with the All-Blacks and was let into their inner-sanctum. His book confirms that the culture of the Maori people is vital to the culture of the All-Blacks.

The Maori culture, through its values, language, story-telling and symbols, provides a unique blueprint that has helped to create the greatest sports team in the World. Using the mantra Better People Make Better All Blacks, a player's on field rugby performance is not the only consideration for selection. This has created a mentally stronger group of players. The philosophy places an emphasis on humility, a sense of leaving the jersey in a better place, moving together like a spearhead; and having calmness under pressure amongst other traits. We could all do worse than start with that type of approach to building a tribe.

In terms of cultural anthropology, each human culture is ethnocentric, meaning that it believes its culture is superior to every other culture. The dangers of this attitude, at their worst, include ethnic cleansing. Tribes and religions can be abused or focused on the wrong purposes. Tribes should be agents for diversity and positive change. Tribal culture has to be genuinely inclusive. Some flexibility and variation has to be permitted.

## *Compromise can be good as long as doesn't jeopardise the tribal plan*

If a vision is shared beyond the tribe, then various cultures and tribes can contribute to the same shared vision and outcomes in different ways. That is when a tribe can become part of a super-tribe or even a nation of tribes, all striving for the same purpose. That type of super-tribe could cross borders, nationalities and religions. If it could become a nation of tribes, it could provide tribal power on a global scale, independent of the institutions and influencers who have control and often lead the fight against meaningful change.

A nation of tribes across the World trying to promote peace, prevent wars, relieve poverty, care for the elderly and infirm, or reduce crime could produce a tribal power that heavily influences, if not leads, governments and religions. That really could be something truly good.

We rely on our politicians to help us deliver change, but career politicians can lack life experience outside Westminster. Everyone can have sympathy for others, but without empathy there is no core understanding of what it's like to live in those circumstances. As a nation we need a blend of politicians who have experience of what it's like to be out of work, paid only the national minimum wage, a business owner, a parent, a student, a carer, a visitor, an asylum seeker, a public sector worker on the front line, or somebody living with a disability. There are far too many characteristics to name them all. Knowing what its like to be in the same situation as someone else creates an empathy for them, which in turn creates a reason for helping them. If we care, we act.

~~~~~

In the Marvel film Black Panther, King T'Challa gives a closing speech in the after credits. It is the call for a super-tribe.

"Wakanda will no longer watch from the shadows. We cannot. We must not. We will work to be an example of how we as brothers and sisters on this earth should treat each other. Now, more than ever, the illusions of division threaten our very existence. We all know the truth: more connects us than divides us. But in times of crisis, the wise build bridges, while the foolish build barriers. We must find a way to look after one another as if we were one single tribe."

~~~~~

Deciding what you stand for and what you oppose is hard. But a tribe has to take a position on the key issues affecting it. It has to chose the option that best that helps it achieve its purpose. Different kinds of tribes will make different kinds of choices.

Subject to the Brexit effect, by 2040 the population of the UK is expected to increase by seven million people to nearly 70 million. Where will everyone live? There is already estimated to be a shortage of two million homes for the current population. If these figures are correct, an immediate, extensive, long-lasting, national construction programme is needed urgently to provide enough homes for 2040.

*As Maslow understood,*
*we all need shelter and safety*

A tribe that's focused on satisfying all those potential home-owners and tenants (such as builders, mortgage companies and estate agents) might ask "How fast can we build all the houses and infrastructure that we need?" A tribe focused on maintaining local views and house prices might ask "How can you justify adding so many new homes into our area?" A tribe focused on party politics or balancing the public finances, might ask "How on earth can we pay for that housing and infrastructure, because we can't afford all the new roads, hospitals and schools to go with them." A tribe focused on immigration might ask "Can we fit all those people on this island? Other countries have far more space than us. Can't they take more people?" All of these potentially competing interests are difficult to reconcile.

The natural countryside of the UK is beautiful, but its rolling hills are becoming steadily eroded. Until what point is our quality of life still being enhanced by new housing and retail development? When does the net benefit tip into a net deficit on our quality of life? Environmentalists and naturalists would say that too many woodlands and hedgerows have already been lost with all the building so far. Historians and archeologists would add that too many historic sites have also been built on or spoiled already. Those tribes might ask a very different question which is "How can we stop all of this building?"

As the hymn says "I will not cease from mental fight, nor shall my sword sleep in my hand, until we have built Jerusalem in England's green and pleasant land." This powerful hymn takes a point of view. It promotes the creation of a way of living and a state of mind, rather than more and more physical buildings. It doesn't use the words "I will not cease from mental fight, nor shall my sword sleep in my hand, until we have built Jerusalem in England's tarmacked and lessened land". So, are the environmentalists right?

According to statistics only about 9% of England has been built on.[110] So on that basis the developers can let loose and build away, can't they? When you hear that the UK has an average of 713 people per square mile[111], you might change your mind. Or if you are told that the vast majority of the 91% remainder is made up of farmland, pastureland, wetland, heathland, parks, forests, mountains, rivers, beaches, reservoirs and domestic gardens your might question the space and practicability of more housing.

On each contentious issue like this you will have a personal view, an established mindset. On each contentious issue a tribe needs to form a collective view. Debating contentious issues should eventually bring a collective view. That may carry everyone along or it might cause a natural splintering. At least where there is a debate and decision you can choose which tribe to belong to.

~ ~ ~ ~ ~

If you want to do more, to be more, then find your tribe. If your tribe isn't calling out to you yet, search for a purpose that taps into an inner-motivation, one which will keep driving you on when things are really tough. Which tribes support that point of view?

When you have your tribe, make sure that its vision, purpose and values are crystal clear and that you communicate them well. Use the key elements and rituals of a tribe, to make your tribe distinctive and appealing to existing and new followers.

## *Clarity is next to tribalness*

Motivate others through stories and involve all your tribe's stakeholders in what you do. Don't try and tackle your purpose all alone. Tribal power only comes when all the tribe's stakeholders are working together for the common good. That means all the tribe's

---

[110] The Land Cover Atlas of the United Kingdom created by Professor Alasdair Rae from Sheffield University's Department of Urban Studies and Planning based on 2012 data.
[111] According to online Worldometers.

owners, investors, officers, workers, managers, trade unions, customers, clients, funders, neighbours, landlords, suppliers, trade associations, creditors, regulators, PR and media agency, government, local community and interested environmental groups working together, collectively, as a group. That wave of tribal power is special and far beyond your own capabilities.

Pulling all of this together will generate tribal power and achieve something purposeful and good. If you think you can do it, you probably can.

## 5.7 TRIBAL ACTION PLAN

What relationships does your tribe have with its stakeholders? Are all their interests aligned? How do you test that? How often do you ask?

With partnerships, joint ventures and alliances, you need to ask "Is there an equality of effort, or does your tribe have to carry too much of the load?" Is it time to add to or change its partners?

# 6. HOW I'VE LEARNED WHAT MATTERS

## 6.1 MY PERSONAL TRIBES

My first tribe instantly became my family. Geographically, through my birth, I became part of the tribes in my local village, from Castleford (where I was born), Yorkshire, England, Great Britain, the United Kingdom, Europe and at the furthest extent the World.

Each of my schools became tribes including St. Olaves and St. Peter's in York. My old school friends remain a core tribe of mine. When I went to University, Nottingham became another tribe of mine for three years. When I moved further South to train as a solicitor, Southampton and Hampshire also became tribes of mine. Through marriage, I've added family connections in Wiltshire and beyond to my list of tribes.

In pure sporting terms I can be found searching for the latest scores for Castleford Tigers, Leeds United, Southampton F.C., Bath Rugby, Yorkshire Cricket and Hampshire Cricket, with a passing glance to Nottingham Forest.

## 6.2 MY WORK TRIBES

I've have worked with and been involved in a wide range of other businesses, committees and community projects in the Solent region over the last twenty-five years.

I have been the Managing Partner and Senior Partner at a leading firm of solicitors called Trethowans LLP, where I have had a strong group of fellow partners and directors to work with. We have all shared the same purpose which was to create a fair, inclusive and motivating place to work, allowing us to do great legal work for our clients.

The Management Team during my time as Managing Partner worked particularly well. In colour terms we had a red, blue, green and yellow working together. Our decision-making process blended everyone's point of view. We were a strong tribe of four within our Firm's super-tribe. Built on trust and putting the Firm first, the Management Team[112] was able to make great progress. We all committed to our purpose and we have all worked tremendously hard.

By working together, we have all benefitted far more than we could have alone. We offer twenty or more different legal services to thousands of different clients. It's a complicated, heavily regulated business which we have turned into one tribe. 'Team Trethowans' is a great place to work precisely because we are a tribe. That's why we've grown from roughly £6M turnover when I joined in 2005, to approximately £18M despite the downturn of 2008 and its aftermath. Prudent financial management and a tribal culture have been the two key pillars behind the firm's success. I acted as the catalyst but acting alone I could not have achieved very much at all. I might not have achieved anything at all on my own. Together we have. This fantastic experience has taught me how to build sustainable teams.

## Built on mutual trust, powered by mutual will

As an employment lawyer I have advised a wide range of businesses, including many household name brands in many sectors including retail, leisure, food and beverage, manufacturing and logistics. I've worked with lots of owner managed businesses, as well as a large number of NHS Trusts, colleges and other educational bodies, local government and charities. Whilst nothing is ever perfect, but there are many excellent practices, benefits and human resources professionals out there. There are so many good people helping their organisations to be good places to work. I've helped and learned from all my experiences, probably in equal measure. Working with high

---

[112] Great credit and thanks go to Andrew Mercer, Chris Whiteley and Garry Treagust.

quality people always brings self-learning and development. That's because learning is a very circular process.

~~~~~

As well as the day job, I have been the Chair of Future Southampton, a board member of the Hampshire Chamber of Commerce Southampton Business Board, a trustee of the Southampton Cultural Development Trust and a committee member of the Business South Environmental Group amongst other formal groups. I have been involved in various skills and education initiatives, chaired three environmental conferences (one featuring Sir. Vince Cable), spoken at business events across the region; and co-hosted the South Coast Business Awards with both Roger Black MBE and Sir. Geoff Hurst. Each one of those experiences has taught me something useful that's helped me to understand collaborative working (and helped me write this book).

I have all spent time inside professional sporting clubs, observing and working with coaching teams. I have done the same exercise with leadership groups in schools; and with boards and executive committees in business. I am very grateful for the trust and opportunities that I've been given. I have in return provided feedback, produced detailed reports and helped to implement positive changes.

## Experience is a great teacher

I have also worked behind the scenes to help mentor over a dozen other leaders. By experiencing their challenges and helping them to overcome them, I have gained a great deal. Having an open-mindset has allowed me to absorb so much more knowledge and experience than a closed one would have done.

~~~~~

In 2011, the economy was really tough. I had the idea to create a business event in Salisbury to help to share knowledge and ideas; and to showcase Salisbury businesses. With enormous help from Claire

Burden (who was instrumental) and Salisbury City Council, James Fry, Simon Ward, Janine Whitty, Eliot Jones and others, we created and ran an annual, three day Salisbury Big Business Event which ran from 2012 to 2017. Each year the event was self-funding. Each year it grew.

The event pulled together the backing of Salisbury City Council, Wiltshire Council, The Federation of Small Businesses, Salisbury Chamber of Commerce, the Salisbury Business Improvement District Blue Frontier, Spire FM and the Salisbury Journal to create a Salisbury super-tribe. We provided free access to seminars, exhibition stands, workshops and one to one mentoring sessions. We attracted a leading keynote speaker every year including: Baroness Karren Brady, Baroness Michelle Mone, Sir. Ranulph Fiennes, Levi Roots (Reggae Reggae Sauce), Wayne Hemingway MBE and Gerald Ratner (who was hilarious).

Every year the SBBE committee adopted an icon to help us advertise the event. These included a key (to help open new doors), a lightbulb (for promoting bright ideas) and a wooden box (to encourage thinking outside it). Each one was branded with the SBBE logo and used to promote the event. Simon Ward took photos of them with celebrities to help raise its profile, including John Challis ('Boycie' from only Fools and Horses).

The SBBE committee was a tribe. We all cared deeply about helping. None of us did it for any money or for any 'thank you's (which was fortunate). We did it to help local businesses. Eventually after six years the same levels of funding weren't available and the event stopped. Whilst it lasted it was fantastic to be involved.

~~~~~

In 2013 I had the idea to create an annual business event in the Solent, as a partnership between Trethowans, Santander, Hughes Ellard (now Vail Williams) and Smith & Williamson. Between us we established The Solent Business Growth Summit. This breakfast event has run from 2014 to 2018 and is still going strong. It offers inspirational business success stories from a local business leader and a national one, together with networking.

Fran Miller at Sky Cycling and Sir John Timpson were just two of the excellent speakers. The combined efforts of the four co-sponsors have provided enthusiasm, insight and encouragement to a range of regional business leaders. The sponsorship provided by all four professional services providers mean that it's been free to attend. It's a community business project, a super-tribe and a pleasure to be involved.

~~~~~

But not every super-tribe works as well as it could. A business committee called Future Southampton was formed in 2014 and I was asked by two participating organisations to chair it. Future Southampton brought together the University of Southampton, Southampton Solent University, Hampshire Chamber of Commerce, Business South, Southampton Airport, the Port of Southampton and Southampton FC amongst other organisations. Between us we tried to generate growth and improvements for the Southampton business community. The idea of a Southampton super-tribe was the vision, but I learned the hard way that the "business community" isn't really a community at all.

The more commercial organisations that are involved in a project, the more agendas there are to try and blend together. As Future Southampton Chair, I was faced with international, regional and local agendas that set differing priorities and in some cases created conflicts of interests. As a result it was difficult to select suitable and inclusive projects. An even bigger problem was the limited resources and funding available. In my experience, independent organisations share a deep suspicion about giving money to a joint project, which is ironic. If only they would share their time, expertise and resources rather than just their cynicism.

*Super-tribes can be hard to form,*
*but try anyway*

Trying to get administrative help and support wasn't easy either. Despite the efforts of a few good volunteers [113] trying to manage progress we weren't able to do very much. We had a good few laughs and we all bonded with the purpose, but we just couldn't get enough traction elsewhere. We did manage to insert a business element into the city's ten year plan and we started the process which led to Southampton's first Business Improvement District (which is now doing a terrific job). [114]

In December 2014, during my time as Chair, I learned that Southampton City Council wasn't going to pay for a Christmas tree and lights for the city centre. Central Government budget cuts had been devastating and a Christmas tree was deemed less important than key public services. I was surprised that the mental wellbeing of the city wasn't viewed as important enough. To me, not having a Christmas tree for the city symbolised a lack of hope. I couldn't let hopelessness be the public face of Southampton. So, I offered to buy the tree for the Bargate and getting it into place. The Daily Echo pledged to share the cost with me and we went halves. Eventually Southampton City Council offered to erect it and provide the lighting without charge.

At the time, Brian Conley was appearing in pantomime at the Mayflower Theatre. Michael Ockwell, the Mayflower's Managing Director and a great figure in the city, generously allowed us to 'borrow' Brian to turn the lights on. A small stage was erected for the switch-on. When the time came, I was ushered up onto the small stage with Brian Conley and Ian Murray (the former Editor of the Daily Echo and another great figure in the city). A small crowd (and I mean small) listened in. Brian's speech was very funny. I remember him referring to the stage as a "mantelpiece" because it was so small and that he'd never turned lights on in front of Poundland before. I also remember feeling embarrassed by how late everything had all been arranged and how little publicity there had been for the switch-

---

[113] Brad Roynon, Trevor Thorne, Christina Nokleby, Henry Pavey and Alex Nelhams in particular.
[114] To his great credit Brad Roynon worked on in a personal capacity to ensure that the BID was secured. He has been a fantastic servant of the city.

on. Fortunately, Christmas in Southampton has been much better ever since.

After about eighteen months of trying to drive things forward, I became frustrated. Without the funding and resources that we needed we couldn't do enough to make all the effort worthwhile. So, with a heavy heart I reluctantly announced that I was folding the committee. I expected immediate resistance and offers of late support. I was hoping for a kick-back that would challenge the decision and allow us to re-engage and go again. But that didn't happen. Nobody said a thing.

After the meeting finished, I sent an email to everyone involved explaining why we had missed a great opportunity. My email ended with Vinny Jones's closing line from Lock Stock and Two Smoking Barrels "It's been emotional." I didn't receive a single reply.

I'm still frustrated that we weren't given the chance to really make that work. Given hindsight I would have agreed a clearer VPV and got clear agreement on the resources we needed, before agreeing to start work. But failure teaches us how to do things better the next time. My projects since then have benefitted from that learning. Alone and separate we are limited in what we can meaningfully achieve. Super-tribes can do so much more. Hopefully someone else might learn from our failure.

~~~~~

I always work hard to build super-tribes wherever I'm involved. It's never been easy, but it's always been worth the experience. Now I'm helping other people to build super-tribes for their organisations.
I hope it has made you think about your own tribes and super-tribes. If you help to build a super-tribe, that could be your legacy.

# REVIEW

Thank you for reading this book. I hope it has helped you in one of the following ways:

- **To better help you re-evaluate your own personal vision, purpose and values (VPV).**

- **To better help you re-evaluate your organisation's vision, purpose and values (VPV).**

- **To better help you understand how you can better influence any of the tribes you are in.**

- **To better help you understand how you can go about starting your own tribe, if you wish to.**

If this book has done any of these things, please will you leave a positive review on Amazon and join the tribe based around the purpose, vision and values promoted in this book. You will be positively helping to promote what this book offers.

If this book wasted your time, or frustrated you beyond measure, then please leave a constructive but honest review explain why. That will help other potential readers understand what this book doesn't offer.

Finally, if this book left you utterly unmoved one way or the other, then please exercise your right to apathy and don't leave a review at all. But if that's the case, just ask yourself one question. What do you care about?

Now go and build your super-tribe!

Simon James Rhodes.

*United you never shall fall*

Printed in Poland
by Amazon Fulfillment
Poland Sp. z o.o., Wrocław